Barcode in Back

MW01121514

RESEARCH METHODOLOGIES IN CRIMINOLOGY

RESEARCH METHODOLOGIES IN CRIMINOLOGY

DAVID A. YEBOAH

Nova Science Publishers, Inc.
New York

NOTICE TO THE READER

The Publisher has taken reasonable care in the preparation of this book, but makes no expressed or implied warranty of any kind and assumes no responsibility for any errors or omissions. No liability is assumed for incidental or consequential damages in connection with or arising out of information contained in this book. The Publisher shall not be liable for any special, consequential, or exemplary damages resulting, in whole or in part, from the readers' use of, or reliance upon, this material.

Independent verification should be sought for any data, advice or recommendations contained in this book. In addition, no responsibility is assumed by the publisher for any injury and/or damage to persons or property arising from any methods, products, instructions, ideas or otherwise contained in this publication.

This publication is designed to provide accurate and authoritative information with regard to the subject matter covered herein. It is sold with the clear understanding that the Publisher is not engaged in rendering legal or any other professional services. If legal or any other expert assistance is required, the services of a competent person should be sought. FROM A DECLARATION OF PARTICIPANTS JOINTLY ADOPTED BY A COMMITTEE OF THE AMERICAN BAR ASSOCIATION AND A COMMITTEE OF PUBLISHERS.

LIBRARY OF CONGRESS CATALOGING-IN-PUBLICATION DATA

Yeboah, David A.
  Research methodologies in criminology / David A. Yeboah.
    p. cm.
  ISBN 978-1-60692-216-3 (hardcover)
  1. Criminology--Research--Methodology. I. Title.
  HV6024.5.Y44 2009
  364.072--dc22   2008041200

Published by Nova Science Publishers, Inc. ✦ New York

CONTENTS

To my late mother Sabina, lovely wife Tracey and very special children Adam and Blake

ACKNOWLEDGMENTS

I express my deepest gratitude and appreciation to a number of organizations and individuals for their assistance with this publication. I am particularly indebted to the various authors whose publications have been mentioned in this publication and who are listed in the reference section of this publication.

I am equally grateful to my colleague and friend, Dr Frank Cibulka, for his strong support, encouragement and advice during the preparation of this manuscript.

I am particularly grateful to my family for enduring the pain of neglect during the preparation of this manuscript and for the immense sacrifice and support they provided. To my wife and children I say "*AYEKOO*".

PREFACE

The purpose of this book is to provide a collection of criminological research methodologies in one volume covering both quantitative and qualitative research together with evaluation, case studies, analysis of existing data, experimental and documentary research. A number of research methodologies exist for criminological research, and this book endeavors to provide details for each methodology. The fundamental principal throughout this book is to simplify the methodologies and make it easy and practical for researchers (both junior and more experienced) to use them in their investigations.

The point of departure of the book from the existing books on research methodologies is the inclusion in one volume a step by step guide to using most research methodologies, the General Research Process, designing and, asking questions, sources of criminological research data and much more. The simplification of the methodologies, the non-traditional areas included (such as asking questions in criminological research and sources of data for criminological research) and the author's pungent style make this book a useful piece for all criminological researchers. Crime is everybody's business and, as shown in chapter one, crime is rising in most jurisdictions around the world and a need continues to exist to find solutions to criminal activity. Criminological research is a sure way of identifying and establishing strategic options for controlling crime and criminal activity.

Chapter 1

INTRODUCTION

This book focuses on criminological research and the question which arises is what is criminological research? Research is the systematic investigation of a specific topic, issue or problem, through a vigorous and scientific collection, analysis and presentation of data with a view to providing more knowledge and understanding of that topic or problem. When this scientific investigation is concerned with an issue of interest to criminology, it falls within the domain of criminological research.

Criminological research can, thus, be defined as the scientific investigation into a criminological issue through the systematic collection, analysis and presentation of data, with a view to providing more knowledge and understanding of that criminological topic. As criminology covers a wide variety but sometimes interrelated issues, criminological research is diverse and numerous with regards to types and potential topics. Criminological research usually covers broad and traditional topics such as analysis of crime, victimization and victim analysis, criminal justice processes including finding of guilt or otherwise, punishment and rehabilitation of offenders.

Other topics which are assuming increasing importance in criminological research include Police studies interrelationships between crime and social factors like culture, education, employment, income and even politics. Another salient point which must be made about criminological research is the increasing importance of the evaluation of criminal justice programs and policies. In most countries today, efforts are being directed at evaluating criminal justice policies, practices, procedures and programs. Nowhere is this evaluation more important than the revaluation of community and prison based rehabilitation programs for offenders. In most countries, resources are being channeled into the evaluation of rehabilitation programs to assess their effectiveness and ensure that areas for potential improvement are identified to achieve the best program outcomes. Needless to add that the ultimate objective of rehabilitation programs is to reduce the incidence and prevalence of recidivism. Thus, criminology is benefiting from evaluation research, benefits which have been achieved for decades by other social policy areas such as education and health.

IMPORTANCE OF RESEARCH IN CRIMINOLOGY

The importance of research in criminology and the criminal justice system cannot be overemphasized. Crime is everybody's business as everybody is at risk of becoming a victim of crime at any time. Research not only provides information for planning, policy and program development, but it also provides data and analysis which enhance our understanding of crime and criminal minds and enable practitioners to work actively to reduce recidivism (re-offending). At a time where the incidence and prevalence of crime and criminal activity are increasing and becoming rife in most countries around the world, criminological research assumes even higher importance. Most law enforcement authorities are striving hard and allocating resources to fight crime. Effective criminological research is essential if not "sine qua non" in the fight against crime in all countries. Evidence from criminological research continues to be used to inform decision making and to support drastic measures and/or strategies to fight crime.

Criminological research is a major source of knowledge on the nature and types of crimes as well as prominent or leading crimes in all jurisdictions, the social, economic, political and psychological impact or cost of crime is rising as overall criminal activity increases. By collecting, analyzing and presenting information on levels and types of crime, patterns and trends are established, paving the way for an enhanced understanding of crime. A good understanding of crime means an improved capacity to develop policies and programs to fight crime and, hence, the importance of research in criminology.. Besides, identifying major crime areas enhances funding decision making, facilitates planning and resources allocation, and provides evidence for the prioritization of programs, facilities and funding.

The increasing importance of evaluation research in the criminal justice systems around the world underscores the overall importance of criminological research. Evaluation research has become significant, not only is it improving programs and policies to reduce recidivism, but it is also important in ensuring the efficiency and effectiveness of preventive measures to stop the onset of criminal activity.

Another area where criminological research is playing a very useful role is punishment. Criminological research has been investigating the best approaches to establishing a balance between punishment and humane treatment of convicted criminals. Most victims of crime would like to see offenders punished severely for their crimes, but there is another side to the story. In the criminal justice system, there is a school of thought which emphasizes treatment and rehabilitation, and some criminological researchers are interested in research which continuously focuses on striking the right balance between punishment and rehabilitation, with a view to achieving the maximum outcomes for reducing crime and protecting the society. Different types of punishment exist in most countries, and include fines, probation, community service, home detention, periodic detention, and prison. Criminological research which focuses on punishment is helping to establish the best or rather most effective punishment for different crimes, without losing sight of the need to protect the community and rehabilitate offenders.

This book provides a comprehensive step by step practical approach to criminological research, covering most of the available research methodologies. In one book, the reader finds information on the importance of criminological research, sources of data, the General Research Process, qualitative and quantitative research methodologies, evaluation research in criminology, ethical issues in criminological research, designing and asking questions in criminological research, the implications of research and other methodologies. These topics are covered in subsequent chapters of the book.

Chapter 2

AREAS COMMON TO ALL CRIMINOLOGICAL RESEARCH METHODOLOGIES

Two important areas which are common to the various research methodologies are discussed in this chapter, namely sources of data for criminological research and the general research process. All criminological research use data – previously collected as in existing or secondary data or newly collected during the research (primary data). Some themes and procedures are common or fundamental to all criminological research methodologies in one way or the other, and these are embodied in what this book calls the General Research Process and what other researchers have called the Basic Research Process. The point is that various aspects of the General Research Process are discernible in the processes involved in criminological research irrespective of methodology (quantitative, qualitative, case study or evaluation research).

TYPES AND SOURCES OF DATA FOR CRIMINOLOGICAL RESEARCH

The discussion of sources of data occurs in two ways. First it focuses on types of crime and the data involved, and this is followed by where the data are found.

Types of Data

Data for criminological research are numerous and diverse, and come from a variety of sources. Data for criminological research include data on the incidence of crime, arrests, the laying of charges and prosecution, finding of guilt, punishment, and rehabilitation. Crime data include types of crime – major or minor, crimes against the person, crimes against property etc. Crime types are specific and include murder and manslaughter, sexual assault including rape, burglary, robbery and theft as well as crimes against property such as arson and other criminal damages to property. Data on the frequency and distribution of these crimes across geographical areas together with information on the socio-economic and demographic characteristics of the perpetrators of crime constitute a useful source of information for criminological research.

The number of offenders who are arrested and their demographic and related socio-economic characteristics provide useful sources of data for the analysis of offenders. These types of data also provide further insights into the interrelationships between the characteristics of offenders and types of crime, enhancing our understanding or criminal minds and criminal activity which, in turn, facilitates policy and program development to fight crime. So also do data on charges and prosecution. Indeed, information on arrests, charges and prosecution permit analyses such as the proportion of arrests which result in charges being laid, the number and proportion of people charged who are prosecuted, the proportion of successful prosecutions and so on, hence the importance of data on arrests, charges laid and prosecution (Brathwaite and Yeboah, 2004).

There is a whole group or criminological researchers whose interests focus on what is called finding of guilt. Finding of guilt relates to the processes of laying charges, prosecution, defense and the verdict, together with the provisions in the criminal justice system and the legal statutes which facilitate the process and guide all the parties involved (the Judiciary, Prosecution and Defense). A number of human rights groups are also interested in these processes to ensure that due process is followed and that the processes and procedures provide fairness and justice to all the parties involved especially the accused and their defense teams.

Data on courtroom practices, the number and proportion of accused granted bail and refused bail, the number and proportion of offenders who receive legal aid or public defense or free legal representation, the number and proportion of the accused who represent themselves and the associated reasons for self-representation, access or non-access to pre-bargain, freedom to change legal representation, opportunity to enter a plea etc provide data for the analysis of finding of guilt and other practices in the criminal justice systems.

Punishment analysis use data on the different forms of punishment available to the Bench, namely warning, probation, fines, house arrests or home detention, periodic detention, and incarceration in prison for diverse terms. In some countries, there are provisions for the Bench to order convicted criminals to a term of residence in a rehabilitation center or facility. While the types of punishment vary within and across countries, they all pursue the balance between punishment and rehabilitation. In countries such as New Zealand, Australia, Canada and the United States most of the punishment options outlined above are available. In other countries, such as the United Arab Emirates (UAE), Barbados, Ghana and other developing countries, the main form of punishment is incarceration in prison, albeit some of the other options may be used to a limited or lesser extent. Another punishment option in the UAE and some other Arab countries is what is locally called "lashes". Convicted offenders may be sentenced to 50 or 100 lashes for selected offences including the consumption of alcohol. Data on the types of punishment enable policy makers to identify and improve upon the sentencing and punishment patterns and trends. It also allows human rights groups to undertake analysis and present evidence to support their case where inhumane or unfair treatment of offenders is seen to exist in the criminal justice system. Sentencing and punishment patterns will, by and large, vary by country and is pretty much defined by the legal and criminal justice institutions and policies of each country.

Sight should not be lost of the data from rehabilitation programs. Most countries have provisions for the establishment of rehabilitation programs and services either within the confines of the prison or within the community or both. With a number of countries experiencing high incidence and prevalence of crime and especially recidivism, the need for rehabilitation has never been more important. Data from rehabilitation programs are necessary for the analysis and establishment of the contribution of rehabilitation to reducing recidivism, albeit they also contribute to punishment and probation analysis, as most convicted criminals released on probation are sometimes ordered to receive treatment or rehabilitation.

Where Are the Data Found?

The actual sources of information for studies of subjects or topics of interests to criminological research fall within two broad groups, namely administrative records and special studies. Administrative information in a number of government and non government departments and/or agencies includes various criminological data. Public sector agencies notably the Police, Courts and Corrections or Prisons, record and maintain data on offenders, types of crime, arrests, prosecution and punishment including fines and prison sentences. It is becoming increasingly notable in criminological research that government sources of information are now more predominant than any other source of secondary criminological data. The information kept includes not only the type of crime and kind of sentence after successful prosecution, but also information on the socio-economic and demographic characteristics of the offenders and, sometimes, their victims.

Police data constitute the single largest source of data on crime and criminal activity in all counties, and include probably the most detailed information on crime.. Data in Police records usually show the number and type of reported cases, their frequency and geographical distribution within police jurisdictions, actions taken and decisions made, number and proportion of reported cases prosecuted and outcomes etc. Needless to state that, in many countries, a large number of crimes, by and large, go unreported and crime data held and maintained by the Police, therefore, do not depict the exact level and nature of crime.

A glance at the administrative records of Courts in every country will reveal among other information, data on offenders appearing before the Courts, their socio- economic and demographic characteristics, the type of crime they were charged with and prosecuted for, finding of guilt and verdict. Like the Police data, Court data will also include date and, most likely, the time the offence was committed. Socio-economic data in both the Police and Court databases include age, gender and related demographical data, marital status, occupational, employment and industry status as well as educational attainment including the highest level of education completed. There is also information on each offender with regards to reoffending and the patterns and trends in reoffending as well as the type of crime committed each time. Data on sentences and sentencing patterns are best obtained from the Courts, especially given the wide variety of sentencing options available to the Bench these days.

Ministries and Departments of Corrections in individual countries are the leading sources of data on punishments such as periodic detention, home detention, incarceration in prison and offender rehabilitation within prisons. In countries where community corrections and prison come under one administrative department of Corrections, such as New Zealand, the Department of Corrections also has the most up to date and detailed information on all forms of punishment including probation and rehabilitation (within and outside of the confines of prison).

Prisons and Prison Departments have data on the number and characteristics of inmates, average daily numbers and changes therein over time, the types of offences committed by the criminals, the dates of entry and exit from the corrections facility, release on probation and conditions of release together with data on prison based rehabilitation programs. Many prisons around the world develop and implement inmate rehabilitation and employment programs and keep data on these programs, especially the number of inmates attending each rehabilitation program and completing rates (proportion of participants completing all aspects of each program), the number and proportion of inmates participating in the employment programs and so on.

The Police, Courts and Corrections or Prisons together constitute one of the leading sources of administrative data for criminological research. There are variations among countries as regards the collection and compilation of data. In many countries, there is one police force, unitary Court system, and one Corrections or Prisons Department collecting and compiling information on crime, arrests, prosecution and punishment, A case in point is New Zealand, Ghana, and Barbados, where there is one police force, a unitary courts system and one prison department overseeing crime and punishment within the country, albeit they have regional branches or offices.

In contrast, there are countries like Australia, Canada, the United Arab Emirates and the United States where there are different State Police forces, various levels of State and Territory Departments of Courts, as well as State Corrections or Prison administration. In countries with federated systems of government and where States, Provinces and Territories have responsibility for crime and punishment, a lot of the detailed crime and punishment data are held by the State government agencies. In some jurisdictions, such as the United States and Canada, there are City Police forces, which maintain law and order within cities. They also have responsibility for collecting and maintaining information on crime and punishment within their individual jurisdictions (e; g; Edmonton Police in the City of Edmonton, in the Provence of Alberta, Canada, or New York Police Department).

In many of these countries, there are national Police forces or some other public agency which compiles information at the national level, but the detail of the data held may not be at the same level as the data held in State, Territory of Provencial administrative records. In Australia, There is the Australian Federal Police (AFP), while Canada has the Royal Canadian Mounted Police (RMCP), and both agencies are major sources of crime data at the national level.

Other Public/Government Agencies

In addition to the principal crime agencies described in the preceding paragraphs, there are many other government agencies which directly or indirectly hold information on crime and punishment within countries. Ministries or Departments of Justice in individual countries and various national security agencies within countries keep diverse information on crime and criminal activity. There are also agencies which hold a variety of data on the population including criminals. These include social policy agencies which collect information of interest to criminological research, such as data on housing and employment for criminal convicts released from prison after serving a term of imprisonment.

National statistical agencies, such as Statistics New Zealand and the Australia Bureau of Statistics, collect, compile and publish data on crime from time to time. A case in point is the Australian Bureau of Statistics which published information on crime in its 2007 Annual Statistical Report on Australia. Information usually published by National Statistical Organizations cover crime statistics including types of crime committed during the year, average weekly or daily prison numbers and characteristics of offenders. They tend to identify major or leading crimes and sometimes distribution by geographical areas as well as distribution or criminals by age and gender.

Non Government Agencies

Criminological research data are also available in the administrative records of some non governmental agencies which provide services for convicted offenders serving community sanctions and probation, as well as agencies providing rehabilitation services for offenders sentenced to rehabilitation or released from prison on probation with a condition to attend rehabilitation .programs. Around the world, there are a number of agencies which provide diverse assistance to prisoners during the period of incarceration as well as after their release from prison, organizations such as New Zealand Prisoners Aid and Rehabilitation Society (NZPARS). Most collect and compile information on the socio-economic characteristics of the convicted criminals who participate in their programs, the crimes they committed, the types of sentences served and their family and cultural backgrounds.

Special Studies

A lot of data for criminological research come from special studies undertaken by researchers. Special studies, such as surveys, participant observation, special case studies and even program evaluation, by and large collect and provide new data for criminological research. For example, sample surveys, designed and implemented to collect information on specific subjects/topics, tend to provide new data on the subject matter. Besides, surveys on topics such as fear of crime, victims' experiences in the criminal justice systems, Police procedures and victimization surveys have been undertaken in many countries including the United States, Britain, Australia and Barbados (Brathwaite and Yeboah, 2004; Yeboah and Brathwaite, 2007). These studies have tended to provide diverse and useful data for further criminological research

The notion that special studies consist of only surveys is a myth. In particular, participant observation (covert or overt), and program evaluation research are important special studies usually undertaken in criminology. Around the world, qualitative researchers are regularly investigating different criminal justice topics, using qualitative methodologies including focus groups. That said, it is necessary to add that quantitative studies using survey research methodologies have traditionally been the leading source special studies data for specific topics or subject matter.

Most of these special studies are the subject matter of subsequent chapters of this book and will be discussed in detail at appropriate parts of the book. Participant observation and focus group methodologies are presented in chapter 3, survey research methodologies in chapter four and program evaluation in chapter five.

THE GENERAL RESEARCH PROCESS

As indicated in the preface and later chapters in this book, criminological researchers use a number of diverse but sometimes interrelated methodologies. The General Research Process shows the procedures and stages involved in criminological research irrespective of the methodology being used. The basic components of this General Research Process are evident in one way or the other in all criminological research methodologies and, hence, the importance of discussing it earlier in this book. Whether a criminological researcher is investigating a particular issue or problem using qualitative or qualitative methodologies, the components of the General Research Process are involved. The procedures of the General Research Process are also evident in investigations using evaluation research methodologies or case studies.

There is a number of logical and sequential stages involved n the General Research Process. It is essential to stress that these so called stages need to be followed in sequential order so as to ensure the successful completion of the specific criminological investigation or research. Broadly speaking, there are 7 basic stages or steps in the General Research Process. These are:

1. Identification and definition of the problem.
2. Review of previously published literature.
3. Identification and definition of research questions or hypothesis.
4. Identification and selection of an appropriate research design.
5. Implementation of the selected research design.
6. Analysis and interpretation of the data collected during the implementation of the research design.
7. Presentation of the results or findings.

Identification and Definition of the Problem, Issue or Subject Matter

Criminological research usually involves investigations into a specific problem, issue or subject matter. The first stage in the research process is to identify what the problem or issue is. In other words, what is being investigated or rather what should be investigated? What is the subject matter for the specific data collection, analysis and reporting? The subject matter of criminological research is not always a problem as such, albeit the usual or commonly used terminology in the first stage of the research process is the problem. For example criminological research can focus on victims' experiences in the criminal justice system, or the evaluation of assessment procedures for parole decision making.

Many a time, criminological research tends to address a specific problem. For example, a research may collect, analyze and present information on why crime is rising. In this case the problem is increasing criminal activity. Again a criminological researcher may study criminal minds with a view to finding out why offenders commit crime. While it may appear technically correct not to use the term problem identification in all criminological research, practitioners and researchers over the years have come to conventionally call the issue or subject matter the problem.

The key point is to establish clearly what is being researched or investigated. It is important to get this right because the details of subsequent stages in the General Research Process will generally depend on the identification of the problem or the subject matter of the research. The subject matter , problem or issue usually arise from diverse sources including existing policies on the topic and their impact on the community (both offenders and victims) or it could emerge from disagreements in the community or among practitioners, recommendations from previous research, request from funding agencies or directives from governments or government agencies. In addition, one government policy can lead to many questions being raised as part of its impact or ineffectiveness, presupposing a need for further investigation into the area covered by the policy. Also, community outrage over a particular parole or sentencing decision can serve as a catalyst to stimulate research into sentencing patterns or trends.

However, a substantial proportion of criminological research arises or emerges from previous and ongoing studies. A researcher may undertake investigations into a topic and subsequently find at the end that there are areas for further investigation. These then become the researcher's next research focus. Other researchers and practitioners see the work and also find areas for further research which have not been covered or which have been inadequately covered.

All told, the first stage in the criminological research process is to define the subject matter of the study, what has come to be called the problem. Once this is done, the researcher can proceed to other stages in the General Research Process making sure that what happens in subsequent stages are first appropriate for addressing the problem and that the stages are linked and focused on the said problem or issue.

Review of Previously Published and Unpublished Literature

No research investigates a topic or problem for which there is no other related or previous work. It is not uncommon to undertake a study which has never been done in a specific geographical area, but it could have been undertaken in another geographical location. For example a criminological researcher in a developing country such as Ghana, Vietnam or St Lucia may be investigating victimization and find that this has never been undertaken in that country. This does not mean that there is no previous work to examine, review or draw insights from.

The point is that such a study could have been undertaken in an adjourning country or in other countries outside the region. While not directly relevant in terms of the demographic, social and economic characteristics of the study country, relevant studies in other countries could still shed some lights and provide further insights into what has been done elsewhere, the problems that might have been encountered, how they were overcome and the results obtained. Even so, many a time, researchers find that there is a previous study of the topic even in the study country.

By reviewing the literature, the criminological researcher is able to discern what has been done on the topic, area and depth of coverage, the exact findings and so on. More importantly, the researcher is able to identify areas, within the broad topic, which are conspicuously missing in the previous research and plan and establish the priorities of the new study accordingly. Even where the researcher is replicating a previous study, a review of the literature on that previous work will provide ammunition for strong and informed decisions on hypothesis and research design including data collection and analysis instruments and which parts of the results/findings should be emphasized.

When reviewing the literature on previous studies, the object should be to find answers to a number of questions including the following:

1. What did the study investigate?
2. What research designs were used?
3. What problems were encountered?
4. How were the problems resolved?
5. What did the study find? What were the results of the investigation?
6. What conclusions were drawn from the results or findings?
7. Did the study identify areas for further research or investigation?
8. Are the identified areas for further study relevant to the current investigation?

Not every study will provide the necessary information to address the above questions. A few will provide information on areas for further research, some will mention problems encountered and how they were overcome, but most will identify the problem, methodologies, results and conclusions. Answers to some or all of the above questions should assist in defining the problem or central issue of the new study, the research questions or hypotheses and the selection of the research design. They may also help avoid repeating mistakes made in previous studies, identify and resolve potential problems in executing the study design, and improve upon the overall performance of the research design and research instruments.

Research Questions or Hypothesis

The next stage in the General Research Process is to refine the problem by making it precise and straight to the point. This is done by clearly identifying a number of research questions to be addressed in the investigation or by developing and stating clearly the hypothesis or hypotheses to be tested in the investigation.

It is essential to ask the correct research questions otherwise the findings may not be effective in addressing the problem, topic or issue initially identified and defined in the first stage of the General Research Process. The basic principles in establishing effective research questions are simplicity and clarity. The questions must be worded such that they attract clear responses for the study. They must also be clear, concise or precise to pin point the types of responses they are expected to attract without any ambiguity (see chapter 8 for more information on asking questions). Questions such as what exactly is being investigated? Or what is the exact issue or problem for which information is sought are useful.

Sometimes, criminological researchers replace research questions with hypothesis. A hypothesis is simply a line of thinking about the relationships between the variables in the study that the researcher intends to test. It usually involves statements indicating the relationship between the variables in one way or the other. For example, a researcher investigating re-offending could have a hypothesis which goes like the following: Convicted young offenders who receive rehabilitation therapy during the period of incarceration in juvenile detention facilities are less likely to recidivate than convicted older offenders who receive the same treatment. There are two types of hypothesis in a study. The first is what is called the null hypothesis and the second is the alternative hypothesis. The null hypothesis is the hypothesis which says there is no difference between the subgroups of the study population, i.e. nothing is happening and no relationship exists. The second hypothesis, alternative hypothesis states the line of thinking of the researcher and proposes that differences exist between the subgroups. It is the hypothesis that the researcher wants to prove, albeit the research data and analysis must first disprove and reject the null hypothesis. The second hypothesis is, therefore, sometimes referred to as the research hypothesis.

The researcher then proceeds with data collection, analysis and interpretation to test both the null and the alternative hypotheses. The usual practice is to find evidence to dismiss and reject the null hypothesis, and follow it up with analysis and evidence to support and prove the research hypothesis, i.e. show if the statement embodied in the hypothesis is true as evidenced from the available data. If the statement emerges to be true and ably supported by the evidence, then there is a Yes Hypothesis. Developing hypothesis may appear daunting for many researchers, albeit that should not be the case. The most effective way to approach the concept and define good hypotheses is to ask questions such as what is being tested and/or what is the likely relationship between the selected variables? A clear line of thinking must be developed and defined as discussed in the preceding paragraph.

Identification and Selection of an Appropriate Design

After defining the problem or topic, reviewing the existing literature and establishing research questions or hypothesis, the next sequential stage in the General Research Process is the identification and selection of an appropriate research design. This is a very tricky stage because the selected research design should allow for the testing of the stated hypotheses .The selected design must also throw more light on and improve the knowledge and understanding of the subject matter.

The selected design should include data collection instruments, data analysis techniques and reporting procedures, what is called together research methodology. Subsequent chapters in this book focus on the diverse research methodologies available to criminological researchers, and only a brief outline is presented here. The available criminological research methodologies include qualitative methods, quantitative methods, case studies, evaluation research, documentary research, experiments and special assessment methodologies to investigate crime and the thinking of offenders as well as other issues in the criminal justice system. Qualitative research methods involve methodologies which are by definition non quantitative and include participant observation methodologies, while the main instrument of quantitative methodology is the sample survey.

The key point is to identify and select the methodology or methodologies which appear appropriate for the circumstances of the researcher and the specific investigation or study (chapter nine). The methodology is deemed appropriate if it is effective in addressing the objectives of the study and in answering the research questions or providing evidence to dismiss the null hypothesis and prove the alternative hypothesis. Other factors to consider in selecting the most appropriate or suitable methodology are cost and funds available, human resources, the ease with which data can be obtained and analyzed, the impact of socio-cultural issues in relation to the community or the study population and so on.

As discussed later in this book, every research methodology has its own advantages and disadvantages, while each methodology lends itself better to specific investigations. Some methodologies are particularly expensive, albeit most research methodologies have varying cost implications. The onus is on the researcher to assess all the advantages and disadvantages, the specific characteristics of the research or investigation and the context of the research (including population and socio-cultural characteristics, cost, funding, the availability of skills required to effectively use a specific methodology) and undertake the investigation.

There are trends in applied criminological research to use multiple research methodologies in what is called triangulation (Patton, 1990). This approach is becoming increasingly important these days because most researchers want to thoroughly investigate the topic and using more than one methodology appears to create avenues for the collection of diverse information on the topic. Proponents of triangulation argue further that triangulation produces more scientific evidence on the problem or issue being investigated and that, in that respect, the benefits outweigh any additional costs of using more than one methodology. It is important not to use each method in the specific triangulation shallowly or superficially. Each methodology involved n the triangulation should have adequate depth to contribute to the data and analysis required. Otherwise the data collected and analyzed are likely to be inadequate for thorough investigation of the subject matter.More rigorous and scientific data are obtained f the criminological research adopts what is called the Scientific Method. The Scientific Method is a series of logical steps which, if followed, allow for the minimization of values, biases and errors in the research and improve data quality and the performanace of the research insruments

Implementation of the Research Design

The logical sequence after deciding on the research design is to implement the selected design. This is to say carry out the research. Carrying out the research involves implementing decisions and procedures on all the parameters of the study including human resources, data collection procedures, assembling and analysis of the data collected etc. In short, this stage is the point where the actual investigation begins.

Every design is different, albeit similarities may be discernible in some cases. This also means that the implementation will vary according to the design. The key point is to collect, analyze and present data as defined in the selection of the design stage. Carrying out the research is a very essential phase. Mistakes made here are likely to affect the results and the outcome of the study. It appears advisable to adhere to the decisions and procedures, unless difficulties arise with some aspects of it to warrant modification as a corrective action.

It is during this phase that the data collection instruments are developed, finalized and implemented, even if a qualitative study is being undertaken. For example, if the research is quantitative, this is the stage where data collection personnel are trained and sent into the field to interview or otherwise collect information. If a qualitative study is being undertaken, this is the point where the researcher collects data using participant observation methodologies (overt or covert).and focus groups. Again, this is the stage where data collected using qualitative or quantitative methodologies, case study or evaluation research are assembled, essential data identified and separated from unnecessary or unneeded data which are subsequently pushed to the background. Data should not be discarded at this point, as data which may appear less useful initially may become important over time and as the analysis proceeds in the next stage.

The stage of carrying out the research goes further than the initial data collection and covers return visits for additional data, clarification of unclear data, and finding answers to any problems (expected or unexpected) that emerge during the implementation of the research. It is at this stage that much of the research funds is used, with funding outlays varying according to the specific research design or designs and whether more than one methodology is used.

Analysis and Interpretation of Data and Results

Decisions on what analysis will be undertaken are usually made during the selection of the research design and implemented during this phase. In practice, it is not unusual for criminological researchers to modify the analytical tools and measures previously determined. This is because criminological research usually involves human beings and human behavior is, by and large, unpredictable or difficult to predict. Responses to specific questions in survey research or focus groups and observations made in participant observation may be congruent to what was expected by the researcher. As a consequence, changes become necessary and previously identified analytical procedures may therefore be subject to changes

This stage of analysis of data, interpreting the analysis and putting results together is very important and must be carefully undertaken. It is during this stage that the researcher attempts to make a sense of all the data collected and analyzed. It is here that the researcher interprets the results or findings from the analysis. The point is that funding agencies, policy makers and practitioners are mainly interested in the findings or results, how they are interpreted, and subsequent conclusions. Thus the interpretation of the results must be undertaken carefully and correctly, without any personal or other prejudice (Scientific Method). All conclusions must be drawn on the basis of the evidence as presented by the analysis and interpretation of the results. A key element of the interpretation is determining the implications of the results for policy formulation, development and implementation as well as the implications for program development and delivery and so on,

Presentation or Reporting of Results

This is the final stage in the General Research Process, characterized by preparation of reports, articles for publications in journals, newspapers and other outlets. It is also the sage where the researcher provides feedback to respondents and funding agencies. Sometimes, the results are presented at conferences, public lectures and workshops. It is not uncommon for researchers to prepare and produce a number of reports for various interest groups. The researcher's job is not completed simply by producing the report. It is during this final phase that the researcher also receives feedback which can be unpleasant sometimes. Sometimes the researcher has to defend the methodologies used, data analysis and interpretation made and the conclusions drawn. That said, it must be pointed out that most research findings are usually well received with minor queries.

Additional Information

With the two essential elements of research common to all methodologies discussed, subsequent chapters of the book proceed to discuss individual methodologies in greater detail. At this point and prior to discussing the detailed features of the research methodologies, it may appear important to examine the differences between the two main research methodologies, i.e. qualitative research methodologies and quantlitative research methodologies.

The notion that qualitative research methodologies are non statistical and does not involve any quantitative or statistical analysis at all is not actually correct in its entirety. So also is the notion that qualitative research methodologies cannot use sampling procedures. Qualitative methodologies have the capacity to use a sample and to analyze data using basic statistical techniques including basic measures of central tendency and basic measures of dispersion. For example in a qualitative study of inmates of a rehabilitation facility using focus groups, the researcher may choose a small group of the inmates to observe (a sample of the rehabilitation facility residents). The researcher may also use basic statistics in the analysis including average age of participants, percentage or proportion of participants who behaved in a particular way or leaned more to a particular therapy etc. By definition, qualitative research methodologies involve small groups of subjects and do not ground themselves in advanced statistical analysis, such as those associated with survey research.

So what are the fundamental differences between these two leading methodologies? The main difference lies in the mode of data collection. Qualitative research is sometimes called observational research simply because of the way data are obtained. In qualitative research methodologies, the researcher observes, i.e. looks, listens and records what is happening. In survey research, the usual practice is to use a pre-designed questionnaire (called instruments) to obtain data from the study population either through direct face to face or telephone interviewing or self completion of the questionnaires by the study population. Thus qualitative research methodologies provide direct first hand practical knowledge to the researcher through the actual observation of the event or behavior.

In contrast, quantitative researchers do not actually see the occurrence of the event, neither do they observe firsthand the behavior of the respondents. They ask questions about the event after it had occurred and sometimes before it occurs. For example, a quantitative researcher studying the patterns of criminal activity of a group of convicted offenders can ask them questions about what offences they committed and why they committed the said offences (after the event). They may also ask the offenders about their potential future criminal activity, using questions such as the following (i.e. before the event): Do you think you will re-offend in the future? Are you sure that you will not return to jail again? Whether, questions are asked about a future event or past event, quantitative research methodologies do not allow for the occurrence of the actual event to be observed by the researcher.

Another salient difference lies in the interpretation and generalization of findings in the two broad methodologies. In quantitative research, the deductive approach prevails, while in qualitative research methodologies, the approach is mainly inductive. Proponents of qualitative research assert that, due to its data collection approach, quantitative researchers are assuming that they know what is important by designing data collection instruments based on what they identify as important. Thus, the deductive approach works from the outside of the event and obtains information from outside the occurrence of the event to draw conclusions and generalize (i.e. after the event has occurred or before the event occurs). On the other hand, in qualitative research, the researcher observes, listens, records and uses the actual information collected during the during the occurrence of the event to define what is importante and to draw conclusions.

Thus, in qualitative analysis, the researcher collects the data first before determining any line of thinking in relation to what is important and what is not. The definition of what is important is coming from within (inductive), while in quantitative research methodologies, what is important is pre-defined and embodied in the research instruments prior to the collection of data (deductive).

More information on the advantages and disadvantages of quantitative and qualitative research methodologies are found in chapters three and four.

Further Reading

Brathwaite, F. S., and D. A. Yeboah (2004): Victims of crime in the criminal justice system of Barbados. Journal of Criminal Justice, Vol. 32, No. 2: 431-442

Patton, M. Q. (1990): Designing qualitative studies: Qualitative evaluation and research methods. London, Sage Publications.

Yeboah, D. A., and F. S. Brathwaite(2007): The nature and impact of criminization in Barbados. The Journal of Ethnicity in Criminal Justice, Vol. 2, No. 5: 55-77

Box 2.1. Summary of Sources of data

1.   Official statistics (Secondary Data), mainly government agencies including
   (a) The Police
   (b) Ministries or Departments of Justice, Prisons, Corrections and Courts
   (c) National Statistical organizations such as Statistics New Zealand or the Australian Bureau of Statistics
   (d) Institutional libraries
2.   Non government sources (Secondary Data)
   (a)   Community based program and service providers (rehabilitation etc)
   (b)   Advocacy groups for prisoners and offenders such as the New Zealand Prisoners Aid and Rehabilitation Society (NZPARS)
   (c)   Other community groups
3.   Special studies (Primary Data)
   (a) Sample surveys (crime, victims etc)
   (b) Program evaluation

Box 2.1. (Continued)

Case study
(c) Prison census
4.   International and regional organizations
(a) United Nations Office for Drugs and Crime

Chapter 3

QUALITATIVE RESEARCH METHODOLOGIES

In this chapter, a detailed discussion of qualitative research methodologies is presented. To ensure consistency throughout the book, the discussion on each specific research methodology focuses on clearly identified headings as follows:

1. Description - what is it?
2. Approaches, practices or processes.
3. Measurements.
4. Analysis and interpretation of data.
5. Advantages and disadvantages.

These headings have been selected to provide a comprehensive coverage of each methodology used by criminological researchers and as identified in this book. With regards to description, an attempt is made to answer the question what are qualitative research methodologies? Within this heading of description, the attributes of qualitative research methodologies are also discussed .The process of collecting the data and the role of the researcher are presented under practices and approaches. How the data collected in qualitative research are measured or operationalized are discussed together with data analysis and interpretation. Measurements and analysis are discussed as part of the stages in undertaking qualitative research. Finally, the advantages (merits) and disadvantages (demerits) of qualitative research methodologies are presented. The discussion of advantages and disadvantages goes further to identify the types of investigations or studies to which qualitative research methodologies lend themselves better.

DESCRIPTION OF QUALITATIVE RESEARCH METHODOLOGIES

Qualitative research methodologies are also called field and/or observational studies. They have evolved over time as a number of researchers seek methodologies which would allow them to observe the actual occurrence of the event and/or the behavior.. As discussed previously, it is the type of methodology in which the researchers directly observe what is happening, listen and record what is occurring together with what is being said by the participants. There are two main types of qualitative methodologies, namely focus groups and participant observation, the latter is used synonymously with qualitative research methodologies. Qualitative research methodologies are characterized by small group studies.

FOCUS GROUPS

Most students and researchers of criminology have heard about focus groups. Using focus groups research to collect data on a subject in criminology is a qualitative research methodology. Focus groups methodology is the type of research in which data are obtained from a selected group of not more than 15 persons from the relevant interest group. The researcher convenes a meeting of the group and uses a series of logically sequential questions to obtain the data. Most topics in the criminal justice system can be investigated or researched using focus group methodology including support programs for victims of crime or the assessment of the effectiveness of rehabilitation programs.

Focus group methodology is a qualitative research methodology which involves interviewing the focus group members. This is distinct from the other popular qualitative research methodology, participant observation, in which data are obtained from the observation of the behavior. Focus group methodology lends itself better to the collection of data on subjective views, perceptions and attitudes in the criminal justice system. Both focus group and participant observation methodologies involve small study groups (compared with survey research) As it involves interviewing, the researcher must have a prepared set of questions to ask the study subjects, and in this respect it is closer to survey research than participant observation (both involve asking questions). It is often the practice in focus group methodology for the criminological researcher to convene meetings of the group and pose the questions to the members during those meetings. A salient feature of focus group methodology is the development of protocols for the meetings, i.e. rules and procedures for the meetings.

The following example will illustrate the practice of focus group research methodology. A researcher is studying the economic impact of victimization. The researcher establishes a focus group of 12 victims and convenes a meeting. The researcher uses a prepared set of questions to obtain data from the focus group, such as:

> What type of crime was perpetrated against you?
> Did you lose a valuable item?
> What was the cost of the item?
> Were the lost items covered by insurance?
> How much reimbursement did you receive from your insurance company?
> How much money did you personally lose?

The research can probe further on responses received on any of the questions to obtain in-depth data. One or more people can dominate the proceedings and different respondents may answer different questions. There is, therefore, no standard data on all respondents (further information on standard data is at chapter four).However the methodology has the potential to produces detailed data on the economic impact of victimization from the study population, i.e. the focus group members. Like other research methodologies, the researcher or interviewer collects data, and any mistakes on their part can and will influence the results. The skills of the researcher or interviewer in asking linguistically and culturally appropriate questions are essential for the successful data collection using focus groups methodology. So also is the ability of the researcher or interviewer to relate well to and deal appropriately with the specific focus group.

Focus group methodology has the advantage of allowing more probing to be carried out and, as a result, the collection of more in-depth and/or detailed data on the subject matter There is also a degree of flexibility in that the researcher or interviewer can briefly ignore the protocols to ask further questions on the responses provided as and when necessary.. Focus group methodology is comparatively cheaper than survey methodology, for example. It also has the added advantage of being effective in studying topics about which little is known. One useful advantage which has not received adequate recognition is that focus group methodology can be used to collect data or develop ideas which can assist in the development of questionnaires for subsequent studies of the topic.

The main disadvantage is that focus group has not been adequately assessed or evaluated as a research methodology. If there is a very vocal member in the focus group, that person can dominate proceedings and, thus, skewing the results. For illustration, in the example above about the economic costs/impact of victimization, one person, say Victim A, can dominate proceedings making the data reflect more the impact on person or Victim A, and overshadowing the impact of crime on the other respondents. This domination can also affect the reliability of focus group methodology. Furthermore, data from focus groups can be misleading as data obtained from the same focus groups at different times and meetings on the same topic may yield widely varied responses.

Besides, it is increasingly very difficult to attempt to use the results from focus group studies for external generalization due to the small numbers involved and the potential bias of the results in favor of one or two vocal and dominating respondents.. Yet another weakness is that, even though focus group methodology involves interviewing, it does not produce standard data on all respondents. Unlike survey research in which all respondents answer the same questions, the situation is different in focus group methodology because respondents are not required to answer the same questions.

PARTICIPANT OBSERVATION

A common terminology used interchangeably with qualitative research methodologies is what has become known as participant observation. The variations in this research methodology center on how the researcher interacts with the subjects or participants and whether the participants are aware of what the researcher is doing. There are two practices in participant observation methodology. In the first practice, the researcher participates in the behavior or event and, in the second, the researcher does not actually participate in the behavior, but instead stands outside of the subjects and observes their behavior and what is happening.

Further distinction can be made between overt and covert participant observation methodologies. Where the researcher participates in the event and duly advises the subjects about the research and what the researcher is doing, the observation is usually referred to as overt participant observation. In the event that the researcher participates in what the subjects are doing, but does not disclose the research and the researcher's role, the methodology is referred to as covert participant observation; in other words the researcher is secretly or clandestinely collecting information from the subjects without their knowledge and/or awareness of what is going on.

The point must also be made that overt and covert participant observation occurs regardless of the researcher participation status. Even if the researcher does not participate in the behavior, the observation of behavior can be overt or covert. The key point is disclosure and whether the researcher informs the participants about the research.. If the researcher does not participate in the behavior or event but tells the participants about the research, that is overt participant observation. Similarly, if the researcher does not participate in the behavior, stands outside of the group but does not inform the participants about the research, the research is described as covert participant observation..

These days the use of covert participant observation methodologies is on the decline. The emergence of research ethics and the requirement placed on researchers to apply the highest ethical levels mean that researchers are increasingly being required to disclose their intentions to their study subjects. Detailed discussion of ethical issues in criminological research is at chapter seven.

Theory

A theory is a series of statements or propositions about a subject matter, which provides better understanding and, in some cases, offers possible explanation of the phenomenon or subject matter. The theoretical underpinnings of participant observation and related methodologies are the avoidance of bias. The inherent idea is to collect data without prejudice, preconceptions or initial data or even line of thinking about the event to be observed. The purpose is to allow for the collection and analysis of data on an event as it occurs naturally, and without prior judgment on what is important and what is not important. So the researcher goes in without any prior ideas, but looks, listens and records information on the subjects as the event occurs. It can safely be called "live data collection" because the behavior and the associated observation are occurring at the same time.. Participant observation research is characterized by the fact that the theories and generalizations which arise from the study actually emerge after the data have been collected and analyzed, not before as in survey research.

In participant observation research methodology, the situation can be described as a stage with the subjects being the actors (see also May, 2001). The researcher looks or observes the act, listens to their speeches and records accordingly. It is paramount for the subjects to talk if participant observation is to be successful. Where the participants are inhibited in one way or the other, they do not talk or act enough and adequate observation may not be made. Sometimes the subjects are shy or do not want to talk about their personal circumstances, and that, by definition, defeats the fundamental tenets of participant observation methodology. For example, many alcohol anonymous and drug anonymous groups have programs which are centered on participants disclosing openly their problem, why and how they arrived at their present situation and demonstrate a commitment to reform themselves.. If the participants refuse to disclose personal and sometimes intrusive information, the rehabilitation may not work. Researchers studying the specific rehabilitation program would not make adequate observation under those circumstances, and much more observation meetins would have to be arranged and organized, resulting in longer period of observation or data collection. Than previously anticipated and planned

The usual practice is for the participants to sit in a circle or something like that, facing each other and talking about themselves. The researcher gets data on a limited number of subjects if any participants refuse to talk or participate fully in the event and adverse effects on the results could occur.

Sometimes, participants talk but do not talk frankly and exclude essential information from their speeches. This can be very frustrating for the participant observation researcher mainly because this methodology allows for theories to be formulated and generalizations to be made only after data collection and analysis. Limited data means restricted analysis and limited possibilities for theory formulation.

It is worthy to mention that participant observation researchers sometimes put themselves at risk working under dangerous circumstances and situations. Imagine a researcher investigating the cognitive attitudes and thinking of convicted criminals serving a jail term. This type of study usually occurs to enable program developers to identify the needs of convicted criminals, understand why they offended or recidivate, and provide appropriate rehabilitation. The convicted offenders' behavior is by and large unpredictable and any of them could attack the researcher if they are not happy with anything the researchers says or does.

The risk is always there and there have been instances when researchers have been attacked by their study subjects, and criminological research is more prone to such attacks than many other disciplines in the social sciences. Where the researcher becomes intimidated, data collection becomes adversely affected and the study results may be compromised, with further potential impacts on the formulation of theories from the study. In the United States, United Kingdom, Australia and New Zealand, gang activity is rife both within and outside of prison. Researchers investigating gang related activities could be working dangerously and putting themselves at grave risk.

The Role of the Researcher

The role of the researcher is paramount in all research but more so in participant observation methodology. In survey research many people have parts to play including the researcher, interviewers, data entry personnel, subjects or respondents. In participant observation research, it is fundamentally the researcher and the participants. In particular, the researcher is solely responsible for data collection. The researcher has to look, listen and record what is happening, the behavior of the participants etc. Any mistake on the part of the researcher could be disastrous and adversely impact on the study and its outcomes. The researcher must win the trust of the participants who will then allow the researcher into their midst to observe the behavior. The researcher is in direct face to face contact with the participants, unlike survey research where questions could be mailed to respondents or interviewers trained and used to collect data without the researcher coming into direct contact with the subjects.

Like the situation with other methodologies, the participant observation researcher's role include problem identification, literature review, preparatory work including making arrangements for the study and contact with the participants, the selection and implementation of research design, data analysis, interpretation and reporting of results.

PROCESSES INVOLVED IN PARTICIPANT OBSERVATION RESEARCH

Participant observation is more unstructured than survey research, albeit a number of stages are discernible. The actual practice of participant observation research involves several stages and processes. Some of these are identical with the stages in the General Research Process, but many are unique to participant observation methodology. Participant observation methodology works on the basis of no preconceptions and/or bias. The researcher is starting from scratch, so to speak. Participant observation methodologies usually do not start with a theoretical basis or theory. The idea is derived from the observed data, and similar to grounded theory. Qualitative research methodologies ground their theories on the evidence from the specific data collection and analysis.

Qualitative research methodologies, such as participant observation, propose data collection and analysis first, allowing any theories or conclusions to be derived from the analysis and interpretation of the data collected, what was described in the previous chapter as induction or inductive logic. Allowing the collection, analysis and interpretation of data to determine any possible theory presupposes a need for a rigorous approach and a clear definition as well as adherence to the principles and stages involved in qualitative research. The research must be scientifically sound to allow for the derivation of theory from the data.

Participant observation methodologies do not examine simple relationships among variables. No variables are defined prior to data collection, and the researcher first observes and records data on the behavior or event. Variables and their interrelationships are derived and defined later. The point is that the subjects are all behaving together and the researcher must be sharp and quick to look, listen and record as the event unfolds. Pre-determination of variables is problematic because there is no prior knowledge of what the subjects are going to do or say, and a pre-defined variable may not feature al all in the behavior of the subjects during the observation. The usual practice, unique to participant observation, is to collect data on as many variables as possible and to sort the data later (separating those needed for the study from those data not essential or not needed for the specific study).

The stages involved in the step by step approach to participant observation study include:

1. Identifying the problem or issue.
2. Reviewing the existing literature.
3. Preparatory work.
4. Deciding the exact design – participant observation, overt or covert. Sampling.
5. Implementing the selected design.
6. Measurements.
7. Analyzing and interpreting the data.
8. Reporting of results.

Identifying the Topic or Problem

All research must have a purpose and the purpose defines what the research is about. In participant observation methodologies, the processes begin with an identification of the topic without any preconceived statement or biases. While participant observation works without initial biases, the researcher must define at this stage at least what is being explored or sought. For example, a participant observation researcher examining a specific community based rehabilitation program for offenders convicted of drug related offences must indicate clearly what subject matter will be investigated in the study.

The researcher has to identify the topic or purpose (the purpose is based on the topic or problem) which can be something like –the general operations of the program, types of therapeutic program and how they are implemented, study subject participation and behavior during participation, participants reception of the therapies, how does the program work etc. The researcher identifies the topic without linking or basing it on any pre-existing theories. The problem or issues being investigated are often presented in a series of statements.

Further insights can be attained from the following illustration. A participant observation researcher attends a gang meeting in prison. The researcher is investigating how gangs operate inside prison and how they are able to organize and operate from within the confines of the prison to cause havoc in the community. The topic to be investigated include mode of communication between gang members in prison and members outside prison, i.e. how are messages transmitted from one environment to the other? Aspects of the subject matter may include one or more of the following: What is the operational structure of gangs in prison? How are decisions made by gangs inside the confines of prison? What is the mode of communication among gang members in prison? How are decisions made in prison, and subsequently transmitted or communicated to gang members outside prison? What channels exist for gang members outside prison to provide feedback to their counterparts in prison?

Thus the participant observation researcher, while avoiding complicating the investigations with preconceptions and biases, must have a clear idea about what the study is investigating or examining.

REVIEWING THE EXISTING LITERATURE

As discussed under General Research Process, literature review is a salient characteristic of research irrespective of the methodology employed. The idea is to establish if any previous studies or similar studies exist on the specific geographical location of the present study. Again, the questions outlined under literature review in the General Research Processes must be answered, but the participant observation researcher must not be overly influenced by findings in the existing literature prior to the observation. The participant observation researcher must avoid the development of preconceptions or biases from the findings of previous studies, not before the observation of the behavior.

One important point to remember about participant observation methodology is that, while the review of literature, should not lead to the development of preconceptions, the review allows the present study to be placed within the context of the literature during the reporting stage. The review of literature also helps to select variables after data collection.

The is because the review may result in the identification of variables on the topic for which no interrelationships have been explored previously, perhaps prompting the participant observation researcher to have a closer look at them during data analysis. On the other hand, the researcher may decide to replicate some aspects of the previous studies and select similar variables after the observation and data collection are completed.

Preparatory Work

Preparatory work is very important in all types of research. That said, sight should not be lost of the fact that in no other research methodology is preparatory work as tedious and involving for the researcher as in participant observation. The successfulness of participant observation methodology to achieve its data collection objectives relies on the trust the participants have in the researcher as well as the participants' confidence and willingness to behave naturally during the observation. Depending on the specific study and its objectives, the participant observation researcher must make many trips to the subjects to be studied and the location prior to the implementation of the research. This is essential for the researcher to establish some level of acquaintance and familiarity with the subjects and the environment where the study will take place. This contrasts the situation with survey research where the researcher may mail questionnaires to study subjects for self completion and return, or send out interviewers to obtain data from respondents they have not met previously, or even undertake telephone interviews.

Thus, during the period preceding the observation, the participant observation researcher visits the location where the observation will take place. The researcher also makes contacts in other ways (telephone, fax, correspondence) with the authorities in charge of the location. If the research is taking place within a specific organization or organized environment, approval must first be obtained from the authorities in charge. Until approval is granted for the research to commence, the participant observation researcher will continuously be explaining the study and the procedures involved to the said authorities. The many visits and the large amount of time spent with the subjects and the environment where the study will take place also allow the researcher to assess security and make decisions on the research design. Specifically, it enables the participant observation researcher to make decisions on whether overt or covert observation will be most feasible and appropriate, and what security measures needed to be taken.

Unlike survey research where the researcher may appear at the door of the respondent in an instance, the participant observation researcher cannot just turn up to observe and record behavior without any prior arrangements.

Selection of a Research Design

As there are different types of participant observation research methodologies, the researcher must identify an appropriate type of design for the investigation. The researcher must decide whether the study will be overt or covert and whether the researcher will participate in the event. The study may be overt or covert, based on the aims and objectives, the nature of the study, and the risks involved in that specific study. If the researcher decides to employ overt observation methodology, then the participants must be told of the research. If the participant observation researcher settles on covert observation, then the participants are not told about the research and the researcher in their midst. The following two examples illustrate the two scenarios:

Example 1. Prison Gang Activities
A researcher is undertaking an investigation into gang activities inside prison. Knowing the risks, the participant observation researcher pretends to be interested in becoming a gang member, and continues to attend organized meetings and activities while quietly and secretly looking, listening and recording information. This is covert participant observation. The gang members or participants, whose behavior the researcher is observing, have no idea about what is going on.

Example 2. Rehabilitation Residents
A participant observation researcher is examining the behavior of residents in a rehabilitation facility for offenders convicted of committing crimes against the person and, in particular, various sexual offences. The researcher visits the rehabilitation facility at various times, and builds and obtains the trust and confidence of those sexual predators. The researcher proceeds to inform them about the research and the researcher's role. This is an example of overt participant observation study.

Sampling

As part of the decision on which methodology to employ, the researcher must decide whether the study would focus on a sample population. Qualitative research usually involves small numbers of participants. Most of the time, there is no need for a sample to be drawn. However, in some instances where large numbers of participants are available to observe, the participant observation researcher may have to decide whether to observe the whole group, or observe a selected sample of the group. If the researcher decodes to use a sample of the participants for the observation, then the whole group of participants will constitute the sampling frame from which the selected sample population will be drawn (see chapter four for detail information on sampling).

For illustration purposes, suppose a researcher wants to investigate the behavior of residents of a rehabilitation facility using focus group. There are about 32 residents in the facility, and the researcher finds this a bit large to observe their behavior at the same time. The researcher decides to select a smaller number of 10 participants. The 32 residents constitute the sampling frame from which the 10 selected residents are selected to become the sample. The sample is used to study the behavior of the residents of the rehabilitation facility. The sample of 10 is a more manageable size for the observation of the behavior of the residents of the rehabilitation facility.

In addition to the practical difficulties associated with observing the behavior of a large number of participants, the effort, time and cost can be enormous. Selecting a sample under those circumstances becomes inevitable. One aspect of sampling in participant observation, which has not been given adequate recognition and which is conspicuously missing in many books on research methodologies, is that sampling is always occurring as part of the observation. The task of the participant observation researcher is to observe and record the behavior of the members of the selected sample or study group They observe some behavior and miss out on others. What the participant observation researcher observes and records is by definition a sample of the total series of behavior taking place at any one time. It must be stated that this type of sampling takes place naturally as the behavior and its observation occur naturally. It may even be argued that the sample observation is not scientific, as the episodes observed naturally are not scientifically selected. Simply put, the participant observation researcher observes and records what is in the researcher's line of sight and not the other behavior outside that line of sight.

In addition to sampling of respondents, sampling in participant observation methodology can cover places, times and events involving the selected participants. The observation can occur in different environments if the participants are required to visit different environments for various program component. The participants are usually required to respond to diverse activities which are programmed during the period of their residence in the rehabilitation facility or the period of incarceration in prison. Besides, there are various events occurring on a regular basis. The participant observation researcher has the flexibility to decide which places or environments to visit for the purpose of the observation, which activities to include and at what times. Indirect sampling is continuously occurring in participant observation

A typical day in a rehabilitation program may involve the following activities at the times and venues indicated:

Monday

Time	Program Activity	Venue/Environment
7.30 – 9.00AM	Breakfast	Dining Room
9.15 – 10.00AM	Group Discussion	Main Hall
10.05 – 10.30AM	Morning Break/Tea	Recreation Room
10.35 – 12.30AM	Residents self-confession	Meeting Room 1
12.30 – 1.30PM	Lunch	Dining Room
1.30 – 2.30PM	Rest Time	Sleeping Rooms
2.30 – 4.30PM	Group Discussion	Main Hall
4.35 – 5.30PM	Exercise/Gym workout	Gymnasium

Tuesday

Time	Program Activity	Venue/Environment
7.30 – 9.00AM	Breakfast	Dining Room
9.15 – 10.00AM	Relapse Discussion	Meeting Room 2
10.00 – 10.30AM	Morning Break/Tea	Recreation Room
10.30 – 12.30AM	Lecture (drug abuse etc)	Main Hall
12.30 – 1.30PM	Lunch	Dining Room
1.30 – 2.30PM	Rest Time	Sleeping Rooms
2.30 – 4.30PM	Group Discussion	Main Hall
4.30 – 5.30PM	Exercise/Gym workout	Gymnasium

[*]Similar program activities at various times and venues for the rest of the week, Wednesday to Sunday.

The participant observation researcher studying the behavior of residents of this corrections facility has the flexibility to sample program activities, times they are held and the venues where the said activities occur. The researcher can decide which activities to visit on

Monday or any other day. The researcher also has the flexibility to sample which days to visit and make the observation of the residents' behavior (say Tuesday or Wednesday) or even decide to visit all day Mondays only. The flexibility is at the discretion of the researcher, but the decision is usually dependent on the aims and objectives of the study as well as the other commitments of the researcher. Thus, sampling considerations can be extensive and cover many aspects of the investigation.

In all these the key point is the ability of the activities, times and venue samples to provide adequate information. A number of indices work together to ensure adequacy in data collection, namely effort, time, physical environment, social and cultural environment and language. For a start, the participant observation researcher should be prepared to put in much effort to ensure that most of the selected activities, times and venues allow the capture of adequate data. Diligence, vigilance and a commitment to capture as much of the behavior as possible are essential.

The second key index is time. The participant observation researcher, unlike other researchers, must be prepared to spend more time with the participants. The longer the time spent on the observation, the larger the potential data that can be obtained, and subsequently the greater the chances of successful investigation and vice versa. Time is even more important when it comes to overt participant observation. When participants are aware of the research and the researcher's role, they sometimes act and behave unnaturally. With time, the participants become comfortable with the researcher, confidence grows and trust is built. Those participants begin to behave naturally providing the researcher with the behavior the research was designed to capture.

The role of the physical environment in ensuring the achievement of adequacy in data cannot be overemphasized. The layout of the venue, for example, could influence and determine what is observed and what is missed. This usually happens when there is a physical object between the researcher and some of the participants or where the participants are seated such that some of them are a bit away from the researcher to allow full observation of their behavior. The physical environment could also influence the behavior of the participants. If participants are cramped in a small room, they may not be able to act or behave naturally or as they would like to. To enable the researcher to put the observation in perspective, it is important for the researcher to record information of the physical environment in which the behavior was observed.

The fourth index is what is called here as social and cultural environment. The participants could come from different social and cultural backgrounds which may influence their behavior, especially in the early stages of observation. In particular, their social circumstances could vary resulting in inconsistent observation. Some may be older, others younger. Some may be married, others divorced, widowed or single, while some may come from rich families and others from poor families. They may also have varying levels of educational achievement and previous employment status. All these impact on their behavior as individuals. The key point is for the participant observation researcher to make every effort to understand the socio-cultural backgrounds of the subjects whose behavior is being observed, and to place their behavior in that context. This understanding must be achieved during the many visits to the participants prior to the actual observation of their behavior.

Finally, there is the issue of language. Do all the participants have the same level of English language proficiency? Are some of the participants from non English speaking background? Is the language proficiency of individual participants adversely affecting their ability to express themselves and subsequently their behavior? Does the participant observation researcher understand the language of the participants?

The researcher must be aware of the potential effects of all these, and quickly try to find answers to those questions. Indeed, in practical terms, the more the researcher understands the linguistic backgrounds of the participants, the more accurate the observation is likely to be. In addition, the social interactions within the group as well as how the researcher interacts socially with the participants are also important.

Implementation of the Selected Design

Once an appropriate observation design has been selected, the researcher has to implement the research through fieldwork. The researcher uses the specific participant observation design as an instrument of data collection and proceeds to collect data through the observation and recording of behavior. The researcher visits the specific location where the participants are performing to observe and record their behavior. If the design requires the researcher's involvement in the behavior of the participants, the researcher must perform with the participants and make the observation and recording of their behavior at the same time. If the selected design does not require the researcher's involvement in the behavior, the researcher stands back and makes the observation and recording of behavior.

Similarly, any pre-selected sampling arrangements must be implemented to facilitate data collection. Needless to add that if a decision is made to use a sample of the participants, only the selected participants should be included in the observation. It is worthy to bear in mind that, in most cases, the number of participants is small, relieving the researcher of any need for sampling.

As the observation is taking place directly at the same time as the behavior is occurring, it is said to be "live". As a result, the participant observation researcher has much flexibility and can modify the process of observation while in the field. For example, the research will make every effort to observe the behavior of as many of the participants as possible. However, if a particular behavior appears special, such as a vocal participant or a participant behavior in an interesting or unusual manner, the observation could, at least for a while, focus on that specific activity.

In overt participant observation, the participants are informed of the research and the researcher's role. There is a tendency for some of the participants to react by not behaving naturally in the initial stages of the observation. This puts enormous pressure on the observing researcher to be alert to identify and distinguish natural behavior from the behavior which is being perpetrated because of the presence of the researcher. This can be very difficult, certainly vitiating the notion that participant observation methodology is an easy research option for which the researcher puts in comparatively less effort. Even so, the researcher must not allow any thoughts of such potential artificial behavior and/or the upped behavior itself to influence the observation and recording processes, neither should there be any adverse effects on the ability of the researcher to capture the natural behavior of the other participants. In practice, the evidence points to a change of attitude over time. As the observation proceeds and as the participants' trust and confidence in the researcher increase, they tend to revert to their natural behavior and responses.

In covert participant observation, the participants are not aware of the research and what the researcher is doing. The participants tend to do their usual routine performance and behave naturally, albeit a few extroverts' behavior could still skew what is observed and recorded. This presupposes the need for the researcher to be alert at all times regardless of whether overt or covert observation methodology is employed.

Measurements

The work of the participant observation researcher extends beyond selection of design, visits to the participants and the implementation of the research design or data collection. The researcher continues to work until a report is produced. Sequentially logical after the data collection stage is the stage of measurement, analysis and interpretation of data. Unlike the attribute of survey research where the researcher can pre-define the measurements and data analysis to be made prior to undertaking the survey, the participant observation researcher does not have such luxury The participant observation researcher must actually observe the behavior, collect the data first and follow it up with the decision on what measurements would be made and what analysis would be undertaken on the basis of the data collected and the aims and objectives of the study.

In participant observation, the measurements to be made can be daunting and complex, given the large array of data that can potentially be collected from the observation of the participants' behavior. Bearing the study aims and objectives in mind, the participant observation researcher must go through the large variety of observational data that have been collected. This can be very tricky and/or confusing due to the massive observations recorded. As the participants behave in a particular way which could or could not have been perceived by the researcher, the actions of the participants usually define the measures to be used in the study, not any preconceived measures as in survey research. In other words, the participant observation researcher must go with the data available and develop measures on the basis of the different aspects of the data that lend themselves better to providing analysis to achieve the study objectives. As the measures are determined by the actual behavior of the participants, they are deemed participant defined, quite unlike researcher defined in survey research.

Analysis and Interpretation of Data

After the observations are completed, the next logical stage in participant observation research is data analysis followed by interpretation. This is the stage where the researcher endeavors to put the observations and their measures together and try to make a sense of all the recordings that have been made. It is not an easy task. All the notes have to be assembled and sorted, bearing in mind the aims and objectives of the study, the subject matter being investigated, the physical settings within which the observations were made and the diverse backgrounds of the participants. For data analysis to be effective, the process must have an end point, and the researcher must accept that the observations are complete and refrain from further observations.

Analysis in participant observation methodology is usually descriptive, with the researcher describing what was observed and the types of behavior exhibited by the study subjects. It should be noted that the participant observation researcher is not able to provide a full picture and description of everything. The enormity of the observations makes this impossible. The approach is for the participant observation researcher to be selective and edit the data collected with a view to describing the behavior of their subjects and addressing the subject matter of the study. Not all the observations made will be necessary for or relevant to the subject matter. Based solely on the observations, the researcher's knowledge about the topic and logic, the researcher must decide which pieces of information can provide further insights into the subject matter and address the issues which led to the study and which the study sought to investigate. Remember that in participant observation, there are no preconceptions or biases, and all conclusions and generalizations are based on the analysis of the observations.

A useful analytical approach or strategy is to undertake limited analysis while in the field. This will allow broad and general behavioral patterns to be discerned early in the research and to be tested further during the stage of analysis. For example, the researcher may notice a specific pattern of behavior in the early stages of observation. When it comes to the data analysis stage, the participant observation researcher can search the data to find out if that specific behavior was endemic and if it prevailed throughout the observations. The researcher will then be in a position for a grounded theory, i.e. to theorize on the behavioral pattern based solely on what is present in the observations. As explained previously, in participant observation methodology, the logic is inductive. What comes out of the observations is what is used to draw conclusions and make generalizations or theories. There is no prior determination of patterns or theories. Diagrammatically, the process appears like this:

Observations → Analysis/Interpretations → Generalizations/Theories
(Inductive Logic)

In participant observation methodology, relationships are examined through the patterns observed. It is not usually two variable interrelationships as many different patterns of behavior are observed at the same time. The participant observation researcher must not explain the behavioral patterns exhibited by the subjects of the study. Instead, the participant observation researcher must allow the subjects to explain their actions. The researcher can add any perceived or observed explanations later, but self explanation by the study subjects must remain paramount as well as the goal. While analysis in participant observation methodology is, by and large, descriptive, causal analysis is sometimes undertaken. It is usual practice for participant observation researchers to specify causal relationships. However, the specified causal relationship must fit within the overall description of the behavioral patterns. As participant observation research does not commence with any prior preconceptions, biases or theories, the decision on which causal relationships to establish is made at a later stage after the observations have been completed.

Interpretation of the analytical results follows closely after the analysis. Again, it is highly essential for the interpretation to be undertaken with an open mind and without any biases. The analytical results have to be interpreted in order to add value to the analysis, and make a sense out of those analyses. Interpretation of the results of data analysis is also important to allow proper, effective and sensible inductive logic to prevail, and to allow for the conclusions to be drawn, potential generalizations explored and theories formulated.

As discussed in the proceeding section on advantages and disadvantages of participant observation methodology, generalizations in participant observation research are very limited and should be undertaken with extreme care and sensible inductive logic.

Preparation and Reporting of Results

The final stage in participant observation research methodology is the preparation and presenting of results. Research is of no value unless the findings from the research are made available through an effective dissemination of the results. The results are normally disseminated through one or more outlets. The results may be made available through internal and external seminars, lectures, workshops, conference presentations, journal articles or books.

It is usual practice to prepare an overall report describing:

1. What the study was about – subject matter or topic.
2. What prompted the research, i.e. the rationale or importance of the study, its purpose and objectives of the study.
3. Review of the existing literature.
4. Methodologies used and, if possible, why.
5. Physical settings and socio-cultural and related backgrounds of the participants.
6. Problems encountered and how they were solved.
7. The main findings.
8. Minor findings
9. Any conclusions drawn as well as any generalizations and theories suggested must also be included.
10. Areas for further research where possible.

A number of factors must be considered when preparing the overall report. These include any specific requests from funding agencies, expressed or inherent interest of practitioners, government and private sector agencies and the general public. The report should also contain materials or information that will add to the existing knowledge of the subject matter, provide further insights into the various dimensions of the subject matter and should appear interesting and informative to readers.

Researchers reach agreements with funding agencies about the nature of the study through the content of the research proposals and funding application. It is crucial that any report produced reflect what was agreed on. In addition, funding agencies sometimes provide explicit expression of their interests and why they are funding the investigation. Under those circumstances, it is paramount that the report provides information on those expressed interests and what was agreed with the funding agencies prior to the commencement of the study.

In the initial parts of the report and possibly in the introduction, there should be statements or paragraphs outlining what prompted the study, its purpose and/or objectives. Research topics sometimes arise as areas for further research from a previous study. Other times they are specifically identified by funding agencies as a priority area for funding. Research topics can also arise from public outcry over an issue , practice or policy, prompting researchers to examine the issue in greater detail. Whatever the rationale or reason for the study, the report should address it a paragraph or so.

The review of the literature, so important in modern research, should be included in the report. The literature review should cover mostly published articles – books, journal articles, conference presentations. However, it can include unpublished articles which can be assessed by readers including PhD and Masters theses (serialized in libraries) and relevant reports from government and non-government agencies. The research should be placed in the context of the literature. If the results confirm results from previous studies as evidenced from the literature review, it should be clearly stated at appropriate sections of the study. If the study findings contradict the findings of some previous studies, this should also be noted and an attempt made to explain the differences.

To place the research in perspective, to facilitate replication and to enhance the understanding of readers, it is appreciable to describe the methodology or methodologies used in the study and any reasons for employing those specific methodologies If a sample was used, it should also be described. As the report is prepared after the investigation, it is appropriate for the participant observation researcher to include any interrelationships among the variables which the study tested or identified without fear of being accused of prior bias. The report should be clear about the stage during the investigation when the interrelationships among and between variables were tested.

The report must place the study within the context s in which it was undertaken. The physical settings and the characteristics of the subjects, especially their demographic, socio-cultural, economic and related backgrounds, must be detailed in the report. These variables have the potential to influence the behavior of the study subjects and, as such, are very important in participant observation research. Besides, participants from different socio-cultural backgrounds may respond differently to different situations and behave in a different manner.

Many a time, participant observation research proceeds smoothly and without any problems or difficulties. Sometimes problems or difficulties arise from participants, authorities or the physical settings where the observations are made. It is important for the overall report to state clearly what the problems were and what the researcher did to overcome them. This is important to bring the problems and their possible solutions to the attention of other researchers using similar methodologies or planning to replicate the study.

In every study, some findings stand out and these are called the main findings. The researcher must state the main findings of the study in the report. Depending on the objectives and purpose of the study, special interests of funding agencies, policy makers, and program developers, the research may include the implications of the main findings for policy formulation and implementation, program development and delivery as well future funding initiatives on the subject matter. In addition any minor or other relevant findings should also be mentioned no matter how brief.

Any conclusions relevant to the subject matter should be discussed in the report. So also should any possible generalizations (no matter how limited) and potential theories explored after data analysis and interpretation. These generalizations and theories should be based solely on the analysis of the observations. They should be explicit to allow readers to identify and understand the inductive logic involved. There is a tendency to provide a summary of the study methodology and findings in the conclusion, but this should be distinct from the drawn conclusion, albeit both could be included in the same part or section of the report.

Finally, any areas for further research should be discussed and possibly explained. Sometimes after data analysis emerging issues arise that do not form part of the subject matter of the study. It is important that the participant observation researcher refrain from delving into it and attempting to superfluously and shallowly address them. Any emerging issues should be identified as areas for further research or funding so the researcher can investigate them in another research, and other researchers can cease upon the opportunity and design a study to examine them. Areas for further research should not be limited to emerging issue only. They may include areas within the broad area of the subject matter which the researcher could not have included in the current study for various reasons.

Advantages and Disadvantages of Participant Observation Methodology

As stated earlier in the discussion of the General Research Process, every research methodology has its own merits and demerits, and participant observation methodology is no exception.

So what are the advantages or merits of participant observation methodology? Participant observation methodologies have the advantage of being live and active during the data collection stage. Participant observation researchers actually observe the behavior when it is happening not before or after the behavior has been exhibited. The observations are actual and original, and the data thus obtained are therefore original.

If the study is successfully undertaken, participant observation methodologies have the added advantage of providing a great variety of fine and detailed data. By making actual observations of the behavior, a lot of diverse data are obtained and assembled, allowing the researcher to select which aspects of the data to use in the specific study.

Yet another advantage of participant observation methodology is its attribute of flexibility. This attribute is very powerful and readily enhances the participant observation researcher's ability to modify the observation procedures during the fieldwork, or to sample study subjects, program activities, the times of observation and so on. It also facilitates the solving of unexpected problems which arise during fieldwork right on the spot, during the observation of actual behavior and as they arise.

In short, participant observation researchers have the flexibility to quickly adjust procedures, practices and observations to suit emerging, unexpected and changing circumstances and field situations.

In addition, emerging issues are quickly noted and relevant data recorded for further research. More importantly, the participant observation researcher can explore new leads which arise during fieldwork and which are relevant to the study. This is essential to enable total and thorough investigation of the subject matter of the research, and improve upon the available information, existing knowledge and understanding of the subject matter.

Participant observation methodology, if well executed, can result in cost savings. Participant observation is relatively and comparatively cheaper than survey research, for example. This is because, there are usually no questionnaires to be printed, interviewers to be trained, employed and remunerated, neither is there any piloting of pre-designed instruments.

The notion of regarding participant observation research methodology as less labor intensive than other methodologies remains debatable. On the one hand it can be argued that only the researcher is actually working and any labor intensiveness relates to the said researcher only.

This becomes clearer if it is borne in mind that other research methodologies, such as survey research, have researchers as well as interviewers who spend lots of time interviewing and obtaining information. The debate centers on the argument proposed in some quarters that participant observation research methodologies are very labor intensive because of the amount of time the researcher spends on the observations and the number of visits the researcher makes to the place of observation. The standpoint taken in this book is that, all told, participant observation research methodology is labor intensive with respect to and on the he part of the researcher, but that is not enough to make the methodologies more labor intensive than survey research methodology.

Despite the many advantages, participant observation methodologies have some disadvantages. By definition and practice, participant observation methodology can only examine or study small groups of participants, throwing into question the ability of the methodology to generalize and theorize from research results. So that external validity of the results of participant observation research is limited.

The accuracy of the data collected trough participant observation depends on the skills of the researcher and the trust, confidence, commitment and ability of the participants to respond well and behave naturally.

The accuracy of data also depends on the researcher's ability and power to make many observations simultaneously and correctly. Anything short of that has the potential to adversely affect the successfulness of the study, and its ability to fully explore and shed more light on the subject matter.

In participant observation research methodology, the role of the researcher is very important. In particular the researcher must interact well with the study subjects as part of the process of building trust and confidence among the participants, an essential ingredient for obtaining accurate data. The disadvantage is that the participant observation researcher has the potential to over interact or interact too closely with the participants, lose focus and become part of the group instead of a researcher from the outside.

This brings the discussion of participant observation research methodologies to an end. The nature, attributes, practices, advantages and disadvantages of participant observation methodologies have been discussed in a practical step by step approach.

FURTHER READINGS

Giddens, A. (1997): Sociology. Cambridge, UK, Polity Press.

May, T, (2001): Social Research..Buckingham, Open University Press.

Teevan, J., T. ED) (1987); Basic Sociology. Scarborough, Prentice-Hall Canada Inc.

Yeboah, D. A (2002): Crime and its Solutions in Barbados. Journal of Criminal Justice, Vol. 30, No. 2:409-416.

Box 1. What studies are Qualitative Research Methodologies most suitable for?

Participant observation methodologies are most suitable for the study of:
1. Small groups.
2. Study of the behavior of residents of rehabilitation facilities.
3. Victimization studies involving small groups of selected victims.
4. Small population and/or community samples.
5. Court room practices.

Questions for readers self reflection

Is participant observation methodology less labor intensive than survey research? Give reasons for your answer.

What should the participant observation researcher do if the participants refuse to trust the researcher?

Sometimes, participants behave unnaturally during overt participant observation even though they trust the researcher. What should the researcher do to obtain accurate data?

Chapter 4

QUANTITATIVE RESEARCH METHODOLOGIES

In the preceding chapter, one of the major criminological research methodologies was discussed. In this chapter, the other leading group of criminological research methodologies is examined in detail. Quantitative research methodologies and their associated attributes and dimensions constitute the subject matter for this chapter. Like the preceding chapter the following broad topics are covered together with a discussion of different types of sampling and measurements usually used in survey research:

1. Description - what is it?
2. Approaches, practices or processes.
3. Measurements.
4. Analysis and interpretation of data.
5. Advantages and disadvantages.

As quantitative research is synonymous with survey research, this chapter focuses on survey research methodologies. It provides a comprehensive, simple, practical, step by step approach to conducting criminological research using survey research methodologies. Throughout the chapter, salient distinctions between survey research methodologies and participant observation methodologies are identified as and when appropriate.

The overarching objective of the chapter is to provide readers with improved understanding of the nature, practices, measurements, sampling, analysis and interpretation of survey research data as well as the reporting of survey research results. Measurements and analysis are discussed as part of the stages in undertaking quantitative research.

In particular, non professional people, junior researchers and those using survey research methodologies for the first time as well as advanced researchers interested in improving their skills would find this chapter very interesting, informative and helpful. Detailed discussion of sampling procedures (essential for survey research), and measurements provide added benefits for the reader with interest in survey research.

DESCRIPTION

Many readers have heard of survey research, but what exactly is survey research? Survey research is used in all countries around the world and it is a very useful source of criminological data. Survey research methodologies are some of the most common and most widespread methodologies ever used in criminological research. Survey research methodologies are used by researchers, government agencies, non government agencies and students. The question which arises is do many of these users of survey research methodologies know what exactly it is and do they employ a step by step approach to undertaking survey research? Do they adopt and use the Scentific Method?

Survey research is a type of research in which information is collected from as many people as possible, usually using a pre-designed standard questionnaire (called the survey instruments). This contrasts the situation in participant observation methodology which by practice concentrates on observing the behavior of small groups of respondents. The key point in traditional survey research is that the same information is usually collected from all respondents and this is facilitated by the use of the pre-designed survey instruments. As discussed later in this chapter, every respondent answers the same questions as found in the questionnaire, especially in face to face and telephone survey research methodology.

The underlying principle is that by collecting information from as many respondents as possible, the researcher is in a position to make as many broad generalizations and/or theories about the subject matter as possible, albeit the accuracy of any such generalizations depends on various factors including sampling procedures and sample size. The main attributes or characteristics of survey research include:

1. Large populations/respondents.
2. Questionnaire design (instruments).
3. Standard data collection for each study.
4. Interviewing in one way or the other.
5. Sampling.
6. Statistical analysis and interpretation.
7. Testing of hypothesis or addressing research questions.
8. Comparative analysis.
9. Exploring relationships between variables.

Criminological surveys, by and large, involve a large number of respondents. Most surveys involve the use of carefully designed survey instruments for data collection, resulting in the collection and availability of standard data. The survey instruments have been called different names, but instruments and questionnaires are the most popular and most frequently used names.

Survey research involves interviewing in one way or the other. The standard data are usually obtained by asking the selected respondents specific questions through interviewing, albeit postal surveys and other survey methodologies are discernible. There is no survey without one form of sampling or another. This is because surveys, by definition, require the use of a selected group of respondents to be identified and questioned. There are different forms of sampling in survey research, and the details are provided later in this chapter. For now it suffices to say that, in survey research, sampling is essential and must be undertaken scientifically where possible to achieve accurate data on the subject matter of the study.

Another feature of survey research, though not unique to survey research methodologies, is the ability to undertake comparative analysis. Comparisons can be made by geographical locations and by characteristics of the respondents. As the same questions are asked of each respondent, responses from respondents of different locations can be identified and compared. Differences in responses by characteristics such as age, educational attainment, gender, employment status and income allow for the comparative analysis of responses. Comparative analysis can even be undertaken by the level and extent of recidivism. Repeat offenders can be grouped by the number of offences committed (e.g. recidivists with less than 5 convictions compared with those with 5-10 and 10 and over convictions). Again, due to the large number of responses, the comparative analysis can be done with confidence and precision, especially where the sample is scientifically drawn. The point must also be made that it is often the practice in survey research to explore potential relationships between the study variables.

Theory

Theory is very important in all types of survey research methodologies – face to face, observational, telephone or postal survey research methodologies. Theory is important because, in survey research, propositions are made about the subject matter under investigation and survey instruments prepared on the basis of those propositions. The propositions are usually in the form of hypotheses or survey research questions. Theory enables the survey researcher to develop a line of thinking about the subject matter, including the interrelationships between the variables which are used to study the subject matter.

For example, from theory the survey researcher is able to discern the interrelationships between population and level of crime, or educational attainment and crime. The researcher can use this proposition to develop a line of thinking about crime called hypothesis (see the discussion of hypothesis in the section on the General Research Process) which goes like "crime increases steadily with population growth". This statement becomes the hypothesis to be tested by the researcher who is examining crime rates over a period of time and has population and level of crime as variables in the study. A number of theory supported hypotheses is usually developed in surveys, depending on the researchers knowledge of the specific theory and its relevance to the research being undertaken. It should further be noted that hypotheses can also be developed from the researcher's own knowledge and understanding of the subject matter.

In survey research, any hypotheses developed arte usually tested during the investigation and the theoretical concepts in the hypothesis are transformed into empirical concepts through data collection and analysis. As explained earlier, in survey research pre-designed instruments with pre-determined content are used to collect information about the subject matter. The pre-designed instruments and their associated pre-determined content are so designed to test the specifically stated hypotheses or research questions, and to provide further insights into the subject matter.

The information collected, analyzed and interpreted allows the researcher to draw conclusions and establish evidence based relationship between the variables. As indicated in chapter two, the first procedure is to undertake data analysis to dismiss the null hypothesis and to prove or confirm the alternative hypothesis. If the analysis and interpretation of data confirm the alternative hypotheses, then it is concluded that the stated hypotheses are true – Yes hypothesis. In the earlier example, this means that the data analysis confirms that "crime increases steadily with population growth. If the data analysis does not support the hypotheses, then it is concluded that the stated hypotheses are untrue and the study is said to confirm the null hypotheses. In the earlier example, it will mean that 'crime does not increase with population growth' and that there is no such relationship between crime and population growth, for example. This could lead to a re-thinking of the theory, resulting in the proposition of a new version or amended version of the existing theory or at least further investigation of the relationship.

Even where specific research questions are stated, these questions are usually developed on the basis of the existing theories, previous research in the literature and the researcher's own knowledge and understanding of the subject matter. The data collected and the analysis which follows must address the questions and confirm or dismiss the theoretical underpinnings of the research questions. For example a researcher studying resident's participation in community based rehabilitation programs may develop the following research questions.

Do prison inmates opt for community based rehabilitation programs when offered, so as to get out of prison?

Do prison inmates who are released to a community based rehabilitation facility actually receive adequate treatment or rehabilitation so that they refrain from recidivism?

The survey instruments must be so designed to allow for the collection of data which will answer these questions. If these questions have been derived from theory, then the conclusions reached and the answers obtained from the research can confirm the tenets of the theory or provide an alternate line of thinking on the subject matter. The key point is to design the instruments such that the questions asked are in a position to provide data which when analyzed answer the research questions. Sometimes, the research questions seek answers on the specific relationships between selected variables. In that situation, the instruments must obtain data which will allow for an analysis to establish the said interrelationships between the selected variables.

These contrast the practice of participant observation methodology in which no prior research questions or hypotheses are proposed. The survey researcher has a well defined objective and mission right from the beginning and goes in to seek information with instruments designed on the basis of the mission. The participant observation researcher, as was noted earlier, has no preconceptions, but collects data from which conceptions are subsequently developed and defined.

TYPES OF SURVEY METHODOLOGIES

There are varieties of methodologies in survey research all exhibiting and employing the basic attributes of survey research methodologies. Survey research methodologies include:

1. Direct face to face surveys/interviews.
2. Telephone surveys/interviews.
3. Postal surveys.
4. Observational surveys.

Face to Face Survey Interviews

Face to face interviews is the most frequently used methodology in survey research. It is also the survey research methodology that many people are aware of. In face to face surveys, the mode of data collection is interviewing. The researcher and/or trained interviewers obtain data from respondents by asking them specific questions appearing in the survey instruments. There is a degree of flexibility in face to face survey research methodology, but prior to the actual data collection phase. The survey researcher can adopt one of three types of face to face research methodologies as part of the research design, namely structured design, unstructured design and semi-structured design.

In structured face to face research design, a structured pre-designed questionnaire is prepared and used religiously to collect the data. The interview is also structured with the interviewer following a strict sequential order of questioning. The interviewer is also responsible for filling in the questionnaires as the responses are given to the questions. Any mistakes made in the completion of the questionnaires are attributed to the interviewer who, thus, has a heavy responsibility of not only asking questions correctly, but also ensuring that responses are accurately recorded on the questionnaire.

As the name suggests, nothing is so structured and pre-determined in unstructured face to face survey methodology. While the questions may be pre-defined, the interview is unstructured so that other questions could be added. The researcher and the interviewer may have and do maintain some ideas for further probing, albeit other questions arise from speci9fic responses. The interviewing itself is so unstructured that the questions are not required to be asked in any specific sequential order. This survey research methodology has the potential to provide a degree of flexibility to the researcher and interviewer, enhancing the ability of both the researcher and the interviewer to probe specific items further as and when necessary. A useful strategy in unstructured face to face survey research methodology is for the interviewer and researcher to note a few prompting points on paper. The researcher and/or interviewer look at the paper from time to time during the interview to make sure that no key issues or points are missed.

A salient characteristic of survey research is the collection of standard data as previously discussed. Strictly speaking, unstructured face to face interviews do not meet this important criterion, largely because probing questions may vary from one respondent to the other. Even so, some level of standard data may still be obtained. On the other hand, probing could provide a variety of additional data on the subject matter because so many different questions are asked or rather could be asked in an unstructured interview. Unstructured interviews are most useful in obtaining data from residents of rehabilitation centers and prisoners.

In practice, most unstructured face to face interviews may have some points sitting at the back of the mind of the researcher and/or interviewer. This leads to what is called semi-structured face to face interviews. In this type of face to face interview, the respondents are subjected to a mix of structured and unstructured questions and interviewing processes. Certain pre-designed questions are put to every respondent and these are mixed with or followed by unstructured interviewing with no pre-determined questions. The unstructured interviewing with no pre-determined questions varies from one respondent to the other. The interview may or may not follow a sequential order and respondents may have to answer different questions as there are no pre-determined questions in the unstructured part of semi-structured face to face survey methodology. . The advantage of semi-structured face to face interview is that it allows for the collection of standard and a variety of other data coming from the unstructured interviewing and the questions which are not pre-determined.

Telephone Survey

In telephone survey research, the methodology involves the use of the telephone as the medium of data collection. It works well in societies where telephones are widely available and easily obtained and accessed. The methodology is similar to face to face interviews except that the researcher or interviewer does not see the respondent and the respondent does not see the interviewer or researcher. Only voices are heard by all the parties involved. Pre-designed instruments are prepared and used to obtain information from the respondents who are selected from the telephones directory, randomly or otherwise. Telephone surveys are fairly structured, and respondents are asked the same questions, usually leading to the collection of standard data. That said, the point must be made that a semi-structured telephone survey is possible.

Telephone survey research methodology is very useful for collecting information on all aspects of the criminal justice system including fear of or concern about crime, Police practices in the community, victimization, recidivism and views of residents of therapeutic rehabilitation centers and their facilities and programs. The onus is on the interviewer to ask questions politely, listen carefully and record accurately the responses provided.

Postal Survey Research

In postal survey research methodology, pre-designed instruments containing pre-determined content are mailed to selected respondents with a request for self completion and return. Stamped self-addressed envelopes are included to enable the respondents to return the completed questionnaires to the researcher without any postal cost to the respondents. While cheaper than face to face and telephone surveys, postal surveys tend to have comparatively lower response rates as many selected respondents do not complete and return the questionnaires.

Like face to face and telephone survey research, postal survey research methodology can be used to collect information on all aspects of the criminal justice system. It is mostly used where research funds are so limited to discourage the use of interviewers for either face to face or telephone data collection. In postal survey research methodology, the researcher does not come into physical contact with the study subjects and no interviewers are used.

Observational Survey Research

Observational survey research methodology is the type of survey research which requires the survey to be undertaken through the observation of the event, phenomenon or activity. It is distinct from participant observation research methodology because the number of incidents or observations is by far larger than what is expected in participant observation, and statistical data not recording of behavior are collected. It is mainly used to obtain information on vehicular movements on specific routes, at roundabouts and traffic lights to provide information for informed traffic policy formulation.

Departmental stores are known to use observational surveys to collect information on patrons as they enter and leave the store etc. Real estate agents also use this methodology to record data on the number of people visiting open homes, without realizing it. No pre-designed instruments and no pre-determined questions are used. The use of observational survey methodology by Departmental stores to collect information on patrons should not be confused with the structured interviews that the stores undertake from time to time. The latter involves face to face interviews using pre-designed questionnaires with pre-determined content to collect specific information from patrons. All the patrons answer the same questions, yielding standard data on the items on which data are sought.

THE ROLE OF THE SURVEY RESEARCHER

The role of the researcher in survey research is similar in a sense to the role of the researcher in participant observation in that they are in-charge of the decisions on the design and other aspects of the research. In criminological survey research, the researcher makes decisions on what subject matter will be investigated, how it will be investigated, how data will be measured and analyzed and how the findings will be disseminated or communicated to interested and relevant parties. The researcher is responsible for reviewing the literature or arranging for the literature to be reviewed and the selection of relevant aspects of that review.

One of the most essential roles of the survey researcher is the weighing of design options and the selection of the most appropriate survey design for the study. The survey researcher must decide whether to use interviewers, undertake face to face, telephone, postal or observational survey as well as make decisions on the use of structured or unstructured interviewing and pre-determined questionnaires. The decisions will, by and large, depend on the subject matter of the investigation, funding and timelines, but it is the research's responsibility to consider all the factors and arrive at a suitable design.

Once decisions have been made on the research design and related issues, the researcher has to make all the preparatory work and implement the design. It is also the researcher's responsibility to find answers to all the problems encountered in the field by the interviewers. In short, the researcher has overall responsibility for bringing the implementation of the research to a successful completion regardless of whether interviewers are used. Issues related to sampling, measurements, data analysis, interpretation and reporting all fall within the realm of the survey researcher's role. So also is the responsibility for the initial contacts with funding agencies, all consultations with the community and attendance to all planning issues.

In comparison with participant observation research methodology, survey research methodology involves a large number of respondents, numerous question items and large data sets. It is the role of the survey researcher to identify the variables which will be considered for data analysis and interpretation, and what types of interrelationships among the variables will be investigated. In survey research methodologies which involve pre-determined questionnaires and structured interviews, these variables are pre-determined by the researcher during the planning stages of the survey.

Finally the researcher has responsibility for the preparation of the final report and other sub reports emanating from the study, the good and the bad. The researcher also has the role of ensuring that the analysis, interpretation, conclusions and any implications for criminal justice policy and program development are accurate and appropriate, defend the findings and answer all criticisms and questions regarding all aspects of the study.

THE PRACTICE OF CRIMINOLOGICAL SURVEY RESEARCH

There are different types of surveys in criminology, each with its own interests and purpose. Criminological researchers undertake surveys on the entire criminal justice system, within prison confines or in the community including the law courts. Unlike participant observation, criminological surveys involve a number of pre-determined items called variables on which information is collected. The interrelationships among the variables are also investigated using various statistical tools.

There are a number of diverse and sequential but sometimes interrelated steps or stages involved in undertaking these criminological surveys. They include:

1. Identification of the problem.
2. Literature review.
3. Selection of survey design or designs.
4. Preliminary or preparatory work.
5. Sampling.
6. Implementation of the survey design.
7. Measurements.
8. Data entry, processing, analysis and interpretation.
9. Reporting of results.

Identification of the Problem

The first stage in undertaking a survey is to identify the problem and the subject matter of the study. Criminological surveys are numerous and varied. There are crime surveys which include level of crime, concern about or fear of crime,, victimization, prison inmates, rehabilitation facilities and their programs and other surveys on specific subject matters within which a problem is identified for investigation. It is sometimes the case that more than one problem is investigated in criminological surveys, covering a number of different subject matters.

It is important for the problem to be well defined. This is because subsequent decisions will be driven and determined, to some extent, by the identified problem. For example, decisions on research design, implementation of the design, measurements, data analysis and reporting of findings will partly be pre-determined by the problem under investigation and associated hypotheses or research questions. A survey of crime levels can also collect data on fear of crime directly or indirectly as respondents make their concerns clear. The reporting of the results will no doubt emphasize the levels or crime established by the study as that was the primary subject matter of that study. Besides, some methodologies lend themselves better to the investigation of specific topics, hence the importance of the identified problem in influencing what research design option is selected. In addition, where many topics are being investigated simultaneously, multiple designs can be used together in what was previously described in the General Research Process as triangulation. (see Patton, 1990; Yeboah, 2000)

Survey topics come from diverse sources. Problems can emerge from a previous study, policy implementation, program delivery or public outcry over a specific issue. It is the responsibility of the researcher to define the exact area of investigation within the subject matter or areas of public concern. Unlike participant observation methodology in which the researcher has a degree of flexibility and freedom to amend the methodology in the field, survey research requires a certain degree of precision about the topic. This is because in most survey research methodologies, structured questionnaires with pre-determined content are used to collect information and there is usually no provision or arrangement for the interviewers to change any part of it.

More importantly, a change of questions by one interviewer means that the overall data collected will no longer be standard. Remember, a salient characteristic of surveys is that every respondent answers the same questions resulting in the collection of standard data. The only potential exception is when unstructured interview is undertaken. Even so, the researcher or interviewer usually has a few essential points noted on paper to prompt them. Hence the importance pinpointing the study problem or topic in survey research methodologies.

Literature Review

The importance of literature review in survey research is similar to the role of literature review in participant observation and a lot of what was said about literature review in participant observation applies in survey research methodologies. However, statements directly attributed to participant observation methodology may not necessarily be applicable to survey research methodologies.

In survey research methodology, literature review assumes additional significance. This is because literature review has the potential, and it often does, to influence the type of survey design selected and the content of the survey instruments. The added significance is based on the fact that the instruments are pre-designed with little flexibility to amend the content in the field, while the literature review assists in guiding and shaping the content of the said instruments.

An illustration will be in order. Imagine a researcher has identified a specific problem for investigation. The researcher has decided to use a structured face to face interview of respondents to obtain the required data on say fear of crime. The researcher reviews the existing published and accessible unpublished literature on fear of crime, especially those covering the specific geographical area of interest to the research. First, the researcher is able to learn what variables were used in the previous studies to enable decisions to be made on whether to use similar variables and/or use completely new variables and the reasons for doing so.

Secondly, the researcher learns from the literature about what methodologies were used in previous studies, what problems were encountered and what solutions were found. This enhances the ability of the researcher to make appropriate decisions on whether to replicate the methodologies or use other survey methodologies. From the evidence on problems encountered and how they were solved, if any, the researcher is able to amend the methodology to avoid encountering similar problems in the field. All these are of special importance to survey research because of the pre-determination of research designs and variables. Like the situation with other research methodologies, the literature review could even assist the researcher in making decisions on which findings to emphasize in the report to avoid repetition, decide whether to re-emphasize important findings recurring in the literature, and/or present new findings on the topic of investigation.

Selection of the Research Design or Designs

After the literature review and with the additional knowledge obtained from that review, the survey researcher is in a position to make decisions on various aspects of the investigation including study design, measurements, data entry and analysis and reporting. The survey researcher must select a design or designs from the variety of survey research methodologies and in doing so, particular attention must be paid to the methodologies which best suit the local conditions, availability of resources (funding and human resources), as well as the methodology which lends itself better to the specific study.

For example, a researcher could initially be interested to undertaking a structured face to face interview. After carefully examining the available resources, the researcher comes to realize that it is not possible to recruit, train and employ interviewers to collect data due to inadequate funding, and opts for postal survey methodology instead. Another researcher investigating traffic accidents and associated criminal offences may settle on observational survey methodology instead of interviewing selected drivers and vehicle users, simply because of inadequate funding, time etc.

Not only must decisions be made on the survey design or designs, but also arrangements for measurements, data entry, storage, processing, analysis and management are to be made during this phase, as they are related to the design. These are essential features of survey research (given the volume of information usually obtained) without which no results can be found and reported. Sampling procedures and sample size must also be determined alongside the selected methodology. Careful thought must be given to the decisions because in survey research, a number of essential component are pre-determined, with little flexibility for change during implementation (depending on the specific survey research methodology).

Preparatory Work

The logical stage after making decisions on study design and other relevant parts of the survey is preliminary or preparatory work. Like other methodologies, this stage involves finalizing arrangements for the actual investigation to commence. Even so, certain aspects are related to survey research methodologies only, including making decisions on the potential number of respondents to be interviewed, their distribution by age, gender and/or any other pre-determined attributes (educational level attained, employment status etc.), obtaining sampling frames and subsequent sampling to determine the study population.

Other activities unique to survey research during this stage include advertising for and the selection and training of interviewers and questionnaire design. Training manuals for interviewing and data entry personnel are also prepared during this stage. Actual field interview manuals and data entry manuals are also prepared during the preliminary or preparatory stage. The training manuals are used to train the selected interviewers and data entry personnel to make them ready for the tasks for which they have been chosen The prepared interview manuals are given to the trained interviewers (after their training) to be used as reference guides in the field to help them cope and to prompt them about procedures etc. The data entry manuals are given to the trained data entry personnel when the task of entering data begins.

In addition, depending on the selected design, it is at this stage that the researcher makes initial contacts with potential respondents and any authorities from whom permission must be sought, if required.

For example, if a researcher is undertaking a face to face prison survey, it is at this stage that initial contacts are made with prison authorities and some of the inmates, familiarization with the prison environments and relevant arrangements made for the interview to take place. If a decision has been made to adopt postal survey as the main methodology for the study, it is during this stage that recipients of the questionnaires are chosen, instructions for completion and return of the questions prepared and arrangements for mailing the instruments to the selected respondents finalized.

A common characteristic of all survey research methodologies is the collection of the same information from a large number of respondents. The result is large data sets containing standard data which have to be managed, processed, analyzed and reported. The survey researcher has an important task to make decisions not only on how the data are to be collected by the trained interviewers, but also how the data will be managed, processed, stored, analyzed and reported. Unlike participant observation research in which the data must be collected first before the variables to be used are selected and defined, in survey research the variables are pre-determined enabling the researcher to make decisions on measurements of the variables, arrangements for data processing and analysis in advance. During the preliminary or preparatory stage, the survey researcher must arrange for the recruitment and training of data processing and data entry personnel, necessitated by the large amount of standard data to be collected. It is often a useful practice to develop and make available data entry and processing manual to the selected personnel to ensure consistency in data entry and processing.

Designing the Questionnaire

Another essential characteristic of this preparatory stage is the preparation of survey instruments. If a pre-designed questionnaire with a pre-determined content is to be used for data collection, it is prepared at this stage. While a full discussion of questionnaire design is presented later at chapter 8, it suffices here to make a distinction between the two main types of questions open-ended questions and closed questions. Most surveys have a combination of open-ended and closed questions. The survey researcher designs the questionnaires and makes decisions on what items will have open-ended questions and what other items will be investigated using closed questions. Sometimes, these decisions are determined by the nature, purpose and objectives of the study.

Open-ended questions are those types of questions without pre-determined responses for the respondent to choose from. Questions such as "How old are you"?, "Where were you born"?, "Why are you concerned about crime? are classified as open-ended because no responses are provided for the respondent to select one.

With closed questions, specifically selected responses accompany each question. For example, the following question and the accompanying responses may appear on a questionnaire:

"How will you describe your fear of crime"?
Possible answers include "Very afraid, afraid, Not Afraid" or High, Medium or Low.

The respondent selects the answer which best reflects their thinking, opinions, perception, views or belief. The question is said to be closed because the answers have been provided and there is no provision for the respondent to provide another answer outside those provided. Sometimes, "Other" is included as a response category to cover responses that fall outside the main response category.

As stated earlier, most survey instruments will have a mix of open-ended and close questions because it creates variety in the interview and works to reduce boredom for the respondent. Diversifying the types of questions also stimulates or serves as a catalyst to let the respondent use their brains, as they may have to think through their answer to the open-ended questions. Open –ended questions are also flexible attracting varied responses. Another advantage is that respondents may see an open-ended question as an opportunity to advance their position on a particular issue. Open-ended questions have the potential to facilitate further probing by the interviewer. In unstructured or semi-structured interviewing, open-ended questions serve a very useful purpose in follow up questions, following a response to a specific closed question.

A number of problems can be identified or associated with open-ended questions. The answers to open-ended questions cannot be assigned codes prior to data collection, and sometimes they are not easy to code because of the variety and length of answers. The way to overcome this problem involves grouping similar responses into categories and coding the categories. For example, respondents may provide 16 – 20 different answers to the question "Why are you afraid of crime"? This is because individual perceptions, attitudes, experiences and beliefs vary, and so also are their responses, The researcher has to make every effort to group the answers into say 5 broad categories of like or similar responses. In addition, the wide variety of potential responses makes the analysis of responses to open-ended question more difficult to undertake than closed questions.

The main advantage of closed questions is that it results in precise answers which are therefore easier to code than the open-ended questions. Closed questions produce data that are easily analyzed and presented. In comparison with open-ended questions, closed questions are cheaper to administer in terms of interview time, and they are also cheaper in terms of data processing. It is faster to process responses to closed questions because they have pre-determined codes which can quickly be entered relative to open-ended questions where the responses have to be assigned codes after data collection. It must also be mentioned that closed questions can help identify discrepancies in responses right in the field.

The disadvantages of closed questions are that a limitation is placed on the potential responses, resulting in less variety. Respondents are forced to choose answers which they may not agree to if they are not happy with any of the pre-determined responses. The pre-determined responses appear to be put in compartments or categories determined by the researcher prior to the data collection, and may not reflect the total picture of potential responses.

SAMPLING

Sampling is 'sine qua non' for survey research, i.e. survey research cannot do without sampling. In participant observation research methodology, the researcher tends to focus on small groups of people and often without the use of a sample. In contrast, sampling is required in all forms of survey methodologies, perhaps except observational surveys. Even in observational surveys the researcher may have tosample traffic lights and roundabouts.. A study which covers the entire population is not a survey but a census. Good examples of criminological studies which cover the total population include prison censuses undertaken periodically by prison officials, justice sector ministries and departments and individual researchers. For example, prisons in New Zealand undertake weekly prison censuses with a view to establishing total number of inmates and available places for new inmates. Prisons and related corrections facilities in Australia, the United States and other countries similarly undertake prison censuses from time to time, with provisions for regular censuses in some jurisdictions.

However, it is not logistically and financially possible to collect information on the total population, especially when undertaking studies on topics such as victimization, crime levels, rehabilitation facilities, corrections and justice sector programs, fear of crime, population's view of police practices and procedures and similar criminological topics; It is, thus, usual practice to select a section of the eligible population, referred to as the sample, and use it in the survey. For this reason, surveys are sometimes called sample surveys.

A number of sampling procedures are available in survey research. Most are scientific and based on probabilities, but some are based on convenience. The decision on which sampling procedures to employ rests with the researcher, but they are sometimes determined by local conditions, prevailing culture and cultural practices, funding availability and requirements of funding agencies, the ease of data collection, goals and objectives of the study and the type of study. The total population from which the sample is drawn is called the sampling frame and, depending on the specific investigation, the sampling frame can be the total population of the country, the total number of prisoners in a particular prison or the total number of prisoners in the whole country, State, Province or Region, the total number of reported crimes or the total number of victims. All cases of the sampling frame are listed and sometimes assigned numbers before sampling is undertaken. In short, the list comprising the total number of cases constitutes the sampling frame from which the sample is drawn.

Face to face interviewing, telephone surveys and postal surveys usually involve the use of a sample population. Observational surveys do not usually involve prior sampling as the researcher surveys all what is happening. If you have ever participated in any face to face interview, you were part of a sample selected for that survey. You may also recall an occasion when your phone rang, you answered and the person at the other end said "I am calling from this business and I would like you to spare a few minutes to answer some questions for us….'. You were probably participating in a telephone survey for which you were a member of the sample.

Types of Sampling

There are many different types of sampling used in survey research. They are broadly classified as probability and non probability samples. Each classification comprises specific sampling procedures. The difference between probability and non probability samples lies in the way members of the sample are selected.

Probability Sampling

Probability sampling, as the name suggests, works on the principle of equal mathematical chance of selection for each member of the sampling frame. The instrument through which this occurs is randomness. When members of the sampling frame are randomly selected to form the sample, the principle of equal chance for all members is achieved. Each member of the sampling frame could be selected. The sample is said to represent the total population or number of cases from which it was drawn, and this is because each member has the same and equal chance of becoming part of the selected sample.

A further distinction is made between simple random sample and cluster sample. In simple random sample, the sampling procedure involves one stage and only one sample is drawn randomly and used in the study. .Cluster samples are popular probability samples used in a number of criminological surveys, depending on the type of investigation and its objectives and goals. In this type of sampling, the researcher engages in multi-stage sampling. A larger sample of the sampling frame is initially selected, called the large sample followed by the selection of a subgroup from this large sample which is usually referred to as the medium sample. Further subgroups are derived from the medium sample and they are called small samples.

For example a criminological researcher, investigating the reasons why inmates of a particular prison committed the crimes for which they were convicted, could undertake various levels of sampling if cluster sampling is employed. . The researcher may first randomly select a specific number of inmates from the total population of inmates in that prison, and this constitutes the large sample.

From the large sample, the researcher undertakes further random sampling by grouping and selecting those with a specific level of educational attainment. Those selected will constitute the medium sample. The researcher proceeds to undertake further sampling from the medium sample using a specific characteristic of the sample members such as employment status, marital status etc. This new sample is called the small sample and it is this sample that the researcher interviews or collects data on.

A distinction should be made between two types of probability sampling, namely sampling with replacement and sampling without replace. In the first type, members of the sampling frame who are selected for the sample keep their place in the sense that the member can be replaced when they leave the sample for any reason. In sampling without replacement, each member can be selected only once and there is no replacement when a member leaves the sample. Sampling with or without replacement can occur in both simple random sampling and cluster sampling.

It must be mentioned that all probability sampling procedures allow for generalizations to be made about the total population using the evidence from the sample. Evidence from simple random sampling and cluster sampling can and is usually used to describe the parameters or the characteristics of the population in the sampling frame in what is called generalization etc. As indicated in the proceeding paragraphs, this is not the case for non probability sampling.

Other Types of Sampling

In addition to probability sampling, criminological researchers have the choice of many other types of sampling broadly known as non probability samples. They include convenience or accidental sampling, purposeful sampling, quota sampling, and snowball sampling..

Convenience sampling is used in studies where it is difficult to get a sampling frame or where it is difficult to get participants or study subjects simply because of the nature of the study or stigma associated with the topic or phenomenon, or because the study is very intrusive of personal circumstance etc. Studies involving prostitution as a crime, families of convicted murderers and serious violent offenders, victims of violent rapes and related sexual assaults, prison gang activity involving interview of gang members and interview of Judges about sentencing patterns and discrepancies in sentences for criminals convicted of similar offences, may all require the use of a sample of convenience, Many potential study subjects in these circumstances may not want to share their experiences with the researcher, believing it to be too personal, painful and/or distressing. The researcher engages only those who are able and willing to provide information and, as such, members of convenience samples are constituted without any scientific selection basis.

In convenience sampling, the sampling frame can be the same as in probability sampling. However, how sampling members are selected is different. As the name suggests, members of convenience sampling are chosen as a matter of convenience and ease of obtaining sample members. You may recall times when you were walking through the square or plaza and somebody approaches and invites you to spend little time to answer a few questions. You were a member of a convenience sample. The researcher or interviewer is accepting any person who is available and willing to participate in the study and there is no prior selection of sample members. It is easy and convenient for the researcher to select the sample in this way, but it is not representative of the population, mainly because each member of the total population or sampling frame does not have the same level and /or equal mathematical chance of being selected.

Another common non probability sampling is what is called purposeful sampling. In purposeful sampling, the members of the sample are selected for a purpose or reason. Purposeful sampling is based on a particular characteristic which is of special interests and relevance to the study. For example, a criminological researcher may be investigating white collar crimes, decides to include only convicted criminals who have postgraduate degrees in the sampling frame and proceeds to select a sample from that sampling frame. Everybody in the sample has been purposefully selected because they have been identified as convicted white collar criminals who have postgraduate degrees, and that is purposeful selection of study subjects. Convicted criminals without a postgraduate degree are purposefully excluded from the sampling frame and, thus, the study. Like other non probability sampling procedures, purposeful sampling does not permit the researcher to establish the level of precision and the findings cannot be used in external generalizations on white collar crimes. In other words, the findings relate to the specific sample population and cannot be used to generalize for the broader population outside the sample, except for population which has the key sample selection criterion, i.e. postgraduate qualifications.

Yet another type of non probability sampling procedure is quota sampling. As the name suggests, quota sampling involves the allocation of a quota to every subgroup of the population who are represented in the sample. It allows the criminological researcher to pre-determine the composition of the sample according to some selected variables such as age, gender, marital status, educational attainment, geographical distribution etc. The researcher determines the number of respondents from identified categories who will be represented in the final sample.

For example, a researcher studying the experiences of victims of crime in the States of New York, California, Wisconsin, and Maine has to determine the number of respondents who will represent each of the States in the study Different reasons are used to determine the level of representation, usually based on the objectives of the study and/or population size. So that out of a sample size of say 5000, the researcher may decide to select 2000 respondents from California, 1500 from new York, 800 from Wisconsin and 700 from Maine or any other distribution. The researcher is placing a limit on how many respondents can be selected from each State while ensuring that each State is duly represented according to the specific quota characteristic of relevance to the study.

Quota sampling is usually used in stratified sampling in which people of different ethnic backgrounds or characteristics are included in the sample. For example, in New Zealand, convicted criminals are classified as "Pakeha" (white or Caucasian), Maori (indigenous population of New Zealand) and other (Pacific Islanders, Africans, Asians etc). A sample for a study of prison inmates can comprise a level of pre-determined representation for each ethnic group.

In this case the pre-determined stratification will be based on the total number of Pakeha, Maori and other groups in the inmate population of that prison, say Christchurch Women's Prison, for example. Quota sampling is useful for ensuring that minor groups are not missed, excluded or overlooked in the study.

Another variation is what is called sampling by proportion according to size. In this type of sampling, the categories of sample members are selected according to their representation (proportion) in the sampling frame. It involves a number of stages.

First the sampling frame is determined and the proportion of each category in the frame is mathematically calculated by dividing the number of potential respondents in each category by the total population in the sampling frame.

Secondly, the researcher determines the sample size for the study. By multiplying the sample size by the proportion for each category, the number of respondents from each category is obtained. The sum of respondents from all categories must be equal to the sample size, while the sum of the proportions should be equal to 1 or as close to one as possible (e.g. 0.99, 1.01).

The following table provides useful step by step illustration. In this illustration, there are 4 settlements named A to D (column 1). The population of each town is in column 2, resulting in a total population of 100 000 in the sampling frame. Column 3 shows the proportion of each town's population in the sampling frame.

The researcher has determined that an overall sample size of 5 000 was appropriate for the study. By multiplying the sample size by the proportion for each town (column 4), the number of respondents for each category is obtained (column 5). The sum of all the respondents selected for the categories should be equal to the sample size. This type of sampling allows for the benefits of stratification to be reaped in that the different strata in the sampling frame are appropriately represented in the selected sample.

Table 1. Sampling by proportion according to size

Settlement	Population	Proportion in Sampling Frame	Proportion X Sample Size	No of Respondents selected in the Sample
Town A	15,000	0.15	0.15 X 5,000	750
Town B	25,000	0.25	0.25 X 5,000	1 250
Town C	10,000	0.10	0.10 X 5,000	500
Town D	50,000	0.50	0.50 X 5,000	2 500
Total	100,000	1.0		5 000

Sample Size is 5,000.

Sampling by proportion according to size is not the same as quota sampling, although both types of sampling allocate representation to each category in the sample. The main distinction is that quota sampling needs not always be done through proportional distribution. The size of each category in the sample can be determined in many other ways, including allocating quotas on the basis of the special circumstances of the study, specific objectives of the study, or on the basis of social, cultural or another relevant characteristic of the study population as determined by the researcher. It is sometimes necessary to increase the representation of smaller groups in quota beyond their proportions to allow for meaningful and effective analysis, or where the study subject matter is associated more with the smaller groups than the large ones.

Snowball Sampling

Snowball sampling is the type of sampling procedure which involves the use of the leaders or at least one member of the study population to reach the other members of the said study population. The approach is to identify and establish contact with the leaders or a member of the group who subsequently leads the researcher to the others. Where members of the study population are known to refuse participation in studies or remain elusive, such as gangsters, prostitutes, and other socially excluded and minority groups, sometimes the only way to reach them is to go through their leaders. The leaders, in particular, are in a position not only to lead the researcher to the subjects, but more importantly to convince or even coerce the members to participate.

Snowball has the disadvantage that study subjects are not only readily available, but also the subjects may not be forthcoming. This approach is very important for investigations involving criminal activity or victimization among refugees, migrants groups, Aborigines, Maori and other minorities and socially excluded groups such as prostitutes. Snowball sampling is also effective for the study of sparsely distributed populations. In this sampling variation, no sampling frame is used because no sampling frame exists. It is impossible to have a sampling frame for prostitutes, victims of crime who are homeless, gang members and so on. Snowball sampling results in a non probability sample because the selected sample members are included as they are reached and as they agree to participate. They are not selected randomly and the use of the findings for external generalization is, by and large, compromised.

It is in a sense similar to convenience sampling, as access or rather lack of access to study subjects is a key issue in both sampling procedures. So also is the unavailability of a sampling frame. Besides, convenience sampling and snowball sampling fall into the category of accidental sampling. Accidental sampling occurs when subjects are not easily accessible and study subjects are selected as they become available and as they agree to participate. A useful merit of snowball sample is that for some of the groups (studied through snowball sampling), such as prostitutes, gang members, homeless people, and other socially excluded groups, may know each other, with an inherent implication that they can provide information on other members and each other.

Systematic Sampling

In systematic sampling, the members of the sample are selected on the basis of a system that the survey researcher decides to use. While, it is possible in practice to arbitrary choose a system, there is an easy, simple and more useful and perhaps more appropriate way of determining the system. For example, a researcher decides to select a sample size of 300 from a prison population of 3000. This means that 1 out of every 10 prisoners in the sampling frame is to be selected. In this illustration of systematic sampling, the survey researcher selects every 10th person in the sampling frame. To make decisions on which system to use, four easy steps must be followed:

1. Develop a sampling frame, i.e. a list of the total population
2. Determine an appropriate sample size (previous discussed)
3. Divide the total number of people in the sampling frame by the sample size
4. The result determines the system which is then used to select the sample.

In the above example of a total population of 3000 and a sample size of 300, if we divide 3000 by 300, the result is 10, hence the selection of every 10th person. The results changes if the sample size is reduced to 100' When 3000 is divided by 100, the result is 30 and this means that every 30th person is selected for the sample.

Systematic sampling is easy and simple to use even where the researcher is not good at sampling. Some survey researchers prefer systematic sampling to random sampling because they can handle it with ease without losing the scientific basis of the sample selection procedures. The key disadvantage is that systematic sampling can result in a biased sample. In the example of prison inmates above, care should be taken in systematic sampling to avoid bias arising from selecting too many sample members with a particular characteristic. Prison inmates live in what is called "wings" within prison. If a list of prisoners is obtained (sampling frame) and every 19th inmate is selected, it is possible to include more inmates from one wing simply because their names are clustered together in the list. Including many respondents from one wing may produce biased data because their responses may reflect more to conditions in their wing. Their problems may be different from those in the other wings, hence the prevalence of potential bias in the sample.

Sample Size and Sampling Error

The total number of people or cases in the selected sample is called the sample size. For example, if there are 300, 000 relatives of murder victims in a study locality and 300 are selected for the sample, the 300, 000 victims constitute the sampling frame from which a sample size of 300 victims' relatives is drawn. There is a general notion in survey research that, for a specific sampling frame, the larger the sample, the better the potential results of the study and the greater the ability to use the parameters of the sample population to describe the total population. This is because statistically the larger the sample size, the lower the potential sampling errors. In simple terms, the sampling error is the error associated with the selection and use of a specific sample, instead of another sample of the same size from the same sampling frame. Remember that the object of sampling is to attempt to use the results or the parameters of the sample for external generalization.

For example, from the above example of 300 cases, at least 10 samples of 30 each can possibly be drawn if there is no replacement .Each sample will have its own variability in terms of the responses provided. The error arising because sample 3 was used instead of sample 7 for example is the sampling error associated with that sample. If sample 2 is used another set of errors may arise in terms of the variability of the responses of the members of that sample, and those errors may not be of the same magnitude as the errors from the other sample. Each sample has its own sampling errors because the members are different and their responses may be different. The sample error denotes, to some extent, the precision of the responses provided. It shows the extent to which the estimates of values of the variables in the study can be made with precision.

The question arises as to what is the optimum sample size. There is nothing like a standard appropriate sample size for criminological surveys In theory, there is a mathematical formula that could be used to determine and calculate the optimum sample size for a specific sampling frame, but this is not covered in this book. However, in practice, many researchers do not use any mathematical formula to determine what sample size is appropriate for their study. In general practice, the sample size depends on many factors including the sampling frame, funding (the larger the sample, the higher the cost), characteristics of the population, type of study, goals and objectives of the study etc. In the real world, these factors sometimes actually determine the sample size appropriate for the specific study. For example, if there is limited funding, the sample size can be compromised and the researcher would have to do with a smaller sample than the level the researcher would have liked. That said it is important to note that the researcher has the responsibility to consider the specific circumstances of the study and all the factors involved to arrive at an appropriate sample size for any particular study.

Other Survey Errors

Generally, there are two main groups of survey errors, namely selection errors and non selection errors. Selection errors include sampling errors, sampling frame errors and non response. Sampling errors are one group of many errors that can potentially affect the survey, but it appears to be the most popular and most highlighted group of survey errors.. Broadly speaking, selection errors comprise sampling errors, errors associated with the sampling frame and non response or inadequate response. Sampling errors have been discussed previously. Sampling frame errors arise as a result of using the wrong sampling frame, including ineligible respondents in the sampling frame or excluding eligible respondents from the sampling frame. Sampling frame errors may also arise from inadequate sampling frames arising from the poor and/or partial coverage of the potential study subjects in the geographical area of the study's scope.

Non response occurs in a lot of surveys and is usually classified as missing data. Many a time, researchers find that selected respondents do not agree to answer all or specific questions resulting in non response. Other times interviewers miss a question or two or fail to record the response to an item, resulting in non response. The problem of non response is exacerbated by the fact that the error is not usually detected until long after the interview and during the data processing stage. Needless to say that, if respondents find a particular question intrusive or uncomfortable to answer, they may refuse to provide a response. Besides, ethical requirements make it obligatory for the interviewer not to pressurize respondents, but to move on to other items/questions. Non response is inevitable in a number of criminological surveys. Where data on vital items are missing, it can create serious problems for the researcher and sometimes it results in additional trips to the field for more data collection.

Non selection errors are those errors that are not associated with the sample or its selection. Most are due to human errors arising from the design of the research instruments through interviewer and related data collection errors to data processing errors It does not happen often, but it is up to researchers to design the instruments appropriately, and include items in the questionnaire which do provide the exact data required, to avoid these survey errors. The research design must provide the data to address the research questions or test the proposed hypothesis. As discussed after this stage, the survey researcher must operationalize the design through data collection, measurements and analysis. In engaging in measurement, the survey researcher must define the estimators to be used and the use of the wrong estimator or measures could and does result in non selection errors.

As alluded to earlier, survey research has the tendency to produce large scale quantitative data which have to be assembled and processed. As a result of the large volume of data, survey researchers recruit, train and employ data entry personnel to input the data into datasets using pre-determined statistical packages, such as SPSS, SAS etc. Data processing errors arise when the wrong data is entered. The stage after data entry is the time for coding. Coding is discussed as part of data analysis later in this chapter. Coding errors and problems arise when data are not correctly coded, i.e. when codes are incorrectly assigned to the items, or where wrong codes are recorded for specific items.

IMPLEMENTATION OF THE SELECTED RESEARCH DESIGN

The logical sequence after selecting a research design and an appropriate sample is to proceed to implement the research design, i.e. proceed to carry out the research. During this stage the survey researcher finalizes many aspects of the study including but not limited to completing training of interviewers, field manuals, piloting of instruments, arrangements for interviews to take place, printing of questionnaires and their distribution to interviewers, reporting arrangements for interviewers and related field staff. .Some of these activities are initiated during the preparatory or preliminary stage but they are finalized at this stage. More importantly, the mechanisms for communication between the researcher and other survey administrative personnel and the interviewers and their supervisors are finalized during this stage.

One very important advantage that survey research has over participant observation is that the survey researcher is able to test the pre-designed instruments before proceeding to the actual data collection phase. As discussed later in the section on measurements, if there are errors and problems with the instruments, there is an opportunity to correct them by modifying the instruments or the way the instruments are administered prior to data collection. If the instrument do not measure what they are intended to measure (i.e. lack of validity), or if the instruments are not producing consistent results (i.e. not reliable), redesign becomes imminent and survey research actually lends itself better to redesign and changes of the instruments as and when necessary, but prior to actual interviewing. Validity and reliability are discussed in greater detail as part of measurement later in this chapter.

Pilot testing can be undertaken in the preparatory stage but many researchers choose to do the pilot during the early part of the implementation stage In pilot testing, the survey researcher selects a mini sample of the study population and the instruments are administered to the members of the mini sample. While the primary objective of the pilot is to pre-test the instruments, pilot testing also allows the researcher to identify potential non questionnaire problems and work at their solutions. For example, respondents may refuse to participate in the pilot for various reasons. This is seen straightaway as a potential problem for the actual survey, compelling the survey researcher to improve the marketing of the survey as well as the way and manner the study subjects are approached. Other times, pilot testing may reveal that arrangements for transporting materials to interviewer or for transporting interviewers to the study subjects are not effective. The survey researcher can then modify these arrangements and other logistic problems prior to the actual data collection. In addition, it should be remembered that any data collection or field problems, identified from the piloting of the instruments, must be addressed before the final data collection exercise.

If face to face interview is the survey research methodology for the study, trained interviewers are used to collect information from the study subjects in the mini sample. If postal survey research methodology is selected, pre-designed instruments are mailed to the selected mini sample for self completion and return. If the research methodology for the study is telephone survey, then a mini sample is selected from the telephone listings. Trained interviewers are used to obtain data from the mini sample. The responses are analyzed, and the instruments as a whole are assessed for their validity and reliability and decisions made whether to amend the procedures, modify the instruments or leave them intact (dependent on the outcome of the assessments).

Following piloting and identification of solutions to any problems arising from the pilot exercise, data collection will then be implemented. The interviewers and their supervisors are sent into the field to interview the respondents selected in the study sample (face to face interviews), or directly to use the telephone to obtain data from respondents (telephone surveys). Similarly, if the survey methodology is postal survey, the finalized questionnaires are mailed to the selected respondents for completion and return.. During the implementation stage the survey researcher can be very busy, relaying information to field staff and receiving information from them. The researcher can also be very busy attending to problems as and when they arise together with any emerging issues.

As part of the project management plan, the survey researcher defines timelines for the achievement of various field objectives including when all interviews are to be completed. When data collection is completed, measurement and data processing (data entry, analysis and interpretation) commence.

MEASUREMENT

Measurement is the medium by which the survey researcher operationalizes the variables, determines and defines how the variables in the instrument will be estimated and/or studied. How the variables will be measured is pre-determined and the decisions are made with the selection of the research design. So that, at the time of data collection, the researcher should have determined the variables on which data will be collected and how those variables will be measured and analyzed. Measurement is the medium through which the study's theoretical concepts and underpinnings (the hypothesis) are transformed into tangible empirical concepts, which can be examined. The key point is to describe the actual measurement procedures to allow for the hypothesis to be tested and/or research questions answered.

The usual practice is for the survey researcher to identify and establish an unambiguous measure for each variable, to allow for the transformation of the data on each variable into something that can be examined and understood, i.e. something more tangible. In simple language, measurement is the way the researcher positions the data on each variable for effective analysis. The process is to place the responses into measurable categories. The choice of categories is essential for effective measurement of the responses, as a correct choice will enhance the testing of the study hypothesis and/or provide answers to the research questions. The wrong choice creates more problems in transforming the theoretical concepts into empirical concepts and may not adequately test the hypothesis and/or answer the study's research questions.

A couple of examples will illustrate and facilitate understanding of measurement. In the first example, which is about a victimization study, a researcher may include the question "have you ever been a victim of crime"? The researcher may operationalize and measure the responses to the question in several ways.

The object is to provide measures which will make it unambiguous for the responses to be categorized, observed, understood and used to test the hypothesis or answer a research question on the level of victimization. Most researchers will select two contrasting categories for the measurement of this question namely Yes and No. Others may go further to include "Don't know or Not Sure". Either way it is possible to put the responses into categories which can be seen and understood, and which allow the theoretical concepts (embodied in the hypothesis) to be tested empirically.

Another illustration involves the use of attitude scales to measure individual responses. For example, a survey researcher investigating victims' experiences with the Police may ask the question "how satisfied were you with the way the Police handled your case"? Attitudinal scaling which includes categories such as Very Satisfied, Satisfied, Unsatisfied and Very Unsatisfied may be used to operationalize and measure the responses provided. Each response will fall under one of the headings in the scale, allowing unambiguous knowledge, understanding and observation to occur. The headings in the scale are the operational definitions which enable the researcher to estimate what number and proportion of respondents were very satisfied, satisfied, unsatisfied and very unsatisfied, and to transform the theoretical concepts in the question and the associated hypothesis into empirical, measurable and analytical concepts.

Levels of Measurement

A brief introduction to the various levels of measurement used in survey research is presented in this section with the sole purpose of making the reader aware of the availability of these measurement levels. Most statistics books will point to four levels of measurement in survey research, namely nominal, ordinal, interval and ratio levels. Nominal level of measurement is simple and less sophisticated than the others, with ratio level being the most sophisticated, followed by interval level which is followed by ordinal level. Most surveys involve one or more of these levels of measurement regardless of the researcher's training and/or experience, and irrespective of the subject matter of the study.

In measurement, the data on a variable are put into categories. Where the categories are not intrinsic (not scaled), they are put into fixed firm categories, and the measurement is said be at a Nominal level. For example in a survey of programs in a corrections rehabilitation facility, the programs may be categorized as recreation, group discussion, lectures, exercises and gym workout. These are non intrinsic categories and the programs have been placed for Nominal measurement. The programs are not scaled in any ascending or descending order. Again, a study of the types of punishment in New Zealand will examine fines, community services, periodic detention and prison terms.. In some countries such as the United States, convicted offenders may be sentenced to other types of punishment such as probation or parole after serving an appropriate portion of a jail sentence. These are not scaled sentences and are as such Nominal variables. The types of analysis that can be undertaken using Nominal level of measurement can be limited.

If an Ordinal level of measurement is to be undertaken, the data on the variable must lend themselves to scaling. The data on the variable must be in one form of ascending or descending order or another form of scaling. Referring to the earlier example on the experiences of victims of crime with the Police, the question was asked –"How happy were you with the manner the Police handled your case"/ A list of scaling responses were provided including Very Satisfied, Satisfied, Unsatisfied and Very Unsatisfied. The levels of measurement are improving or increasing from Very Unsatisfied to Very Satisfied and the measurement is said to be done at the Ordinary level. Responses or data measured using categories like this allow for more sophisticated analysis than Nominal level of measurement.

Following Ordinal level of measurement in terms of sophistication is Interval level of measurement. In Interval level of measurement, there is the possibility to determine the difference between two measured cases quantitatively. The object is to introduce and establish a unit of measurement that will allow the quantitative differences to be explained qualitatively. For example, prison inmates, undertaking a course in science as part of their educational training, are tested at the end of the course. Prisoner A achieves a mark of 90% and prisoner C obtained 30%. In interval level of measurement, it can be said that Prisoner A obtained a mark three times higher than that of Prisoner C, but it cannot be said that Prisoner A was three times as good in science as Prisoner C. A number of qualitative factors can explain the difference in marks including their individual levels of understanding of the specific test items, their intelligence differences, and their personal circumstances on the day of the test. Besides, if a different set of questions had been used in the test, Prisoner C could have done better. In practice, interval level of measurement is not widely used in criminological survey research.

The final level of measurement is what is called Ratio level. The Ratio level is the most sophisticated level of measurement, the values or data on the variable are scaled and may be put into ratios, enhancing the possibility of undertaking a more detailed analysis and with precision. It is given greater attention here because of its very high level of sophistication. In addition, there are fewer restrictions on the Ratio level of measurement which also increases the ability to undertake detailed and sophisticated analysis. The minimum value, zero, is firmly fixed and non arbitrary, and subsequent values increase from it. . Examples of Ratio level of measurement include age, number of programs completed by inmates, number of victims per population of the suburb they live in etc. To fully appreciate the level of sophistication of Ratio level of measurement, let us look at table 2. In a study of criminal victimization in four towns –A, B, C and D, the survey researcher decides as a central theme to establish which of the towns have the highest victims per population (table 2).

The towns are listed in column 1, population in column 2, victims per 1000 in column 3 and victim per population rank column 4. By dividing the number of victims by the population of the town and multiplying by a constant of 1000, the number of victims per 1000 population is obtained. The sophistication of the ratio level of measurement is demonstrated in the fact that if no ratio is computed, the conclusion may be drawn that victimization is highest in Town D. However, if the figures for number of victims per 1000 population are examined, it is evident that Town C has the highest victim/population ratio, i.e. the highest concentration of victims per 1000 population (5.0 per 1000 population), followed by Town A (3.3 per 1000 population). Victimization is more prone or dense in Town C than in any of the three other settlements. In this specific Ratio level of measurement, we have standardized for population. The average number of victims per 1000 population for the four settlements is about 2.6, so that Towns A and C are above the average and Towns B and D are below the average. Thus, various analyses can be undertaken using ratio level data.

It is also possible to compute what this book introduces as the Density of Victimization, i.e. the number of victims per square area (kilometers or miles). Density of Victimization is similar to the concept of population density in demography. A glance at table 3 reveals that column 2 contains data on area in square kilometers and column 3 has the number of victims, and column 4 number of victims per square kilometer. This presents another level of sophistication for Ratio level of measurement. Column 4 shows the density of victimization (i.e. number of victims per square kilometer), and the number of victims per 1000 square kilometers is shown in brackets. It is evident that the ranking also changes allowing the researcher to undertake varied analysis to add value to the study results.

Table 2. Illustration of Ratio Level of Measurement

Settlement	Population	Number of Victims	Victims per 1000 population	Victims per population Rank
Town A	15,000	50	3.3	2
Town B	25,000	60	2.4	3
Town C	10,000	50	5.0	1
Town D	50,000	95	1.9	4
Total	100,000	255	2.6	

Table3. Illustration of Ratio Level of Measurement using Density of Victimization

Settlement	Area in Sq. Km	Number of Victims	Victims per Sq Km	Victims per Area Rank
Town A	5 000	50	0.01 (1.0)	4
Town B	2 000	60	0.03 (3.0)	3
Town C	10 00	50	0.05 (5.0)	2
Town D	8 000	95	0.01 (11.9)	1
Total				

*Figures in brackets indicate victimizations per 1000 sq. km(Column 4).

Discrete and Continuous Variables

In the measurement of survey data, a further distinction is made between discrete and continuous variables. The underlying objective is to distinguish between those measurement numbers or variables that can fall within a continuum from those that do not. Discrete variables can be counted in precise numbers and are not presented in a continuum. For example the number of criminal traffic accidents during a specific period was 20 in Town A, 30 in Town B and so on, or the number of reported crimes was in a particular year 500 in Town A, 400 in Town B and 350 in Town C. The numbers stand on their own and there is no continuum. In contrast, continuous variable fall within a continuum and can be anything within a range or interval. Examples of continuous variables in criminology include the ages of inmates in a particular corrections facility, say James Fort Prison in Ghana, Glendairy Prison in Barbados or Rimutaka Prison in New Zealand. The ages fall within an interval and can range from 17 years to 80 years. The ages of the prisoners are in a continuum and that is continuous data or variables. In criminological survey research, both discrete and continuous variables are widely used, with each lending itself to diverse analysis.

Validity and Reliability

With measurements come the concepts of validity and reliability. Are the measures actually measuring what they are intended to measure? If they are, they are said to be valid measures or that the measures have a fair or high validity (depending on how well they are measuring what they are intended to measure). If the measures are not measuring what they are set up to measure, they are classified as not valid. In surveys a number of questions are asked on various variables. It is expected that those questions will provide valid measures on the variables. For example, a criminological survey researcher is investigating concerns about crime in the society. The researcher employs fear of crime as a variable to establish concerns about crime. The survey respondents are subsequently asked the question "Are you afraid of becoming a victim of crime"? This is followed by a scaling question such as "How afraid are you of crime"/, or "Will you describe your fear of crime as Very High, High, Moderate or Low"? If responses to either or both questions provide a measurement of concerns about crime, then the variable fear of crime has a high validity and is said to be a valid measure of concerns about crime. In other words, the variable fear of crime is measuring what it was intended or set up to measure.

Reliability is closely related in a sense to validity and the two concepts are usually discussed together. However, a clear distinction exists between the two concepts. A measurement of a variable is said to be reliable if it consistently measures what it is intended to measure. If a measurement is reliable, then it must always produce about the consistent results every time it is used, irrespective of the sample used for the data collection. As discussed in the previous section on implementing the selected design, survey researchers tend to test their instruments in the field prior to the actual data collection in what is called pilot testing. If survey instruments are piloted and they consistently produce about the same results, then the instruments or items in the instruments are said to be reliable. If the results obtained from different administration of the same instruments are not consistent, the instruments are subsequently said to be unreliable or lack reliability.

Validity and reliability are very essential in survey research. They establish confidence in the measurements and the overall criminological survey instruments. There is no point in pursuing a survey in which the validity and reliability of the variables and their measurements are not high, especially if there is little to no validity and reliability. The concepts are not of the same level of importance in participant observation. This is because in participant observation, the data are collected first before any analysis, whereas in surveys the instruments can first be carried out in a pilot testing and their validity and reliability established. If the measurements are found to be of low or no validity and/or reliability, they can be redesigned or modified to improve their validity and/or reliability before the actual data collection begins.

Bias and Variability

Bias and variability are two other attributes of measurements in survey research and they are briefly discussed in this section. The meaning of bias in survey research is similar to the general meaning of the word in the English language. The inherent philosophy or concept is prejudice. Bias in survey research is the situation where there is consistent prejudice in one or more directions for or against the measurement. Sometimes, bias occurs where instruments are pre-designed to produce consistent results in a particular direction for any reason, or because the researcher invariably wants those results. Other times, bias occurs from the interview process when interviewers directly or indirectly push respondents to answer in a particular direction. Where the results are biased, the conclusions of the study many not be accurate.

In criminological survey research, it is often found that the measurements exhibit some degree of changes or variability. These are usually identified from the discrepancies in the measurements. These discrepancies are neither predictable nor easily explained. It must also be mentioned that variability is not identified in a single measurement, but rather from a number of interrelated measurements. The extent of variability depends on the level of reliability of the measurements. Higher variability is found in situations where the measurements are not reliable, i.e. where the measurements are producing inconsistent results.

DATA PROCESSING

Following data collection is the stage of data processing. The main tasks during this stage are data entry, storage, management, analysis and interpretation. Decisions made on data processing during the selection of design stage are implemented during the data processing stage. During the preparatory stage or during the actual data collection phase when the interviewers have been dispatched into the field, the survey researcher trains the data entry personnel. Using pre-designed training manuals, the survey researcher prepares the data entry personnel for the huge task ahead and gets them ready for their upcoming duties. Data entry arrangements are made during the selection of design stage and implemented after data collection.

Data entry is a very important task and must be undertaken with due care, hence the need for training of data entry personnel. It is also essential for all the data entry personnel to be trained so they can enter the data in a consistent and uniform manner. Inaccurate or partial entry of data will adversely impact on the results and conclusions of the study. Even where professional data entry personnel are employed, some level of training is still necessary, mainly because every survey is different and has its own design, measurements and dimensions.

How the data collected are stored and managed is also very important. In most surveys, the researcher assures the respondents of the confidentiality of their responses. This presupposes a need for the data to be stored securely and managed properly to ensure that the confidentiality assurance given to the respondents prior to and during data collection is maintained.

Coding

After data collection, interviewers return the completed questionnaires to the researcher (telephone and face to face interviewing) or self-completed questionnaires are returned (postal survey). The data on the questionnaires must be transferred to the pre-design electronic databases. To facilitate this transfer, the responses are assigned numerical values called codes. In its simplest example, suppose a researcher working on criminal victimization poses the question "Have you ever been a victim of crime? Yes or No. responses are expected and sometimes Not Sure is added. To facilitate data transfer into the databases, numerical values are assigned as follows: Yes 1, No 2 and Not Sure 3. These values are entered into the databases reflecting the responses and are called codes. The process of assigning codes to responses is what is called coding in survey research.

Coding occurs in two ways, namely before data collection and after data collection. Coding which is done before data collection is referred to as pre-survey coding or pre-coding while coding occurring after data collection is known as post -survey coding or post-coding. In general, closed questions lend themselves better to pre-coding and open-ended questions can only be post-coded because the variety of responses are not known until after data collection. In closed questions, pre-design responses are provided for the respondent to select the one which best suits the respondent's situation or view. Codes can therefore be assigned in advance because the responses have been identified and specified. Sometimes questions are designed to seek multiple responses. Whether single or multiple responses are sought, the responses provided must be coded.

In the following table, a researcher is investigating victims' experiences in the criminal justice system and, in particular, their experiences with the Police, Prosecutors, Court Room practices, the Bench, the Verdict and the sentence. Respondents are asked the question "With regards to your victimization, how satisfied were you with the following? Four responses are provided as indicated in table 4.

Table 4. Victim's satisfaction with the criminal justice system

Variable	Very Satisfied	Satisfied	Not Satisfied	Not Very Satisfied
Police		2		
Prosecutors		1		
Court Room Practices			3	
Judges/Magistrates			3	
Verdict	1			
Sentence				4

It is usual practice in survey research for the interviewer to have the responses on a card which the interviewer shows the respondent. Pre-coding has been carried out and the four responses are assigned codes of 1 to 4, with 1 representing Very Satisfied and 4 Not Very Satisfied. In this specific illustration, codes are assigned in accordance with the respondent's answers. The respondent was satisfied with the Police and this attracts a code of 2. The respondent was very satisfied with the Prosecutors and the verdict so a code of 1 has to be assigned to each of them. The respondent was unsatisfied with Judge/Magistrate and very unsatisfied with the sentence so codes 3 and 4 have to be assigned to the two variables respectively.

It is often found in survey research that respondents have not answered some questions or that an interviewer has not recorded an answer to a question or questions. There is no data for the question or variable and this is called missing data. Even where there are missing data, codes must be assigned instead of leaving it blank. Codes which do not interfere with the other codes in the questionnaire are assigned to missing data. As no variable or questionnaire item is likely to attract 99 varied responses, 99 is the usual code assigned to missing data.

Where feasible and depending on the extent of missing data, some researchers opt to go back to the respondents for the missing information. Any new data must be coded correctly using the same codes as for the responses from the study subjects who answered the questions.

Coding is very important in survey research and must be undertaken with due care. Codes must be correctly assigned and once codes are assigned, the responses from each study subject must be coded. It is the researcher's responsibility to train coders to assign the codes to each question on each questionnaire.

Any mistakes made in coding may affect data analysis as well as the study results and conclusions, especially in proving or disproving the hypothesis. It is usual practice for the researcher to check a randomly selected sample of questions from each coder to ascertain if coding is being carried out correctly.

Data Entry, Storage and Management

Once all responses on all the questionnaires have been coded, data entry begins. The information on the questionnaires is transferred to the data sets and files in accordance with the researcher's specifications. Inaccurate data entry is a major source of non selection errors in survey research, presupposing a need for the data entry to be carried out with care and with serious attention to detail. Data entry can be carried out manually or in the form of semi-automated and automated input of data. Manual data entry is very common in survey research and involves the use of trained data entry personnel, but the process is slow and time consuming, labor intensive and costly. Manual data entry is more likely to produce inaccuracies and errors because the input is made by persons who can or has the potential to make mistakes, irrespective of their level of training. Hence, the increasing use of semi-automated or automated data entry.

Semi-automated and automated data entry procedures involve varying degrees of automation with semi-automated entry showing a mix of manual and automated data entry. The researcher determines which aspects of the data will be manually entered and which other parts will have automated entry. The easy to enter codes such as items which require two code responses including Yes and No are easily entered manually. For example, a response of Yes or No will be provided to the question "Have you ever been burgled"? The responses could be pre-coded (usual) or post-coded (sometimes) as 1 and 2 for Yes and No respectively. It is not difficult for the codes 1 and 2 to be entered for a simple question like this. In contrast, the information in table 4 is not as easy to enter as the Yes or No responses, and data entry errors can inadvertently be made.

In semi-automated or automated data entry, the data are transferred by scanning the questionnaires and saving the scanned data in files which are set up in the survey data sets. In recent times, a more sophisticated scanning mechanism has become available. Known as Optical Mark Readers (OMR), this mechanism allows only the answers to the questions, clearly marked in specific areas of the questionnaires, to be electronically detected and recorded in the data files. Semi-automated and automated data entry are faster to input, and, thus, less time consuming, less expensive and less prone to errors relative to manual data entry. Whatever is recorded in the questionnaires are automatically transferred to the data files. One problem remains. If the interviewer has made a recording mistake, it may not be detected until the data analysis stage when semi-automated and automated data entry is used. However, in manual data entry, the detection of inaccurate recording of data can sometimes be detected during the process of entering the data, at least the potential for early detection of the error is higher in manual data entry than in semi-automated and automated data entry. For example, if information on age and occupation of a victim of crime is recorded, errors are detected where the data on age and occupation are not compatible. A case in point is where a victim who is aged 15 years and is also recorded as working as an Engineer. Errors such as that are picked up by the data entry personnel during the data input process, and addressed before the analysis stage. There are various data entry computer software that facilitate electronic data entry of survey data.

After data entry, the data files must be carefully stored and continuously managed .As indicated in chapter seven, it is becoming increasingly necessary and imperative for researchers to advice respondents that the information they provide will be stored, managed and used with confidentiality. This has arisen as a result of strict ethical requirements for the collection, storage, management and analysis of unit record or individual data. It has also become important because of the skepticism of many respondents about providing personal information. The data sets should have limited access, and access should be restricted to the researcher and any other personnel to whom the researcher gives access privileges partially or in full.

Data management continues unabated throughout the post data entry phase. Following the completion of data entry, the researcher must check and clean the data files. As part of data management, data may be arranged in specifications and rearranged over time to suit the proposed data analysis. Data management also includes checking the data files for internal and external consistency, identifying errors and addressing those errors. A salient feature of data management is the continuous process of cleaning the data sets. The data in the data sets are checked and any errors or unwanted information is cleaned out. In addition, other aspects of data management involve the assignment of numbers to each respondent to ensure privacy and confidentiality and to avoid the identification of individual respondents. In this way each respondent becomes a number, and all respondents are numbered in a sequential order according to when the questionnaire containing their responses, were entered into the data files. If postal survey was the methodology employed to collect the data, checking is usually done immediately the self completed questionnaires are returned.

Once the data sets have been checked and cleaned, the researcher is ready to proceed to the data analysis stage. Decisions made earlier during the selection of design and preparatory phases about data analysis are implemented at this stage of the exercise. Depending on the study subject, the type of data, goals and objectives of the study and the skills of the researcher, slight modifications of the previously determined data analysis procedures can be made.

QUANTITATIVE ANALYSIS OF SURVEY DATA

The analysis of survey data is an important stage in the entire survey. The purpose is to make sense of the huge quantitative data collected and processed as part of the survey. The objective is to put various aspects of the data together to enable the provision of accurate, scientific, credible and persuasive information to address the problem identified at the beginning of the survey, and the associated research questions and/or hypotheses. In the analysis of quantitative survey data, data are transferred into information, i.e. put together to make some kind of sense and enhance the interpretation of the results of the analysis. One important point worthy of mention here is that the researcher has to make a decision on the unit of analysis and the level of aggregation of the data. This decision will determine the extent to which responses are analyzed so as to eliminate or minimize the potential for any response to be traced back to any respondent. In addition, the unit of analysis and the level of aggregation of data allow the ethical requirement of privacy and confidentiality to be met.

The types of analysis in survey research depends on the objective and goals of the survey, contractual obligations, the types of data collected and processed, skills of the researcher, funding and other factors. As survey research results in massive quantitative data, the analysis often takes the form of quantitative or statistical analysis. The subject matter of this book is not statistics. It introduces readers to the various quantitative analyses that are often undertaken by the criminological survey researcher. Computational procedures are beyond its scope and can be found in the books and articles listed for further reading. Only the computational procedures for fundamental measures are included.

Two broad types of analysis are undertaken in survey research, namely descriptive analysis and non descriptive analysis. However, it should be noted that most survey data analysis will involve both descriptive and statistical analysis. In fact, a mix of descriptive and non descriptive analyses enriches the analyses, provide variety in the analyses, provide credible and persuasive data results, and strengthen the survey's conclusions. The standpoint taken in this book is that criminological survey researchers should make every effort to undertake both descriptive and statistical analyses of survey data to strengthen the contribution of the specific survey.

Descriptive Analysis of Survey Data

In descriptive analysis, the survey data are put together and aspects of it are described to provide further insights on the topics. The basic dimensions of descriptive analysis of survey data include some of the following:

1. Frequency distributions
2. Statistical summaries
3. Proportional analysis
4. Narratives
5. Quotations and citations from the responses

Frequency Distribution, Proportions and Statistical Summaries

The most widely used analytical measure to describe survey data is what is called frequency distribution. It is very difficult to find a criminological survey which would not include frequency distribution of one sort of the other. Frequency distributions provide total counts of the number of cases or responses for each variable in the study and are presented in the form of two or three column tables listing the variable in the 1st column and the total counts for each response category in the 2nd column (table 5). A survey of fear of crime in a community obtains data from 5000 respondents. The distribution of the respondents by age, gender, level of educational attainment and employment status are presented in tables 5 and 6.

Table 5. Frequency distribution of survey respondents by age

Age Group	Frequency	Proportion (%)
15-24	850	17
25-44	1,800	36
45-84	1,350	27
64 and over	1,000	20

Sample size for this survey is 5000.

What is learned in table 5 is that there are 850 respondents aged between 15 and 24, years, 1800 aged from 25 to 44 years and 1350 and 1000 respondents aged between 45 to 64 years and 64 years and over respectively. These counts constitute the frequency distribution of survey respondents by broad age groups. Similarly, table 6 shows the frequency distribution by selected personal characteristics of the survey respondents. Of the 5000 survey participants, 2800 were males and 2200 were females, 2000 have high school as the highest level of educational attainment and 3000 have completed post high school education, 3500 were employed and 1500 were unemployed. These numbers are the frequencies for each of the variables relative to the respondents.

Table 6. Proportional distribution of survey respondents by selected variables

Variable	Frequency	Proportion (%)
Gender	5,080	
Male	2,800	56
Female	2,200	44
Educational Attainment	5,000	
High School	2,000	40
Post High School	3,000	60
Employment Status	5,000	
Employed	3,500	70
Not Employed	1,500	30

*Sample size for this survey is 5000.

Proportions indicate the share of any response category in the total number of responses for the particular variable. Proportions are normally provided in percentages, albeit they can be computed relative to 1. The sum of the proportions should be equal or close to 100% or to 1. Sometimes, proportions can be slightly below or above 100% as a result of rounding. Proportions are associated with frequencies and they usually come together with the frequency distribution as part of the statistical output. Major statistical analysis packages, such as SPSS and SAS have provisions for the production of frequency distributions. The 3rd column of tables 5 and 6 show the proportions in percentages for the various response categories. In table 5, the variable is age and the response categories are broad age groups. A glance at table 5 reveals that the largest proportion of respondents are aged between 25 and 44 years, followed in descending order by respondents aged 45 to 64 years, 64 years and over and 15 to 24 years. Similarly, the proportion of males in table 6 is 56% compared with a female proportion of 44%.

Another descriptive analytical tool is statistical summaries. As implied in the name, statistical summaries provide abridged one static summaries of information on a variable or the responses obtained on a variable. Total number of respondents, total number of respondent in specific categories and average or median age of respondents are all statistical summaries. Statistical summaries are used to describe various as aspects of the survey. As indicated later in this chapter, even interrelationships between variables can be analyzed with statistical summaries such as X^2 and R^2 and other one statistic Summaries.

Narratives

Survey research data can be described using narratives. In this approach, the survey researcher simply narrates what the data are saying or revealing. The criminological survey researcher describes in words what evidence is emerging from the data. For example, a survey researcher can narrate responses to the question on why are you afraid of crime as follows:

> "Many respondents stated that they were afraid of crime
> because they had previously been victims of crime, a friend
> was killed during a burglary, their parents home was torched
> by arsonists. Others explained that they had been witnesses to
> crime, had their vehicles taken from them at gun point and suffer
> from the trauma from previous crime against them".

The survey research is using words to transform survey data into information that can be clearly understood. The researcher could also put these responses into categories or groups and assigned codes to the responses. The researcher could have followed up with statistical analysis of the responses after assigning the codes to the data. Narratives can be used to describe most responses or data obtained from survey research. However, open-ended questions lend themselves better to narrative analysis. This is generally because open-ended questions can potentially generate many diverse responses. Narratives are regularly used in survey research reports to put emphasis on specific responses which the survey researcher finds significant or to be of special interest or relevance. As discussed earlier in this chapter, the analysis of survey data often involves both descriptive and statistical analysis. Narratives are usually found in the descriptive analysis parts of many survey reports, stressing and drawing attention to special points.

Quotations

Quotations appear in survey reports from time to time. The approach is similar in a sense to narratives, except that in quotations the exact response is cited or stated. In the example above, the report will have the exact statements as follows:

Question:	Why are you afraid of crime?
Answers:	"My junior brother was murdered."
	"My parents' home was torched by arsonists."

"My friend was raped."
"My car was stolen at gun point."

Similarly a criminological survey researcher posed the following question to a sample of convicted criminals serving time in prison:

Question: Why did you commit the offence for which you were convicted?
Answers: "I could not control myself."
                 "The victim made me very angry."
                 "This is the second time my car has been
                    stolen, I just shot him."
                 "She encouraged me."

In analysis using quotations, these responses are cited as they are given by the study subjects without any rewriting or changes. The statements are attributed to respondents without identifying the respondent for each specific response. In the above mentioned example, the analysis will include "asked why they committed the offences for which they were convicted", one criminal stated "I could not control myself". Another said "this is the second time my car has been stolen and I just shot him" Unlike narrative analysis where the responses are described in words (words used by respondents, researchers or a mix of both), in quotation analysis the exact statements of the respondents must be reproduced. Quotations add variety to the reporting while stressing important or significant points. Like narratives, analysis involving quotations appear in many criminological survey research reports. Some variables may appear to be of central interest or relevance to the problem of investigation or subject matter, and responses on such variables usually attract quotation analysis. Some responses may appear astonishing, strong or peculiar and attract quotation analysis.

NON DESCRIPTIVE ANALYSIS OF SURVEY DATA

Non descriptive or quantitative analysis of survey data involves using statistical tools and measures to analyze the data obtained from the respondents. In non descriptive or quantitative analysis of survey data, a number of estimates or measurement areas are usually addressed including the following:

1. Measures of central tendency.
2. Measures of dispersion.
3. Cross-tabulation.
4. Single variable and Multivariate analysis.
5. Standardization of variables.
6. Analysis of inference.
7. Measures of association.

Measures of Central Tendency

Measures of central tendency are regularly used in the analysis of survey data. They constitute some of the simplest, convenient but useful measures that are available to the criminological survey researcher. Measures of central tendency are statistical summaries but discussed separately because of their usefulness and importance. They provide one statistic, summary information on the variable. In so doing, they provide information on the average and/or most typical characteristic of the variable. There are three main measures of central tendency which are commonly used in survey research, namely the mean, median and mode. The mean is the most popular measure of central tendency appearing in many criminological survey reports.

The mean, by definition, represents the center of a set of numbers. It is the arithmetic or numeric average of a set of numbers and provides a summary measure of those set of numbers. If the values for a variable are added up and divided by the number of values, the mean value for the variable is obtained, i.e. the average value of the variable is obtained.

The mean appears a lot in survey reports, but it has the disadvantage of being distorted by extreme values, The highest and lowest vales in a set of data will influence the mean and distort its value. In criminology, the mean is used in many instances including average age of criminals convicted for a specific offence, average length of time spent in a rehabilitation or other corrections facility, average age of victims of crime, average wage of prison employees etc. The mean is used interchangeably with arithmetic averages in many instances.

The median is the middle value or the average of the two middle values in a set of numerical data arranged in ascending or descending order.. For example, looking at the following numerical data, what is the median? To enable the median to be determined, the data must be arranged in an ascending or descending order. From the column marked "Ages in Ascending Order", 29 is the middle value in the ages of the victims of crime. The median age of those victims of crime is, therefore, 29 years.

Ages of 9 victims of crime	Ages in Ascending Order
25	25
26	26
30	27
28	28
31	29
32	30
27	31
33	32
29	33

The mode is the most frequently occurring value in a set of numerical data, e.g. economic cost of victimization reported by various victims in a survey, ages of prisoners, number of recidivism reported by various convicted offenders in a study etc. The following numerical data show the ages of various prisoners. They have not been arranged in an ascending or descending order because arranging them in order is not needed to identify the mode.

Prisoner	Age
1	22
2	45

3	20
4	35
5	20
6	42
7	18
8	35
9	20
10	21

A glance at the numbers or ages reveals that 20 is the most frequently occurring age and thus the mode. The mode is not very much used in surveys relative to the mean and the median. It is sometimes used in numerical analysis to complement the mean, especially when the mean is influenced by extreme values, i.e. extreme highest and lowest values.

Measures of Dispersion

Unlike measures of central tendency which focus on the center of the numerical data, measures of dispersion provide information on the variety and spread of the numerical data. The main measures of dispersion are the "Range, Variance and the Standard Deviation". The range shows the difference between the highest and the lowest values and is the simplest, easiest to compute and most comprehensible measure of dispersion or variability. The range is also very easy to interpret. The standard deviation indicates the average distance of the values from the mean, while the variance is a measure of the variability or dispersion of the numerical values for a variable. In the previous illustration using the ages of prisoners, the ages of the inmates are between 18 and 45 years, yielding a range of.27 years.

For readers interested in the computation of the frequently used measure called standard deviation, the following six steps must be followed:

1. Compute the mean
2. Calculate the difference between each value or score and the mean computed in the first step (deviations from the mean)
3. Compute the square for each difference or deviation
4. Add up the computed squared deviations
5. Divide the sum, thus obtained, by the number of values for the variable
6. Take the square root of the figure calculated in step 5

Alternatively, if the variance of the values is known, the square root of the variance is the standard deviation.

To compute the variance for a set of numerical data, steps 1 to 5 must be followed. The result in step 5 is the variance, the measure of variability or dispersion of the values or scores. These days, a number of statistical software is available to assist in making these computations. Simple commands in SPSS or SAS software will produce the range, variance and standard deviation for the criminological survey data without any further effort from the survey researcher.

Cross-Tabulations

In detail analysis of numerical data, it is often inevitable to include cross-tabulation of one form or the other. Cross-tabulations, sometimes called contingency tables, show summary measures for two or more variables, indicating the frequency distribution for each combination of variables. Most analyses of survey data include tables, and cross-tabulations are one of the most commonly used tabular formats in criminological surveys, presenting findings in a combination of variables in one table instead of many single variable table formats. Each summary measure is represented in a cell of one of the rows and columns. By combining information on multiple variables, it is possible to discern the interrelationships among the variables from cross-tabulations. Much of the information in cross-tabulations are descriptive, hence cross-tabulations are best suited for descriptive analysis of survey data. Cross-tabulations are very useful and powerful analytical tools or measures for descriptive analysis of survey data.

Table 7. Cross-tabulation of bio-data of convicted criminals

Variable	1st Conviction	2nd or More Convictions
Age in Years		
19 - 24	1,200	2,100
25 59	1,450	3,000
60 and over	550	600
Gender		
Male	2,000	3,000
Female	1,400	2,500

*Total number of convicted criminals is 8,900.

Theoretically, it is possible to include many variables in cross-tabulation. In practice, it becomes increasingly difficult to interpret the data in the cells as the number of variables exceeds four or five. Large cross tabulations exist, but the problem is how to define and interpret the interrelationships among the variables in the table. Cross-tabulations format is illustrated in table 7 This specific cross-tabulation has four variables, namely Age, gender, offenders with 1st conviction and offenders with 2nd or more convictions. Each cell in columns 2 and 3 shows some relationships between the variable in column 1 and the corresponding variable in column 2 or 3 as appropriate. It shows further the number of combined cases for each of the values in the variables in column 1 and the other two columns.

Translating the data in table 7 into comprehensible information, it can be said that there were 1200 convicted criminals who were aged 19 to 24 years and who were convicted for the first time, compared with 2,100 convicted criminals of the same age who have been convicted for a 2nd time or more. Of the convicted criminals aged 25 to 59, 1,450 were convicted for the first time and 3,000 of them had two or more convictions. The other variable which is cross-tabulated with 1st conviction and 2nd or more convictions is gender. Of the total male offenders of 5,000, 2,000 were convicted for the first time and 3,000 have been convicted for a 2nd or more times.

Similar 1,400 and 2,500 females have been convicted for the 1st or 2nd or more times respectively. In this way, the number of males convicted for the 1st time and those convicted for 2nd or more times are compared, and a similar comparison is made for females. Cross-tabulations are so useful and powerful that the interrelationships can be identified in another way, such as comparing males and females with specific number of convictions. For example, from table 7, it is discernible that 2,000 males were serving time for their first conviction compared with 1,400 females and that another 3,000 males had two or more convictions compared with 2,500 females who recorded two or more convictions..

Single Variable and Multiple Variable/Multivariate Analysis

In survey data analysis, a distinction is made between single variable analysis and multiple variable/multivariate analysis. Depending on the survey design and objectives, important or relevant individual variables are analyzed. Single variable analysis involves discussion of frequency distributions for each selected variable, together with proportional distribution of the categories/values/responses for each of the variables. Single variable analysis can also include measures of central tendency such as mean as well as measures of dispersion such as range. For example, in criminological surveys, age of convicted criminals is analyzed as a single variable. Measures, such as frequency distribution of the subjects accordingly to various age groups or ages, mean or median age of the offenders under study, age of criminal initiation (i.e. age of first criminal activity), are analyzed. So also are measures of dispersion such as the range, the difference between the highest and lowest ages. In this example, the single variable is age.

Other single variables often explored and analyzed in criminological surveys are gender, recidivism and victims. However, any variable in the survey data files can be analyzed on its own depending on the type of study, the relevance of the variable to the survey objectives and the hypothesis or research questions.

In contrast to single variable analysis, multiple variable or multivariate analysis involves two and usually more variables. Like single variable analysis, multiple variable analysis can also involve frequency distributions. In its simplest form, multiple variable analysis is explored in cross-tabulations. In table 7 and the preceding paragraphs, it was shown that simple two variable analysis can be undertaken for age and 1st conviction or age and 2nd or more convictions. The two variables in this example are age and 1st or 2nd and more convictions. It is also possible to examine a multiple variable analysis involving age, gender and 1st conviction or 2nd or more convictions.

Multiple variables or multivariate analysis can be more complex than the above mentioned examples. Even in cross-tabulations, three, four or five variables could be explored together at the same time. For example, in table 7, if data are available, we could explore a multivariate or multiple variable analysis involving age, gender, 1st or 2nd or more convictions together with other bio-data at the same time. More complex multiple variables analysis occurs in the analysis of inference, multiple regressions and, to some extent, measures of association. These statistical techniques are discussed briefly later in this chapter).

Standardization of Variables

In criminological survey data analysis, comparisons among variables are sometimes undertaken. Many a time variables being compared have not been measured in the same way, i.e. the variables have been measured using different units of measurements. This can distort or adversely affect the comparisons and it usually does. To reduce or eradicate these problems of measurement, standardization techniques are employed. Standardization is simply the processes of bringing different units of measurement for different variables into comparable units of measurement for all the variables. The result is a more effective and appropriate comparison and the variables become known as standardized variables.

Analysis of Statistical Inference

It has been mentioned earlier that in survey research, the methodologies involve the selection of a sample from the list of all potentially eligible study subjects, called sampling frame. Refreshing our memory, suppose a citywide victimization study of New York City is to be undertaken, all the residents of the City of New York are the eligible members of the sampling frame. Each resident, can potentially be included in the sample and subsequently participate in the study. Different types of sampling procedures have also been discussed previously. Irrespective of sampling procedure, the end result is the selection of a sample, and data are then collected on the sample members. If 5000 people are selected from the population of New York City for the study, the 5000 people become the sample for the study.

Depending on the sampling procedures used, the 5000 people are said to constitute a representative sample for New York City, especially if they are randomly selected. In statistical inference, the estimates and parameters for the total population is inferred from the estimates and parameters of the sample. The data collected and analyzed for the sample population and any conclusions reached are used to describe the population in the sampling frame in what is called external generalization (discussed previously as part of sampling). It must be stressed that the sample should be a probability sample (random or cluster) to allow any generalizations to be appropriate.. If the sample in the New York City example is random, the data collected on the 5000 sample members are said to reflect or represent the total population in the sampling frame. Any conclusions, reached from the analysis and interpretation of data are extended to cover the entire population of New York City. The information on the total population of New York City has been inferred from the information obtained from the 5000 selected New York City residents.

Inferential statistics also allow for the establishment of differences between subgroups of the sample relative to any specific variable. Any parameters can be used in inferential statistics to identify and establish differences between subgroups within the study sample, including summary statistics such as the mean, median or range.

Interrelationships among Measurement Variables

In the analysis and interpretation of criminological survey data, as it is in other areas of social research, it is essential to explore and include the relationship between and among variables.

This is undertaken in many different ways depending on the type of study and its objectives, and include employing statistical techniques such as cross-tabulations, measures of association, including the Chi Square ($\aleph^2$) statistic, and regressions including correlations. For example, a value of zero means that the measure of association finds no relationship between the variables while a value of 1 denotes maximum strength relationship. Such valuable data are not available from cross-tabulations.

Using cross-tabulations to explore simple relationships between variables was discussed earlier. Attention is now focused on the other statistical tools for investigating the relationships between variables.

As previously stated, this book does not purport to focus on statistics and the computational procedures for measures of association and regressions are outside the scope of the book. Only a brief introduction is presented here and more information is found in the list of items in further reading. Besides, simple commands in statistical software such as SPSS and SAS will produce these measures or statistics.

How Measures of Association and Regressions Establish Relationships between Variables

Relationships discerned from cross-tabulations are basic and simple. They do not allow the exact strength of the relationship between the variables to be established. In relation to nominal measures, the measures of association address the said inadequacy in cross-tabulation, provide an improvement and establish a better measurement of the relationship. The use of measures of association to study relationships between variables depends on the type of variable – nominal, ordinal and ratio level variables. With regards to nominal values, measures of association establish the strength of the relationship using the $\aleph^2$. The $\aleph^2$ statistic is particular powerful in establishing relationships between two nominal variables. If the statistics falls between -.96 and +.96, then there is a relationship between the two nominal variables.

Correlation is the measure which explores relationship between ratio level variables. In most regression analysis, the relationship between the variables is partly established by examining the correlation values or scores. Again a simple SPSS command will produce the correlations matrix which has zero as no relationship and 1 as maximum strength relationship. So that, regardless of the + or - sign, the closer the value is to 1, the stronger the relationship. An example of an arbitrary correlation matrix for the variables age, gender, employment status, income and number of convictions is presented in table 8 for illustration.

Table 8. Correlations matrix for selected variables

Variable	Age	Gender	Employment Status	Income	Number of Convictions
Age	1.000	.113	-.203	-.151	.692
Gender		1.000	.554	-.541	.505
Employment status			1.000	.766	.616
Income				1.000	.423
Number of convictions					1.000

In terms of ordinal variables, measures of association explore the relationship between variables using regression analysis involving dependent and independent variables, for example. In regression analysis, it is often the practice to identify one variable as the dependent and another as the independent. The dependent variable is so called because a unit change in the value of the independent variable changes the value of the dependent variable, while the proportion in the variance of the dependent variable explained by the independent variable also changes. In other words the values or scores of the dependent variable depend on the values or scores of the independent variables. The exact strength of the relationship is measured by the power of the independent variable to predict the value or score of the dependent variable in the regression equation, and the extent to which the independent variable explains variance in the values or scores of the dependent variable.

Other Dimensions of the Analysis of Survey Data

So far the focus has been on the numerical analysis of survey data. There are other ways of representing and analyzing survey data. Two of them are presented in this section, namely histograms and shapes. Histograms and shapes allow for quantitative survey data to be analyzed in diagrammatical form. It must be stressed that, in even the most basic analysis of survey data, a combination of numerical analysis and some form of pictorial or diagrammatical analysis is often found.

Histogram

A histogram is a pictorial or diagrammatical representation of data. Instead of having tables containing data, histograms present the data in various graphs, pictures or diagrams Histograms have also been called charts. Histograms graph the frequency distribution of the scores appearing in assigned categories. While SPSS, Microsoft Word, Excel and other statistical software will produce histograms, histograms can be produced manually as well. To create a histogram the following steps are essential:

1. Divide the range of the data into intervals to create categories (e.g. category 1 is 1 – 4, category 2 5-9 etc). Remember the range is the difference between the highest and the lowest scores or values. The number of categories is the number of bars or segments (pie charts)
2. Establish firm categories for the scores or values (1-4, 5-14, 15-49 etc)
3. Count the number or scores or values for each category (frequency distribution previously discussed)
4. Draw a bar or other graph for each category making sure that the length or height of each bar is proportionally represented, i.e. the height of each bar is proportional to the count of the scores or values of the category represented by the bar (step 3 above).

Figure 1 provides an example of a histogram showing recidivism and other characteristics of prison inmates. Prisoner 1 has 15 previous convictions, Prisoner 2 10 previous convictions, and Prisoner 3 has only 2 previous convictions. Prisoner 1 is 20, Prisoner 2 is 44 and Prisoner 3 is 33 years old, Prisoner 1 has completed 10 rehabilitation programs while Prisoners 2 and 3 have completed 7 and 12 programs respectively. The last category represents the number of fines the prisoners have been sentenced to pay fines.

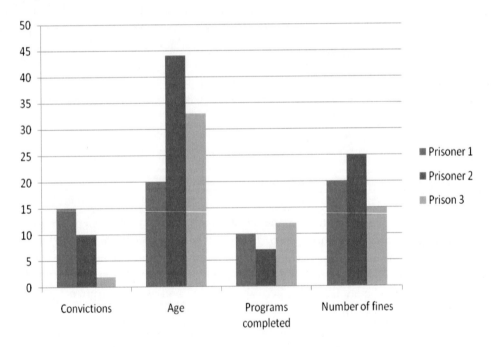

Figure1. A histogram of recidivism among prison inmates by selected features.

So far, histograms have been presented as they appear in bar graphs. Bar graphs are the most popular histograms, but there are other types of histograms. The most notable of these charts or histograms are line graphs and Pie graphs or pie charts as it is sometimes called. Line graphs present quantitative survey data in the form of lines. They are mostly used in criminological research to portray trends and changes over time, such as crime rates. In the illustration in figure 2m crime rates of countries A, B and C are shown using line graphs The crime rates per 1000 population were 100, 120, 150, 155 and 160 for 1993, 1996, 1999, 2002 and 2003 respectively for Country A. The corresponding data for Country B were 100, 110, 130,140, and 150 for the 5 years respectively, while in Country C, the crime rates declined from 150 per 1000 population in 1993 to 135, 120, 110 and 100 in 1996, 1999, 2003 and 2005 respectively.

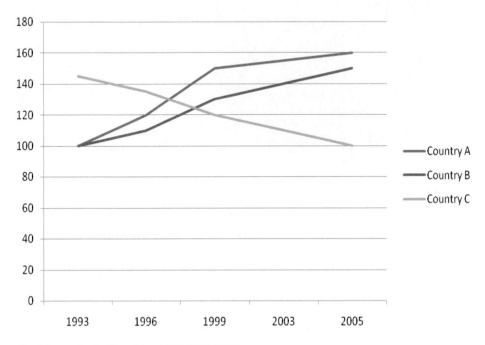

Figure 2. Crime rates in Countries ABC 1993-2005.

Line graphs are very useful in quickly presenting a picture of the trends. In this case a glance at the line graphs shows clearly which countries are recording increasing crime rates over time (Countries A and B) and which of the countries is recording declining crime rates (Country C). In this way, line graphs have the added advantage of enhancing comparative analysis of crime data.

Pie charts, as the name suggests, appear in the form of a circle (pie) divided into segments according to the frequency for each category. Like other graphing methods, proportions (%s) or actual numbers may be used. For example in a study of the number of programs completed by residents of an alcohol rehabilitation facility, it is found that Resident 1 has completed 10 programs while Residents 2, 3. 4 and 5 have completed 12, 8, 5 and 2 programs respectively. A glance at the pie graph reveals that Resident 2 has the largest segment and Resident 5 the lowest segment. Pie graphs are most useful in the graphical representation of scores or categories for a single variable, such as number of programs completed, number of convictions, density of victimization for various locations etc.

Programs completed

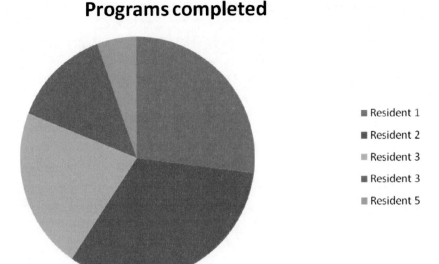

Resident 1
Resident 2
Resident 3
Resident 3
Resident 5

Figure 3. Number of programs completed by residents of a rehabilitation center.

Pie graphs or pie charts as they are sometimes called and the other graphical methods represent and analyze survey data in the same way, but use different graphs to represent the said survey data. All the various bar graphs represent and analyze data using bars, line graphs use lines and pie charts use circle in representing and analyzing survey data.

Shape Analysis

Shape is another way survey data is graphically presented and analyzed. When quantitative survey data are plotted, specific shapes emerge or are obtained and these shapes may subsequently be subject to further analysis. A number of shapes are discernible, and each shape portrays a particular picture. It must be mentioned that the type of shape usually depends on whether the data is symmetrical or asymmetrical. If a line is drawn through the plotted data set and the shape on either side of the line is the same, the data is said to be Symmetrical. In contrast, if a line is drawn through the center of plotted numerical data, and the shape of the data on one side of the line is different from the shape of the data on the other side of the line, the data is asymmetrical.

A distinction is drawn between unimodal and bimodal (or sometimes multi-modal) shapes. Unimodal shape is the situation where the plotted data have only one most frequent score or mode, while in bimodal shape, there are two modes in the data set. Most survey data sets will be unimodal, even though bimodal shapes appear in many survey data analyses.

In many data sets, when the data are graphed, it is found that there is a concentration of values or scores on one side. The data are said to be skewed. If the scores are concentrated on the left side, the data are said to be skewed to the left, and if the concentration is on the right side, the data are said to be skewed to the right Skewing in essence shows how spread the data are.

Testing Hypothesis and Addressing Research Questions

In survey research it is usual practice to define and test hypotheses. Inferential statistics are used to test the hypothesis and in particular to undertake analysis which enhance decision-making on whether to reject the null hypothesis and prove the alternative hypothesis.. As discussed earlier under hypothesis and research questions, the null hypothesis works on the basis that there are no differences between subgroups within the sample. It is often the practice for survey researchers to endeavor to dismiss the null hypothesis and to prove that empirical differences exist in the survey data. Even where no major effort is made to reject the null hypothesis, the researcher must analyze the data so as to identify some empirical evidence to either support or dismiss any alternative hypothesis defined at the beginning of the study.

So how is hypothesis tested? Testing hypothesis involves selective analysis of data on variables which have some relevance to the hypothesis. For example, if the previously stated hypothesis "crime increases with population growth" is to be tested, data must be obtained and analyzed to indicate whether there is population growth, if crime is increasing at the same time and finally if a link exists between the two variables. During this process, the test statistic (the measure which indicates links between population growth and crime) must be derived from the analysis and used to determine if the null hypothesis is true or false before proceeding to prove the research hypothesis. Subsequently, the researcher makes decision on whether to reject the null hypothesis and present analytical evidence to prove the research hypothesis which was stated at the beginning of the study.

Survey Report

The end product of the survey is the report. After all the analyses have been completed, the researcher must put everything together in a report. The report is prepared along the lines discussed in the section on General Research Process with modifications depending on the specific study, its methodologies and objectives together with any funding or stakeholder requirements. It is also usual practice to prepare an overall report describing.

1. What the study was about – subject matter or topic?
2. What prompted the research, i.e. the rationale or importance of the study, its purpose and objectives of the study?
3. Review of the existing literature.
4. Null hypothesis and Research hypothesis/Research question.
5. Methodologies used and, if possible, reasons for using the specific methodologies.
6. Problems encountered and how they were solved.
7. The main findings.
8. Minor findings.

9.   Any conclusions drawn as well as decisions on the null hypothesis and the research hypothesis or answers to the research questions.
10. Any internal and more importantly external generalizations and theories arising from the data analysis.
11. Areas for further research where possible.

ADVANTAGES AND DISADVANTAGES OF SURVEY RESEARCH

Survey research has a number of advantages and disadvantages. The main advantages are that survey research allows for the collection of detail information on large population groups, producing standard data on all respondents to enhance comparative analysis. Also, Multiple topics can be investigated in a single survey.

Unlike participant observation, survey research has the added advantage of external generalization, especially if the sample population was statistically selected. In other words, the parameters or estimates of the sample population can be extended to the total population in the sampling frame.

Survey research has the demerit that it does not involve the observation of the actual event. Criminological survey researchers do not have the opportunity to observe the behavior of the study subjects, but ask questions and obtain data after or before the observation occurs. Even though survey research is efficient in terms of cost per data collected etc, it is still more expensive. The initial outlay of funds is large covering training and use of interviewers, data collection on large groups (reward if offered to participants could add enormously to cost), printing of a large number of questionnaires and the entry of large amounts of data. Yet another disadvantage is that survey research can be time consuming taking a long time to complete.

In survey research, it is not possible to ascertain the truth of the responses provided by respondents as the data collection takes place after the event or sometimes before the event. An example of seeking response to a future event is to ask " are you going to stay away from criminal activity in the future"?. More surveys focus on past event and questions such as "Did you assault the victim?, Did you steal the handbag? Etc. are usually asked.

FURTHER READINGS

Aldridge, A., and K. Levine (2001): Surveying the social world. Buckingham, Open University Press.

Brathwaite, F. S., and Yeboah, D. K. (2004): Victims of crime in the criminal justice system of Barbados. Journal of Criminal Justice, Vol. 32, No. 2: 431-442.

Cramer, D. (2003): Advanced quantitative data Maidenhead (England), Open University

Giddeons, A. (1997): Sociology. Oxford, Blackwell Publishers.

May, T., (2001): Social research. Buckingham, Open University Press.

Teevan, T. (1987): Basic Sociology. Scarborough, Ontario, Prentice-Hall.

Utts, J. M. (1999): Seeing through statistics. Pacific Grove, Brooks/Cole Publishing Company.

Yeboah, D. A., and F. Brathwaite (2007): The nature and impact of criminal victimization in Barbados. Journal of Ethnicity in Criminal Justice, Vol 5, No 2/3: 55-77.

Box 1. Main characteristics of survey research methodologies

1. Large populations/respondents
2. Questionnaire design (instruments)
3. Standard data collection for each study
4. Interviewing in one way or the other
5. Sampling
6. Statistical analysis and interpretation.
7. Testing of hypothesis or addressing research questions
8. Comparative analysis

Box 2. Types of survey methodologies

1. Probability sampling
Random
Cluster
2. Non probability sampling
Convenience
Purposeful
Quota sampling
Snowball
Systematic

Box 3. Types of data collection methodologies

1. Direct face to face surveys/ interviews
2. Telephone surveys/interviews
3. Postal surveys
4. Observational surveys

Box 4. Questions for readers self-reflection

1. What is the role of the criminological survey researcher?
2. Distinguish between structured and unstructured data collection.
3. Distinguish between probability and non probability sample.
4. What is the null hypothesis?
5. Name the 4 levels of measurement.
6. What is the difference between numerical data analysis and graphical data analysis?

Chapter 5

EVALUATION RESEARCH

In this chapter, evaluation research, the 3rd major group of methodologies used in criminological research, is presented. In the criminal justice system, as it is in other social policy areas, evaluation research takes the form of policy and program evaluation. Policy and program evaluation research in this chapter focuses on the following topics, with specific emphasis on program evaluation:

1. Importance of evaluation in criminology.
2. Definition and description of evaluation (including models of program evaluation).
3. Types of program evaluation.
4. Evaluation methodologies.
5. Types of data used in program evaluation.
6. Step by step guide to program evaluation.
7. Analysis of cost.
8. A word on Program Logic or the Logical Framework.

IMPORTANCE OF EVALUATION IN THE CRIMINAL JUSTICE SYSTEM

There are a host of programs in the criminal justice systems, including public sector and private sector programs. With rising recidivism in many countries, it is becoming increasingly imperative for criminologists and the criminal justice policy makers to investigate the effectiveness of crime prevention policies and programs as well as rehabilitation and corrections programs designed to reduce the perpetration of crime, i.e. programs to reduce recidivism. A number of strategies exist to undertake successful evaluation of criminal justice policies and programs. Program evaluation provides one of the most widely used means to assess policy and program effectiveness and efficiency in many societies.

The importance of program evaluation in the criminal justice system cannot be overemphasized. Every year hundreds of millions of dollars are allocated by Governments around the globe to fight crime and make the society safer for all residents. Large numbers of people are also employed in the criminal justice system and other areas of law enforcement. Substantial proportions of the funding goes into developing and implementing policies and programs intended to reduce the incidence and prevalence of crime. Many programs are designed and delivered every year in both the community and within the confines of prisons.

Despite this, new criminals appear all the time and recidivism continues unabated. A need exists to assess and establish the effectiveness of the policies and programs in the justice sector. Evaluation provides a sure process of undertaking the said assessment to ascertain or establish if the programs and policies have been successful in achieving their stated objectives.

Besides, there is enormous cost to victims of crime, including physical, economic and emotional or psychological cost (Yeboah and Brathwaite, 2007). The physical injuries sustained by victims of assault, the economic cost arising from theft and burglary, in particular vehicles, jewelry, and other valuable personal items, the emotional and psychological costs endured for a long time by victims of sexual and physical assault exacerbate the need to develop policies and programs to reduce criminal activity. Most governments actually respond with policies, funding and programs. The question arises as to how to find out if the policies and programs, thus developed to reduce the incidence and prevalence of crime, have been successful. The answer lies in the evaluation of those policies and programs. Policy and program reviews do not exhibit the same level of detailed analysis of effectiveness and efficiency as do policy and program evaluation.

In short, evaluation provides information which serves as a useful resource base for making all sorts of policy and program decisions Findings from program and policy evaluation serve as sources of information for informed decisions on new policy directions and the reinforcement or abolition of existing policies. For example, if an evaluation of the decision making process of the Parole Board in a country finds that the process has not been effective in stopping recidivism by convicted offenders released on parole, policies on the existing process may be abolished or amended on the basis of the findings from the evaluation and exploration of new policy directions will becomes imminent. Evaluation findings also provide valuable data and sometimes recommendations for decisions on whether to continue or discontinue funding of a program. Most evaluations in recent times include cost benefit analysis and, in the government sector in particular, cost benefit analysis is now central to funding allocation decisions. Given the competing demand for limited funding and other resources in both government and non government sectors, it has become important for programs to be evaluated not only to assess their effectiveness, but also to make funding decisions and to establish their impacts on the community.

Quite often, government sector and some private sector organizations tend to replicate specific programs in various geographical locations. Evidence from program evaluation provides support for replication of programs where the evaluation finds that the program has been successful in achieving its objectives, and cessation of the program where the program evaluation produces adverse findings. In practice, where adverse evaluation findings are made, efforts are often directed at amending the program to eradicate or substantially reduce the problems which affected the success of the program. That said it is worthy to note that program funders can withhold funding at any time if the evaluation findings show that nothing or very little was achieved from the huge investment. With rising recidivism in many countries, the effectiveness of rehabilitation programs is brought into question in many areas and program evaluation provides answers to the questions on program effectiveness.

Another area where evaluation has demonstrated so much importance is the formative evaluation of new programs. In all jurisdictions, there are prison based and community based rehabilitation facilities which provide offenders with therapeutic programs and services. Formative evaluation, as discussed later in this chapter, is the type of evaluation which aims at identifying areas for improvement during the early stages of a program. Formative evaluation findings provide useful information on problem areas, their potential solutions (sometimes options for addressing the problems) as well as areas where improvements could be made. Similarly, process or implementation evaluation provides data that guide program developers to avoid repeating mistakes as they attempt to replicate programs in other locations. If some aspects of the implement are found to be deficient through evaluation, corrective actions are usually devised and implemented before the program is replicated elsewhere.

Specifically to government sector programs, evaluation ensures better accountability. Evaluation findings usually provide information on various components of the program and their performance. Non performing components may be identified and leaders of those components held accountable for what has happened.

DEFINITION, DESCRIPTION AND MODELS OF PROGRAM EVALUATION

Evaluation is the systematic collection and analysis of data to establish facts about a policy, program or activity with a view to identifying their effectiveness, impacts and efficiency. Specifically to evaluation research, evaluation may be defined as the continuous process of data collection and analysis with the objective of establishing internal and external validity.

This chapter focuses more on program evaluation because there are more program evaluation activities than policies, and this is due largely to the availability and provision of more funding to program evaluation than policy evaluation. This situation presupposes a need to assess program effectiveness and efficiency through program evaluation. Program evaluation can be undertaken in two ways, namely internal evaluation and external evaluation. Internal evaluation occurs when the program evaluation is carried out by the program personnel or by other personnel in other areas of the organization. For example, a rehabilitation program for prison inmates can be evaluated by the prison officers delivering the program or by other personnel within the Prison Service such as personnel of the Research Department or the Policy Division. External evaluation is the situation where the evaluation is carried out by hired consultants and other evaluators who are not employed by the organization. In the above mentioned example of the prison rehabilitation program, the program can be evaluated by evaluators who are not employed by the Prison Service, but who are contracted to undertake the evaluation.

A number of organizations in the criminal justice system need program evaluation. They include government sector organizations such Prisons and Prisons Departments, Community Corrections Department (Community Probation), Ministry or Department of Justice, Department of Courts, the Police etc. These agencies develop and administer policies and programs which need to be evaluated. Many of these agencies also provide funding to private sector consultants or organizations to develop and implement various programs which need to be evaluated.

Private sector organizations working in the criminal justice system need to have their programs evaluated irrespective of the source of funding. A number of private sector organizations provide assistance to prisoners when they are released back into the community. Assistance is often provided in the form of direct cash, housing, employment, education and training referrals and other settlement areas. The object is to assist the released prisoners to resettle properly back in the community and, thus, reduce their potential to recidivist. There are also programs to help young offenders with a view to stopping them from graduating into adult full time criminal offenders, while many other programs are developed to assist offenders who are sentenced to community probation, community service and/or fines.

It is worthy to mention that a number of organizations do not evaluate or arrange for the evaluation of their programs and, where they evaluate their programs, many do not pay adequate attention to the findings of the evaluation. Several factors influence or rather determine the use of evaluation by organizations. They include lack of funding, evaluation perceived as irrelevant, departmental inertia, lack of skilled evaluators within the organization, and a lack of effective mechanisms to disseminate evaluation findings.

Models

A number of program evaluation models are available including

1. Traditional or fundamental model.
2. Objectives and/or purposes based model.
3. Funding based model.
4. Accountability and performance model.
5. Improvements based model.
6. Open concept model.

The traditional evaluation model epitomizes what evaluation was in the past. Traditionally, program evaluation has tended to focus on the organization developing and delivering the program, assessing organizational arrangements, management, finances and overall program performance. This was particularly prevalent in the evaluation of justice sector program providers such as community based rehabilitation centers, youth justice activities and prison programs. Unlike other models of evaluation such as accountability or performance models of evaluation, the traditional evaluation model does not focus on staff performance and accountability.

With regards to the objectives based evaluation model, the emphasis of the evaluation is the assessment of goals and objectives pre-determined by the evaluator. The said goals and objectives are in a sense the evaluation goals and objectives and are partly aligned with the objectives, purpose and goals of the program under evaluation. Most criminal justice programs have clearly defined goals and purposes which are usually stated in program documents. In designing program evaluation, which includes objectives based models, evaluators have to identify the objectives and goals of the program and assess their achievement in the evaluation. The evaluator often examines program documents and records the objectives and goals of the program. These objectives and goals are subsequently inculcated in the evaluation goals and objectives which are usually defined before the evaluation is actually carried out.

The funding evaluation model, also called the fiscal model, is particularly important in these days of limited financial resources, fiscal restraints, cost-benefit analysis and the policy push towards the reduction and minimization of waste in program delivery. In this model, the focus is on assessing the complexities of funding effectiveness, cost effectiveness and program efficiency partly based on the analysis of the cost and benefits of the program. For example, an evaluation of a rehabilitation center for alcohol and drug addicts will examine the financial investments made on the program as well as the benefits from the program. The funding model looks at factors such as how much funding was received, how much went into direct program activities, how much was invested in staff and program administration, how much was the overall cost per resident etc. These types of analysis, inherent in the funding model, allow for conclusions to be drawn on funding and the returns on the funding, leading to informed or evidence based funding decision making.

Yet another program evaluation model is what this book calls accountability and performance model. This model operates with the underlying philosophy that programs are successful in their purpose, effectiveness and outcomes if each component or activity performs well. In this model, different program components are held accountable for their performance and leaders of the components responsible for the failure or success of the component. In its simplest form, the model focuses on program performance, including budget performance, performance against time, outcomes against expenditure etc. It is by and large an audit of program activities or components, examining their performance in terms of deadlines or timelines, goals, objectives and efficiency.

Improvement based models are evaluation models which focus on collecting and analyzing data to improve program performance, efficiency and effectiveness. They are the models on which formative evaluation is based, except that while formative evaluation concentrates on the early stages of the program, improvement based models focus on identifying areas for further improvement throughout the entire life of the program. They are particularly useful where there is an intention or decision to replicate the program elsewhere.

Open concept or no goals models approach evaluation without any prior knowledge of the goals of the program. The object is that, by operating without any knowledge of the program goals, the evaluation can be independent and concentrate on many diverse areas. Even so, this model leads to the collection of considerable amount of information and lacks precision and focus. Models which operate with prior knowledge of program goals tend to have direct focus in assessing whether program goals and objectives have been achieved by comparing stated objectives and goals with the goals and objectives achieved in the outcomes.

The Role of the Evaluator

Like the other research methodologies discussed in preceding chapters, the role of the evaluator is essential for successful program evaluation. The evaluator is responsible for the success or failure of all aspects of the evaluation from design to the production of the final evaluation report. The evaluator makes all arrangements for the evaluation to occur, makes decisions on design including models and types of evaluation and implements decisions made on the design, data collection, analysis and interpretation. That said it should be noted that sometimes the type of evaluation is pre-determined by the funding agency. This is true of both internal and external evaluations. Some funding agencies may be interested in the implementation of the program and commission a process or implementation evaluation. Others may be interested in program outcomes and commission outcomes evaluation and so on. The type of evaluation assumes more prominence if it is clearly stated in contract documents, i.e. the agreement between the evaluator and the agency commissioning the evaluation.

A key area where the evaluator's skills are brought into question is consultation. There is a lot of internal and external consultations in program evaluation as discussed later in this chapter. The evaluator must have good oral and written communication skills as well as negotiation, interpersonal and liaison skills to deal with the variety of stakeholders and interested parties. The evaluator talks and negotiates with funding agencies for funding and types of evaluation and to get some additional ideas on what the evaluation is expected to cover. Even after the initial report, the evaluator must liaise with the stakeholders and other interested parties to finalize and defend the results, especially where adverse findings are made. In the event that adverse findings are made, the evaluator has the added responsibility of nogiating the acceptamce of the evaluation report.

The evaluator is also responsible for identifying, contacting and seeking the agreement of the study subjects to participate. If a sample is to be used, the evaluator is responsible for obtaining or developing sampling frames, determine an appropriate sample size and decide on an appropriate sampling procedure or sampling methodology. If the data collection involves an interview of study subjects using pre-designed questionnaires, the instruments are developed by the evaluator. In addition, the evaluator is responsible for undertaking data analysis and interpretation and for producing the evaluation report.

Sometimes the evaluation is undertaken by the evaluator. Other times the evaluation is carried out by a team of researchers led by the evaluator. In the latter circumstance, the evaluator has the added task of identifying team members, building and nurturing the team, assigning responsibilities to the team members and managing the team. In situations like this, the evaluator is called the principal evaluator or lead evaluator, and is the spokesperson for the team and the project. The said principal evaluator attends to all queries and makes media statements on behalf of the team.

Another role of the evaluator is the monitoring of the progress and performance of the evaluation activities, and decisions on corrective action where problems arise. Monitoring may indicate emerging problems which may include delayed evaluation activities or components, overspending in terms of achievements against expenditure and/or expenditure against evaluation budget.

TYPES OF PROGRAM EVALUATION

There are many types of program evaluation with their distinctions based strongly on the objectives and goals of the evaluation and the measurements carried out in the evaluation. A distinction is made between short term and long term evaluation, which establishes a time dimension to evaluation. As the name suggest, short term evaluation systematically collects and analyzes data to assess the effectiveness, impacts, efficiency and related costs and benefits in the short term (6 to 12 months) while long term evaluations do the same things but over a long period (e.g. 3 years and over). Long term evaluations assess long term programs and are characterized by the production or periodic summary reports as essential phases of the program evaluation are completed. Lying somewhere between short term and long term evaluation is medium term evaluation. Which usually can be anywhere between one year and three years.

The following different types of program evaluation exist. They can be short or long term and may involve one or more evaluation models:

1. Process or Implementation evaluation.
2. Formative evaluation.
3. Outcome evaluation.
4. Summative evaluation.
5. Impact evaluation.
6. Effectiveness evaluation.

Process Evaluation

Process evaluation is also called implementation evaluation. In process evaluation, the emphasis is on the implementation of various aspects of the program, hence the reason for being called implementation evaluation. Process evaluation assesses how the program was implemented against stated implementation procedures, identifies mistakes made if any, and makes recommendations for corrective actions. The successful outcomes of a number of programs depend partly on how the program was actually implemented and hence the importance of process evaluation. Sometimes, mistakes are made in the implementation of the program, agreed or stated procedures and processes are not followed, corners are deliberately cut to achieve savings on funding allocated to program implementation etc. Sometimes, the best program staff are not recruited leading to program delivery problems. Process evaluation assesses all these possible problem sources as part of the evaluation.

These days many government and non government agencies tend to replicate their designed programs in many geographical areas to save money on reinventing the wheel. Mistakes made in the initial implementation of the program are most likely to be repeated in other locations if there is no process evaluation of the initial program implementation and associated procedures. Process evaluation provides a strong information base for making decisions on amendments or modification of the program before it is replicated. Sometimes, decisions on whether to completely discontinue with a program all together because of extensive structural difficulties are based on or supported by process evaluation findings.

Formative Evaluation

Formative evaluation focuses on identifying areas where improvements could be made during the early or formative stages of the program. Formative evaluation is particularly important for the delivery of new programs. There is always a potential for teething and related problems to arise when a program is first implemented, but more so if the program is new. In formative evaluation the evaluator has a responsibility to find out if any such problems have arisen, and provide options and recommendations for corrective action. The point is that problems in the formative stages of the program could have adverse effects on the outcomes of the program, if not resolved. In addition, if problems in the formative stages are not identified and addressed, they will be carried over to other locations where the program is replicated.

Outcomes Evaluation

This type of evaluation examines the program in terms of its achievements and outcomes. Programs in the criminal justice system in all countries tend to have stated expected outcomes in addition to objectives. Outcomes evaluation assesses the program to find out if the stated expected outcomes and objectives have been achieved. Outcomes evaluation covers the entire life span of the program and is usually undertaken after the completion of the program. It should further be noted that there is always the potential for delayed effects and outcomes evaluation must give consideration to any potential delayed outcomes.

For example, a community based rehabilitation center may have its stated outcomes as follows:

1. Prepare residents for successful resettlement in the community
2. Change the cognitive aspects of the residents, especially the thinking which increases their propensity to commit crime
3. Teach the residents to seek help from the facility or other community help lines if tempted or find themselves in difficult situations
4. Reduce recidivism among the residents of the facility

Outcomes evaluation will seek to find out if these stated outcomes have been successfully achieved. Indeed, outcomes evaluation is not by any means restricted to the stated program outcomes. Any other outcomes, desired or undesired, and intended or unintended consequences must be noted with the stated outcomes. Outcomes evaluation is very important because of the competing demand for limited resources in both government and non government organizations. Funding agencies are now more interested in the outcomes of the programs they provide funding for than anything else. In addition, different funding sources require a clear statement of expected program outcomes in all funding applications, and applications failing to do so may not be considered.

Summative Evaluation

One type of evaluation, which has been receiving substantial attention, is summative evaluation. As the name suggests, summative evaluation focuses on all aspects of the program from the beginning through to the end, covering process or implementation evaluation, formative evaluation and outcomes evaluation (i.e. the sum of the different types of evaluation).The findings of summative evaluation provides a strong information resource base for program areas and funding agencies, largely because of its broad coverage (implementation, formative and outcomes evaluation). The strong information base it produces serves also to assist with decisions on program improvements, replication, and further funding .However, summative evaluation is slightly tedious and takes a much longer time, effort and funding than the other types because summative evaluation, by definition, covers all of them.

Impact Evaluation

Impact evaluation focuses on the impact of programs on the participants, their families and the society as a whole. Program developers are being required to include statements on potential impact of the program on the participants and the community as a whole Impact evaluation examines the program in terms of any identified potential impacts as well as the actual impact of the program or policy. Program impacts can be diverse and may include social impacts, economic impacts, emotional or psychological impacts and, in some cases, physical impacts.

With the advent of consumer groups and prisoners aid and advocacy groups (such as New Zealand Prisoners Aid and Rehabilitation Society), the assessment of program impacts has assumed enormous importance. In the criminal justice system, the assessment of the impacts of corrections and justice programs for offenders extends beyond the offenders, and includes their families, victims and the community as a whole (as it is the community which endures recidivism). Governments are continuously being held accountable for their criminal justice policies and the justice sector programs they develop or provide funding for. This presupposes a need for governments to pre-test or pilot programs and assess the potential impacts of the programs prior to making them permanent parts of the criminal justice system. For example, the New Zealand Government piloted two major national programs, namely home detention and the Habilitation Centres Pilot Program. The aim included the assessment of the programs in terms of impacts, effectiveness and efficiency beforemaking them permanent punitive options in the counry's criminal justice system.

Governments responsiility or accountabioity for thc impacts of their criminal justice programs together with the unintended impacts of various criminal justice policies and programs provide the underlying reasons for the emergence and importance of impact evaluation in the last two decades or so.

Effectiveness Evaluation

Every policy or program in the criminal justice system will have some effects in one way or the other. These effects may be pre-determined, intended or unintended and desired or undesired. The effects may also be seen in relation to the offenders, victims and/or the community. Either way, a need exists to identify and discuss these effects. Effectiveness evaluation is that type of evaluation which focuses on the effectiveness of the programs. Program effectiveness is usually measured in terms of program objectives or purpose, stated outcomes and its successfulness in achieving what it was set up to do .However, other measures may be used depending on the nature and objectives of the evaluation as well as the type of program. Where the program is new and its effectiveness is being assessed for the first time, the evaluation is sometimes called efficacy evaluation.

Meta Evaluation

Meta evaluation is the type of evaluation which involves multiple evaluation goals and the assessment of a number of factors. In meta-evaluation, the focus is on the assessment of technical quality, cost effectiveness and efficiency, usefulness and appropriateness as well as other dimensions depending on the goals of the program and the objectives of the evaluation.

EVALUATION METHODOLOGIES

Various evaluation methodologies are available for criminological researchers interested in program evaluation and include the following:

1. Surveys
2. Focus groups
3. Discussion groups
4. Participant observation/ field work
5. Analysis of existing data
6. Experiments

A leading group of methodologies in the evaluation of programs in the criminal justice system in many societies is the survey. The different survey methodologies were discussed in the preceding chapter and include face to face, postal, observational and telephone survey methodologies. Depending on the goals of the program, funding, skills of the evaluator, timelines and the purpose of the survey, the researcher determines which survey methodology will be used. For example, an evaluator of a community based rehabilitation program for released prisoners may decide to obtain information from the residents using face to face survey methodology or employ focus group research methodology.

Focus groups methodology us used in a number of evaluations. Focus groups methodology, as discussed in chapter three, is the type of evaluation in which data are obtained from a selected group of not more than 15 persons from the relevant interest and/or eligible group. The evaluator convenes a meeting of the group and uses a series of probing questions to obtain the data. Most programs in the criminal justice system can be evaluated using focus group methodology including support programs for victims of crime and investigation of why criminals commit offences or rehabilitation programs.

Closely similar to focus groups is what is called discussion groups. Discussion group methodology is the same as focus groups in situations where the researcher sets up groups and convenes meetings of the group. However, discussion group methodology goes beyond that and involves the researcher putting a topic to the meeting for the participants to talk about without asking participants specific questions as in focus groups methodology. While no specific questions are used as such, the researcher can add leading ideas here and there. With the advent of modern technology, the discussion which is expected to provide information for the researcher, can take place using the internet. A discussion group from the eligible population can be set up on the internet with selected topics to address the evaluation objectives and members of the discussion group can subsequently provide their views on the items. To be very effective, discussion group methodology must be used with one or more other evaluation methodologies.

Participant observation methodology is another evaluation methodology and was previously discussed in greater detail in chapter three. In this methodology, the evaluator obtains data to address the evaluation questions and goals by observing the study subjects behavior in relation to the program. It is most useful in evaluating rehabilitation programs in both prisons and the community. The skills of the evaluator are crucial in making and recording the appropriate behavior so as to obtain adequate data for analysis and interpretation. The evaluator must also seriously take notice of the physical and other contexts of the observation. Participant observation is an effective evaluation methodology if combined with the analysis of program records.

The analysis of existing data is another methodology available to criminological researchers interested in program evaluation. Substantial data exist in program records and other administrative records. The methodology best suits cost benefit or fiscal type of evaluation. Funding agencies hold data on funding provided to the program developers and the itemization of the funding. Program developers hold data on funding received, actual itemized expenditure and the outcomes from the said expenditure. Depending on the type and goals of the evaluation, a lot of data held in government agencies may be accessed and analyzed in the evaluation. Program records constitute leading sources of information on resident numbers and characteristics, program components, program participation, completion and drop out levels or rates. Thus, program records are useful for effectiveness, impact and efficiency evaluation as well.

The final evaluation methodology presented in this book is what is described as experimental evaluation methodology. In this methodology, an experiment is designed to collect data for the evaluation. Experimental evaluation methodology is usually used to evaluate an intervention, such as an intervention to stop young offenders from graduating into adult offenders or an intervention to change the way criminals perceive crime and criminal activity. The experimental evaluation methodology works best in organizational settings with an engaged audience of study subjects, such as participants of specific corrections program. The practice of experimental evaluation involves using the engaged members of the program as the study group and identifying other people with similar characteristics as the control group. The control group does not receive the intervention and does not participate in the intervention or program. Comparative analyses of the data subsequently obtained from the two groups provide information to address the evaluation questions and goals. In the case of the participants of the corrections program, the offenders who receive the intervention, i.e. participate in the program, become the study group, and other offenders who do not participate in the intervention program constitute the control group. More information on experiments as a criminological research methodology is found in chapter six.

TYPES AND SOURCES OF DATA FOR PROGRAM EVALUATION

The various types and sources of criminological research data discussed in chapter two are applicable to program evaluation as well. In addition, there are certain types and sources of data that are unique to program evaluation and they are presented briefly in this section.

These include program data held by services providers, data provided by program beneficiaries, data held by the funding agency, relevant government organizations etc.

Program areas hold data on diverse items such as number of participants, their bio-data (age, gender, marital status, employment status etc), number of program components offered, number and proportion of participants completing listed components of the program, number of staff by gender and related characteristics, budget and funding received, itemized expenditure against budget, recidivism while attending the program, supervision arrangements especially at night and more. Program beneficiaries or participants are in a position to provide information on the effectiveness of the program from their individual perspective, what they have learned, whether they are able to avoid further recidivism, areas within the program which are not helpful, areas which are particularly good and areas where further improvements can be made, overall delivery and operation of the program and any problems they have encountered and so on.

Funding agencies hold data on funding applications including itemized budget sought and what was provided, reasons for refusing aspects of the proposed itemized budget, arrangements for releasing funding to the service provider, whether funding was provided in bulk or periodically in specifically apportioned amounts, any conditions attached to the allocation of funding and any breaches of those conditions and so on.

There is also the group of potential data providers called "significant others'. The "significant others" is the classification given to the people who have close contacts with the offenders who are released back into the community after completing the rehabilitation program. In corrections and other criminal justice programs, the object is to change the behavior, thinking and attitude of offenders by making them attend rehabilitation program. These offenders have people who are important in their lives including parents, spouses/partners, children, siblings and other family members as well as friends. These people can sometimes provide useful data for evaluation, especially in relation to outcome, impact and effectiveness evaluation. They can identify changes in the offender who returns home after completing the program, and can provide evaluators with data on the impact on the offenders and themselves, and if they believe that attendance at the program has made a difference and is helping the offender to stop recidivism.

The data on program staff, data from program records and any other data collected during the evaluation process may be analyzed and the results used to evaluate the program. Depending on the type and goals of the evaluation, the data can be used to undertake process, formative, outcome summative, impact or effectiveness evaluation of the program. A word of caution on data obtained from service providers and program developers will be in order. When collecting and using data provided by service providers or program developers, it should always be remembered that those areas have vested interest in the evaluation findings and the potential to be biased through selective reportingcannot and should not be ruled out.

STEP BY STEP GUIDE TO PROGRAM EVALUATION

Program evaluation is not a simple task. There are a number of steps and procedures in the design and implementation which have to be followed to ensure successful completion of the evaluation.The steps include the following stages:

1. Establishing the evaluation topic and coverage.
2. Planning the evaluation.
3. Literature review.
4. Consultation with stakeholders and relevant organizations and individuals.
5. Deciding the type of evaluation.
6. Selecting an evaluation methodology/design including sampling if required.
7. Implementing the selected design.
8. Data processing, analysis and interpretation including measurements.
9. Producing the evaluation report including further consultations.
10. Dissemination of the results.

Establishing the Evaluation Topic, Purpose and Scope or Coverage

The first step or task in program evaluation is to determine the nature of the evaluation in terms of subject matter and scope/coverage. Corrections and other criminal justice system programs are numerous and varied. For each program, different aspects are discernible. It is therefore essential that the subject matter for the evaluation is identified and clearly defined. In the evaluation of public service programs, the subject matter may be based on questions raised by Ministers or Parliament, or a direct Cabinet instruction. The evaluator may also define the subject matter in consultation with the funding agency, or define the subject matter around the objectives and goals of the program.

Closely related to the subject matter is the precise definition of the purpose or objectives of the evaluation It is often the practice for the evaluation to address the objectives of the program as part of the purpose of the evaluation, albeit this depends, to some extent, on the type of evaluation. For example it is not feasible to address the program objectives if an implementation or process evaluation is undertaken, unless the program objectives include implementation outcomes. The purpose of the evaluation may vary and is specific to each program. However, it could be to provide information for policy and program development decisions, funding allocation decisions, performance assessment and/or to assess accountability. The purpose may simply be to identify areas where improvements can be made or an assessment of the program for replication in other localities.

The subsequent logical step is to define the scope or coverage of the evaluation. In terms of the specific subject matter, the extent of coverage including aspects of the subject matter, which are deemed relevant to be investigated, should be identified and stated. The scope of the evaluation must include areas such as:

1. Geographical coverage (one area if the program is located at one place or multiple geographical areas if the program under evaluation has multiple locations).
2. The parts of the program's duration which will be covered by the evaluation, partly pre-determined by the type of evaluation (e.g. process evaluation covers only the implementation phase).
3. Indication of relevant groups involved in the program that will be covered in the evaluation, i.e. whether program managers will be included, or if selected participants or all participants will be covered etc.

4. Timelines for the completion of specific components of the evaluation as well as the possible date for the completion of the entire evaluation project..
5. There should also be a statement or two about which individuals or organizations or community groups, outside the program personnel, program participants and funding agency, that the evaluation will be interested in interviewing.
6. Type of evaluation and any evaluation models identified.
7. Limitations of the evaluation and a brief statement on the potential topics or subject matter excluded from the evaluation.

The subject matter, purpose or objectives of the evaluation are sometimes pre-defined by the funding agency. This is particularly so in commissioned evaluation where a funding agency contracts an evaluator to carry out the evaluation of a program. Prison officials may commission an evaluator to evaluate a specific prison program. They are likely to state which areas they have specific evaluation interests, which may be the effectiveness of the program, for example. At other times, the subject matter and evaluation purpose may be pre-determined by the type of evaluation and the evaluation models to be used. For example, formative evaluation may dictate the subject matter for the evaluation including "the identification of areas where improvements could be made during the early or formative stages of the program".

The evaluation must subsequently be designed to allow for the collection, analysis and interpretation of data to address the subject matter and objectives of the evaluation. That said it should be noted that the evaluator may decide to do more than addressing the purpose or objectives of the evaluation. Interesting issues may arise which require the attention of the evaluator and, depending n the type of evaluation, there could be a degree of flexibility for the evaluator to investigate those issues.

Terms of Reference

In the preceding paragraphs, it was stated that the subject matter for the evaluation is sometimes pre-defined by the funding agency. The medium through which the subject matter is so determined or defined is called the "Terms of reference". The terms of reference is an essential part of the agreement between the evaluator and the organization commissioning the program evaluation. The terms of reference state clearly the key issues to be investigated as well as what is expected from the evaluation including the following:

1. Purpose of the evaluation.
2. Specific topics or subject matter to be investigated.
3. Non specific or other issues which can potentially be investigated.
4. Timelines for completion (sometimes).
5. Scope of the evaluation.

Planning the Evaluation

Planning is critical for successful evaluation. Evaluation has so many dimensions, many of which have to be attended to prior to the actual evaluation. The evaluator has to plan every aspect of the evaluation in advance. The aspects include preparing the proposals, contacting funding agencies and programs areas, identifying and having informal conversation with program participants, undertaking literature review, consultation with stakeholders and identifying evaluation design options (the last three are discussed under separate headings later in this chapter). During the planning phase, the evaluator must also determine if the program can be evaluated at all, and establish what relevant data already exist. The existing data include program records, data held by funding agencies, data held by justice sector agencies such as the Prisons Service, Community Corrections/Community Probation Service, Department of Courts, Department of Corrections and the Ministry of Justice. The Departments may vary by name in individual countries but, no matter what they are called, the organizations hold a large volume of mainly quantitative data which may be relevant to program evaluation.

The evaluator must also establish a medium for liaison between the evaluator and other parties such as the evaluation team. In the public service, it is usual practice to form an evaluation advisory committee or what is usually called the Steering Committee, comprising representatives from relevant public sector organizations and other stakeholders. This Committee must be consulted regularly during the entire evaluation.

The planning stage is the time during which the evaluator assesses what resources will be needed, if the resources are available and how they will be accessed. Costing for the evaluation may be undertaken at this stage and a budget prepared prior to the application for funding or prior to the signing of the agreement for the commissioned program evaluation. Most funding agencies prefer itemized budget and the probability of securing the evaluation contract improves significantly if the evaluator submits an itemized budget to the finding agency.

All negotiations are commenced and possibly completed during this stage, and the desire should be to complete all the negotiations during the planning stage. The negotiations should not cover only funding, but also access to existing data, program participants, program records and related matter.

It is during this phase that the researcher mulls the idea of what the potential problems and issues are likely to be and what plans are made to resolve them. A number of unanticipated problems may arise during the evaluation and the evaluator may not know them in advance. However, some potential problems are usually discernible and the evaluator can work on those problems during the planning phase. Some problems come to the evaluator's attention through literature review and/or through discussions with program personnel etc.

Another salient feature of the planning stage is the establishment of an evaluation team. During the planning stage, the evaluator must ask and answer the questions "am I going to undertake the evaluation on my own" or "am I going to involve other people in the form of an evaluation team?

If the evaluator decides to involve an evaluation team, it is at this stage that the team is set up. The evaluator must decide what personnel will be required for the specific evaluation, what skills will be needed, where they will be found, what the cost is etc., and build the evaluation team. Sometimes, the evaluator may have to provide training to the members of the team. Communication between the evaluator and members of the evaluation team (where there is an evaluation team) is crucial for the success of the evaluation. The team members must have knowledge and understanding of the agreed communication medium and mechanisms as well as the chain of command in forwarding queries and information to the evaluator, especially if trained interviewers are employed to collect the data.

In addition, this is the stage where the evaluator makes data processing decisions and plans as well as any specific reporting plans. The reporting plans must include the channels which will be used to disseminate the evaluation findings including the final written reports, journal articles if allowed under the agreement with the funding agency, presentations to the funding agency, program personnel, the public etc. as permitted by the funding agreement.

Literature Review

The importance of literature review in program evaluation is similar to survey research and participant observation, and along the lines of the general research process. In Program evaluation, literature review assumes additional significance. This is because literature review has the potential, and it often does, to influence the type of evaluation, evaluation design and models. The added significance is based on the fact that most evaluations involve the use of multiple methodologies (triangulation) and the literature review can provide valuable information on which blend or combination of methodologies worked best in previous studies. More importantly the literature review is likely to throw more light on the methodologies which have been ineffective or combinations which failed in previous evaluations, and which methodologies and combinations to be avoided. The literature review can also assist in guiding and shaping the pre-determined content of the evaluation instruments if focus group or one of the survey methodologies is chosen.

To illustrate, imagine an evaluator has been commissioned to undertake the evaluation of a particular program. The evaluator initially decides to use a structured face to face interview of respondents to obtain the required data. The evaluator reviews the existing published and accessible unpublished literature on the evaluation of similar programs, especially those covering the specific geographical area of interest to the evaluation. First, the evaluator is able to learn what evaluation methodologies were employed and the degree to which they were successful. This information from the literature review enables decisions to be made on whether to use similar methodologies and/or use completely new methodologies.

The literature review is also a useful source of information for identifying any theories relevant to the operation and/or performance of the specific program Sometimes, the literature review can provide further insights into empirical non-methodological problems (logistical) encountered in the evaluation of similar programs, thus enabling the evaluator to avoid them.

Initial Consultation with Stakeholders

There is much more consultation in program evaluation than most other research activities. This is largely because there is far more interest in program evaluation including interest from funding agencies, program and service providers, organizations in the justice sector and families of program participants etc. It is absolutely necessary for the evaluator to identify the key stakeholders, and other interested organizations and individuals that are to be consulted during the evaluation of the program. Generally speaking, stakeholders include any individual or organization with specific interest in the program. The main stakeholders include the funding agency, the organization providing the service, the participants of the program and the government in the case of the evaluation of public service programs. The justice sector organizations with interest in the evaluation usually include the Police, Prison Service, Community Corrections, Ministries or Departments of Justice, Courts, Corrections etc.

Corrective programs, such as those designed for convicted offenders (community or prison based) tend to have some impact on the family members who have to live with and cater for the program participant after their release, and they must sometimes be consulted.(determined by the nature of the corrective program and what changes it is expected to make to the participant). Stakeholders may be consulted any time during the evaluation, but it is critical to contact the stakeholders at the beginning and at the end of the evaluation before the report is finalized. Contacting the stakeholders at the beginning will provide information to the evaluator, information which will help make many decisions including evaluation subject matter, type, design, implementation and reporting.

Contacting or consulting the stakeholders during the preparation of the final report enables the evaluator to receive comments and to decide which aspects of the data analysis and interpretation should be included and emphasized. It also marks the beginning of the negotiations on the acceptance of the final report, while all potential queries on the final report could be signaled by the stakeholders during consultations. In short, the evaluator becomes aware of what the stakeholders are interested in, i.e. the topics and questions they would like answered in the evaluation report. It must be stated that consultation does not mean that factual information in the report should be changed, especially adverse findings should be maintained. Consultations should be a process of receiving feedback from stakeholders on the areas they would like to see emphasized in the report, relevant issues which should not be missed. In some instances, stakeholders would require regular updates on the progress of he evaluation.

Examining Evaluation Design Options and Selecting an Appropriate Design

After reviewing the literature and consulting with stakeholders, the evaluation progresses to the next logical stage, identification and selection of the research design. This is a crucial stage because the selection of the wrong or inappropriate design would most definitely have adverse effects on the evaluation and its findings. The evaluator must have a strategy to select the most appropriate design for the specific study. The evaluation design will to a large extent be determined by the type of evaluation, the goals and objectives of the program to be evaluated, funding, ethical considerations, concerns of stakeholders and the skills of the evaluator and/or the evaluation team.

There are different designs available to the evaluator including participant observation, focus groups, surveys, the analysis of existing data in particular program records, and other methodologies. The evaluator must weigh the pros and cons of the different methodologies and decide on the appropriate methodology or the appropriate combination of methodologies for the specific program evaluation. Most evaluations involve at least two methodologies in some form of triangulation. Most evaluations involve the analysis of program records and one of the prominent designs (surveys, focus groups or participant observation). Experiments have been used in some cases, but the use of experiments to collect data for program or policy evaluation has not been as widespread as the three prominent methodologies. Most evaluations these days tend to focus on methodological or design issues related to appropriateness, effectiveness or efficacy, efficiency and impact of the program. Considerations of these issues affect the decision on what evaluation methodology or methodologies to use.

There are different designs for evaluations involving issues of appropriateness, effectiveness or efficacy, efficiency and impact of corrections and other criminal justice programs. The evaluator must decide on an evaluation methodology or design depending on the emphasis of the evaluation, objectives and goals of the program. Assessing program appropriateness requires responses to various questions including:

1. Why was the program established?
2. Is there a need for the program? Is the program serving community needs?
3. What reasons were given for providing funding for the program?
4. Are there accessible alternatives?
5. Is the program likely to achieve its objectives?
6. Are there any unique program objectives?
7. Are there any unique or special program characteristics?

Answers to questions such as those mentioned above will most certainly provide useful information to determine the appropriateness of the specific criminal justice program. If the evaluator decides to undertake an appropriateness evaluation, a design which will allow for the collection of data to answer these questions will be in order.

With regards to the assessment of program efficiency, a number of questions may be asked and a design which would provide data to answer the said questions would be a better design. Efficiency, by definition, is the achievement of the same program output with less resources or program inputs over time. For example if it cost $10 000 to provide rehabilitation program for 5 residents in year one, and $5 000 and $3000 to rehabilitate the same number of offenders in years two and three respectively, the program is said to be efficient, i.e. the program uses lower program inputs to achieve the same outputs or results over time. The converse is true in that if program cost or resource use to rehabilitate the same number of offenders increase, the program is deemed inefficient or that the program is not achieving efficiencies.

In assessing program efficiency, a number of questions need to be answered including:

1. How much funding was provided for the program?
2. How much was used to implement various components of the program?
3. What was the initial cost per program participant?
4. Did the initial cost change over time?
5. If yes to question 4, did the initial cost increase or decrease over time?
6. Did the program make any savings from the budget?

Answers to these questions will determine if lower amount of resources or inputs were used to achieve the same program outputs over time and allow the evaluator to discern the exact level of efficiency achievement or lack of efficiency achievements. An evaluation design which allows for then collection of data to address the questions will be appropriate. A design, such as the analysis of existing data, especiallyfunding agency data and program records on budget and expenditure may be more appropriate.

An evaluation of the efficacy or effectiveness of a criminal justice program will need a design which will enable data to be collected to answer specific questions. When a program is being tested for the first time, efficacy is the appropriate term, while if the program has been tested previously, then effectiveness evaluation applies. Evaluating efficacy or effectiveness involves measuring outcomes and costs (cost effectiveness) as well as the achievement of program objectives. Cost effectiveness is distinct from efficiency measurements. Cost effectiveness is measured by cost per capita regardless of any changes over time which is efficiency. For example, in assessing cost effectiveness, the total cost of the program will have to be established together with the total cost per participant. For example, a rehabilitation program may cost $40 000 to operate and there were 400 participant completing the program in that year. In the analysis of cost effectiveness, the cost per participant is established as $100. Cost effectiveness is useful in comparing similar programs.

Answers to the following questions may be required: in assessing efficacy or effectiveness: including cost effectiveness:

1. Did the program have any effect on the participants?
2. Were the objectives of the program achieved?
3. Is there a need to modify the program to achievement the objectives?
4. Is there a need to modify the program to improve overall program performance?
5. How much did it cost to achieve the observed program outcomes?
6. What was the cost per capita? What was the overall cost per participant?

The answers will also assist the evaluator to select an appropriate evaluation design if the object is to assess program efficacy or effectiveness.

The assessment of program impact requires answers to questions similar to those identified in the preceding paragraphs for program effectivneses. In particular "what was the impact of the program on the participants, their families, and the community? With increasing criticism of the impacts of many government funded programs in various jurisdictions, impact evaluation is assuming increasing importance. Most agencies are now required to provide an indication of the potential impacts when applying for funding for new programs. They are also required to provide data on actual impacts through program evaluation after the implementation of the program. Needless to say that data from impact evaluation is usually used to assess the suitability of replicating a program.

It is at this stage that evaluator finalizes the formal decisions on whether a team will be involved in data collection and the evaluation as a whole, and whether a sample will be used. Detail description of sampling types and procedures were provided in the previous chapter and will not be repeated here, except to say that the evaluator has to decide whether to collect data from a sample, and what type of sampling procedure will be best for the evaluation. Some criminal justice programs involve a small number of participants, and others have a large number of participants. With regards to programs with a small number of participants, the usual practice is to collect data on all the participants, because the small number of participants makes that feasible. Where the program participation is high in terms of number of participants, iit is logistically and financially difficult to collect data on all the participants, and identifying and employing a suitable sampling procedure becomes inevitable.

In addition, during this phase the evaluator must also give considerations to the data processing strategy for the program evaluation. This involves decisions on measurements of the variables, how data will be entered into data files, and how the files will be maintained. Considerations must be given to, and decisions made on, the types of data analysis that will be undertaken and strategies for the interpretation of the results from the data analysis. Strategies which allow data to be collected, analyzed and interpreted so as to achieve the objectives of the evaluation and answer the evaluation research questions must be identified. Depending on the type of evaluation and the expected amount of data, decisions must be made on whether to employ data entry personnel and what type of training would have to be provided to them.

IMPLEMENTATION OF THE SELECTED EVALUATION DESIGN

The logical sequence after selecting the program evaluation design and an appropriate sample (if applicable) is to proceed to implement the selected design, i.e. proceed to carry out the evaluation. During this stage the evaluator finalizes many aspects of the project including but not limited to completing training of the evaluation team (if applicable), interviewers, field manuals, piloting of instruments (i.e. If survey methodology is chosen for the evaluation), arrangements for interviews to take place, printing of questionnaires and their distribution to interviewers, reporting arrangements for interviewers and related field staff etc. Some of these activities are carried out during the evaluation planning stage but they are finalized at this stage. More importantly, the mechanisms for communication between the evaluator and other survey administrative personnel and the interviewers and their supervisors are finalized during this stage.

If focus groups or participant observation methodology is selected, arrangements are made in the planning stage must be implemented. These include establishing the focus group members or participants for observation, establishing data collection venues and times and actually proceeding to collect the data. The evaluator subsequently proceeds to obtain data through the interviewing of the focus group members or the observation of the behavior of participant observation subjects.

If survey methodology is selected as the evaluation design, implementation procedures described in detail in chapter four are followed. One very important advantage that survey research has over participant observation in terms of evaluation is that the survey researcher is able to test the pre-designed instruments before proceeding to the actual data collection phase. The evaluator using survey methodology as the evaluation design may avail themselves of this advantage. As discussed previously in the section on measurements, if there are errors and problems with the instruments, there is an opportunity to take corrective action and modify the instruments accordingly before data collection.Following piloting and identification of solutions to any problems arising from the pilot exercise, data collection will then be implemented. The evaluator commences data collection by sending the interviewers and their supervisors into the field to interview the respondents selected in the study sample, or the evaluator undertakes the data collection personally.

It is at this stage that the evaluator requests data from program records for analysis. The data sought may include program data on participants/clients, program management, staff data and information on program components. Other relevant data include the number and proportion of participants completing each program, number and proportion of participants completing the whole program as well as funding and expenditure data, number and types of recidivism etc. The data, thus obtained from the program authorities, are subsequently analyzed alongside the data obtained from other sources.

As part of the project management plan, the evaluator defines timelines for the achievement of various field objectives including when all interviews and/or observations are to be completed. Sometimes, funding agencies request progress reports during the implementation of the evaluation and the evaluator obliges by providing reports indicating how various activities and assigned timelines are being met. When data collection is completed, measurement and data processing (data entry, analysis and interpretation) commence.

Data Processing and Measurements

Following data collection is the stage of data processing, measurements, analysis and interpretation At this stage, data would have been obtained from various sources including program beneficiaries, program providers, funding agencies and relevant observers of the program. All the data must be entered into data files according to data processing decisions made during the planning and selection of an evaluation design stages. The step after data entry is data analysis and interpretation. The first step in data analysis is the measurement of the variables. Measurement can involve single variable or multiple variables as discussed in chapter four.

In program evaluation, specific measures must be developed for each of the broad sources of data, namely beneficiaries, program and service providers, program records and funding agencies where appropriate. Measures for program beneficiaries include the following:

1. Actual responses from beneficiaries are to be measured using the approaches described in chapter two if participant observation methodology was used or in if either focus group or survey methodologies were used (chapter four).
2. Indexes must be developed for different responses foe each question(focus group and survey methodologies) or for different observations for the same variable (participant observation).
3. Level and rate of recidivism as reported by the program beneficiaries.
4. Number and rate of breaches of program rules, regulations and procedures as reported by the beneficiaries of the program.

In undertaking program evaluation data on program staff are essential and every effort should be made to obtain and analyze service personnel data. Data on service providers include:

1. Number and bio-data of program managers.
2. Number and bio-data of service personnel (non managerial).
3. Qualifications of service providers.
4. Resident/staff ratio, i.e. number of residents or participant per unit staff.

5. Dace to face contact hours of staff with residents, i.e. staff time per resident contact (group or individual).
6. Number of other contacts, e.g. phone contacts.

Equally or more important is the actual data on the operations of the program and the participation of the residents as evidenced from program records.

1. Number of participants during the period covered by the evaluation (total and mean or average per week/month).
2. Number of participants as a proportion of overall capacity or total number of available program places.
3. Types of program activities.
4. Number of programs available.
5. How many programs must each resident complete to meet the requirements of rehabilitation and become eligible for release?
6. Number and proportion successfully completing individual components of the program.
7. Number and proportion successfully completing all aspects of the program.
8. Itemized budget (actual).
9. Itemized expenditure.
10. Shortfalls in the budget/over expenditure.
11. Savings or budget surplus.

In addition, funding agencies can provide data on funding applied for, funding approved etc. Other administrative records from prisons on the residents of the rehabilitation facility may be sought, especially history of breaches and recidivism.

In addition to the data and measures described in the preceding 3 or 4 paragraphs, the new data collected through participant observation, survey of clients, focus group or a combination of methods must also undergo further measurements and analysis. Data are obtained on a number of variables including demographic and personal data on the participants (bio-data), knowledge variables (responses to specific questions or observations of specific behavior), attitudinal, self-rated capacity to settle in the community, cognitive skills (criminal minds and thinking), level of motivation to lead normal life style etc. Depending on the purpose and type of evaluation and the goals of the program, the evaluator may obtain, analyze and interpret data on many more variables.

After measurements the data must be analyzed. The analyses must be such that they allow for the evaluation goals and objectives to be achieved regardless of what type of evaluation and what methodologies were employed. Closely associated with data analysis is the interpretation of the measures and analysis. It is from the interpretation that evaluation findings are made and firm conclusions drawn. The interpretation must be made carefully, so that accurate conclusions can be reached. .When all relevant data have been analyzed and interpreted, the evaluator proceeds to prepare the report containing the findings and any proposed recommendations.

It is important to remember that the analysis and measures presented in chapters three and four for participant observation and survey research methodologies are applicable to program evaluation depending on the evaluation design, goals and objectives. If survey research methodology or focus group methodology is used, the measures and analysis presented in chapter four may be used. These include coding of open ended and closed questions, numerical and graphical analysis of data and the various measures used in numerical analysis and histograms. Frequency distributions, cross-tabulations line and bar graphs can be used to analyze and understand evaluation data obtained using survey design or focus group research methodology. Relationships between survey data variables may be tested through chi square, causation or correlations and related methods.

Evaluation Report

The end product of the evaluation is the report. After all the analyses have been completed, the evaluator must put everything together in a report. The report is prepared along the lines discussed in the section on General Research Process with modifications specific to program evaluation, especially the goals and objectives of the evaluation. It is also usual practice to prepare an overall report containing and describing all or some of the following:

1. What the evaluation was about – subject matter or topic.
2. Goals and objectives of the evaluation.
3. Review of the existing literature.
4. Evaluation design and related methodologies.
5. Main sources of data.
6. Stakeholders, organizations and individuals consulted.
7. Problems encountered and how they were solved.
8. The main findings.
9. Minor findings.
10. Any conclusions drawn, especially as they relate to the evaluation goals and objectives.
11. Recommendations
12. Any other items of relevance and interest to the evaluation and.or stakeholders.

A unique feature of program evaluation is the consultation with stakeholders during the drafting of the evaluation report. Stakeholders are interested in receiving information and possibly recommendations on various aspects of the program from the evaluation. The evaluator must consult with the stakeholders to ensure that the report addresses the specific issues and/or concerns of interest to them. For example, funding agencies would be interested in knowing if the funding was appropriately used and what the outcomes of the program were. Funding agencies would usually like to see in the evaluation report analysis of cost effectiveness and efficiency and in particular a recommendation or recommendations on whether funding for the program should be continued or discontinued and why.

Program areas or service providers would like to know if the goals and objectives of their programs and services have been achieved. They would also like to learn about areas where further improvements can be made including the implementation of the program or service. Program providers may even be interested in receiving recommendations on which program components or activities should be discontinued, for any reason, which activities should be modified and which components were strong enough to be kept as they are or reinforced. Other stakeholders could be interested in the overall performance of the program, including weaknesses and strengths of the program and accountability of program staff. Sometimes, the evaluator will have to produce a draft report and seek comments on the draft report before finalizing the evaluation report (this is actually recommended). Seeking comments on draft reports is becoming increasingly imperative for the evaluation of public service programs or government funded programs where stakeholders have a bigger say on the issues to be included or rather addressed in the evaluation report.

Consulting with stakeholders should not be taken to mean that factual information should be deleted or manipulated to please stakeholders. Well, some stakeholders including service providers may not be happy with adverse findings but the evaluation must report the good with the bad findings (if any). The key point is that the evaluation findings must be balanced, objective, fair, and true (what this book introduces as BOFT).The evaluation report should also be able to withstand scrutiny and other critical tests. There is no worry for the evaluator if the analysis, interpretation and conclusions have been done scientifically, correctly and appropriately (Scientific Method). Any preconceptions and prior beliefs and expectations should not overshadow the actual findings arising from the collection, analysis and interpretation of data. There is no room for biases in the evaluation report. The evaluator should be aware that there will be queries about the report and that the need to scientifically defend the evaluation findings is an integral component of the entire evaluation process. In other words, the evaluator should be in a position to use evidence based arguments to defend the report and to address any questions asked of the evaluation report (i.e. evidence from the evaluation).

Dissemination of Evaluation Results

The final stage in the continuum of aevaluation ctivities is the dissemination of the results. How the evaluation results are disseminated or who receives copies of the evaluation reports are sometime defined in the contract between the evaluator and the organization commissioning the evaluation. Nonetheless, program providers, funding agencies and other key stakeholders must receive copies of the evaluation reports. Where there are no restrictions, the evaluation findings must be widely disseminated using outlets such as the local newspapers, journal articles, public presentations and lectures. Copies of the reports must also be sent to many organizations, libraries and program providers wanting to provide a similar program or service.

ANALYSIS OF COSTS

Most program evaluation reports would contain varying analysis of costs regardless of the goals, objectives and types of evaluation. Cost analysis is becoming a salient feature of program evaluation for a number of reasons. First, it provides useful information for funders to make funding decisions. Secondly, it provides information about whether funding has been effectively used. Third, it informs both program providers and funding agencies about achieved efficiencies and budget savings, or the lack of savings and budget deficits. The fourth and perhaps the most important reason is that we live in a world of limited resources and competing demands. Prudential management of available funding is now essential and funding will not be allocated to program areas unless there is some indication that the program will be successful in yielding some desired outcomes. Undertaking cost analysis in program evaluation provides the required indication of the success or failure of the program.

Cost analysis in program evaluation demonstrates if the program achieved cost effectiveness and efficiency, and if funding should be continued. Indeed, no program evaluation will be deemed comprehensive and appropriate without an analysis of costs, and governmental sources of funding are particularly interested in cost analysis and subsequent funding recommendations. Another reason which has not been given adequate recognition in the literature is that cost analysis in evaluation shows what financial resources are needed for programs to be successful and viable, and avoid or reduce under-funding of programs and budget deficits. It is for these reasons that a special section is allocated to cost analysis in this book, albeit it was mentioned briefly in the section on reporting of evaluation findings.

There are different types of cost which can be analyzed in program, evaluation. A distinction is usually made between the two broad areas of variable and fixed costs. Fixed costs are cost of setting up the infrastructure and relate to cost incurred during the setting up of a facility. For example the building, beds and other items required for setting up a prison are fixed costs.

They must be incurred before the prison can start operations or receive its first inmate. Fixed costs change very little even though, by definition, they should not change. Variable costs are those other costs which do change during the operation of the prison including salaries, costs of maintaining the prison and providing food, water, electricity to the inmates and the irregular running cost of the prison as a whole Fixed costs are sometimes called capital costs while variable costs also called ongoing or recurrent costs During the establishment of a prison, fixed cost may be incurred once, while the variable costs are ongoing.

In undertaking cost analysis as part of evaluating a criminal justice program, two other types of costs are discernible, namely incremental and non-incremental costs. Incremental costs include ongoing costs, costs that must be incurred regularly to ensure the smooth operation of the prison or corrections facility, including staff salaries, electricity and water costs, pay or wages for inmates who work in the prison, food and other supplies which have the propensity to increase with time. These costs are not only ongoing or recurrent, but they also increase with time. A salient feature of incremental costs is that they do change over time. Salaries of prison staff have built in annual or periodic increases, the costs of food and other supplies may rise over time and the cost of maintaining the facility may change regularly. Staff remuneration packages tend to incude agreed increments which are implemented over time. Inflation also affects the cost of maintaining the facility include food and water supplies and so on. Non incremental costs are those cost which are expended usually once and most importantly costs that do not increase on a regular basis.

Other costs include hidden versus obvious costs, direct versus indirect costs and opportunity costs. Obvious costs, as the name suggests, are those cost that prison or program officials are aware of, and hidden cost include unexpected costs which crop up during the operation of the program or facility as well as expected costs which are sometimes forgotten. For example, in budgeting for a new corrections facility, the costs of the physical infrastructure may be included, but sight could be lost of the cost of feasibility studies as well as the cost of some supplies required for the smooth operation of the facility, i.e. hidden costs.

Direct costs are those cost that are directly associated with providing a service, and indirect costs include accidental cost and related unexpected costs that are incurred to support the operation of the facility. For example, a rehabilitation program must have counselors, social workers and experts in the program components or activities. The salaries and other remuneration costs of these staff are direct costs. The cost of transporting a recidivist resident to and from Court is an indirect cost, i.e. not directly related to the operation of the rehabilitation program.

For the successful operation of the program and the facility, the program and the facilities must be managed. The costs of managing the program, including salaries for non program staff, i.e. administrative staff, also constitute the indirect costs of the program (e.g. receptionist, cleaners etc). Opportunity costs in program evaluation follow the logic and concept of opportunity costs in economics. Simply it operates on the basis that there are a number of programs and choices. By selecting a specific program or service, other programs and services are forgone and the lost of the opportunity to secure one of the other programs is the opportunity costs.

In program evaluation, analyses of variable, fixed, incremental and non incremental and the other costs provide further insights into the financial operations and the financial health of the program. They also assist in cost benefit, efficiency and cost effectiveness analysis, and enable the evaluator to make fiscal or financial recommendations. It is becoming increasingly imperative and paramount for program evaluation to include some cost analysis.

Cost Effectiveness

Cost effectiveness relates outputs to the cost of producing the outputs which led to the outcomes. It is simply theunit or per capita cost of producing a particular output and subsequent outcome. In program evaluation, there is always a need to establish the overall cost of the program relative to the outcomes of the program in order to ascertain if there has been value for money and if the outcomes are those which are intended. If the funding has yielded the expected outcomes within the budget in terms of program goals and objectives, then the funding has been well spent and the program is said to be cost effective. Cost effectiveness analysis demonstrate the productivity of the program and is measured by computing one or more indexes including a ratio of the overall costs to achieved outcomes. Cost effectiveness is not an indicator of the efficiency of the program, and does not usually include savings over time.

Efficiency

Efficiency is related to cost effectiveness but it is quite distinct from its cousin. Efficiency indicates the differences in achieving the same outcome over time using a decreasing level of resources input. So that if a program achieves the same outcome with lesser resources, then the program is efficient, and vice versa. For example, suppose a corrections facility is set up to provide rehabilitation programs for offenders convicted of alcohol and drug related crimes. In the first year of operation, the facility expends $50 000 to rehabilitate 25 inmates, but expends only $25 000 in the following year to rehabilitate another 25 offenders using the same program components. The program is said to be efficient or achieving efficiencies because it is using a lesser amount of resources to achieve the same output/ andoor utcome. Most service providers are under increasing pressure from funding agencies to avoid waste, make savings within the budget and achieve efficiencies. Program evaluation should include efficiency assessments as an essential component of cost analysis.

Cost-Benefit Analysis

Intertwined in cost effectiveness and efficiency is cost-benefit analysis. Most people have at least heard of cost-benefit analysis. Similar to cost effectiveness, cost-benefit analysis pinches the total cost of the program to the program outcomes. It denotes the relationship between the benefits obtained from expending a certain amount of resources to the resources expended. Cost-benefit analysis is becoming increasing important in program evaluation for various reasons. First, there is competing demand for limited governmental and private sector funding. Funding agencies are asking for better use of resources and the identification of savings through the minimization of waste, in particular, those programs, which receive regular annual funding or continuous funding, have to show that the continuous funding is appropriate and valuable in the sense that the benefits from the program outweigh the cost of the progam.

Cost-benefit analysis addresses the following questions, for example:

1. What was the total funding of the program?
2. What was the actual expenditure of the program?
3. What were the outcomes or benefits?
4. What is the actual cost per outcome or identified benefit?
5. Was the outcome worthy of the funding? Is it worthy to expend that level of resources for the actual or achieved outcomes?
6. Do the benefits outweigh the costs?
7. If the benefits do not outweigh the costs, do they in any way justify the resources put into the program?

The evaluator must undertake cost analysis to answer those questions and establish the cost-benefit analysis for the program. In the process of assessing the cost-benefit analysis, it is sometimes useful to use the cost-benefit analysis from similar programs as benchmarks, and to undertake comparative analysis.

Types of Program Costs

In undertaking cost analysis in program evaluation, it is important to identify and analyze various types of data on program cost. These include all the costs associated with the program and the delivery of program components such as:

1. Staff salaries (professional staff such as counselors and social workers and all other staff such as receptionist and cleaners).
2. Non salary cost of interventions and related program components.
3. Equipment and other infrastructure costs.
4. Cost of maintaining the facility.
5. Cost of supplies (food, materials etc).
6. Cost of electricity, gas and water as appropriate.
7. Other costs (hidden or obvious).

One of the biggest program expenditures is personnel costs. Without the personnel, the program cannot be delivered. Professional staff are needed to deliver and manage the professional aspects of the criminal justice program including counseling and discussion group sessions. Non professional staff are needed to provide administrative and other support to allow the program to function properly. A substantial proportion of program funds is usually expended on program personnel, albeit the preferred option is to minimize program personnel costs.

Non recurring costs such as cost of securing the physical facility, equipment, beds, tables and other items can be expensive but they are not incurred on a regular basis and most are incurred usually once. It takes a long time for the physical and related infrastructure to be replaced.. Non salary recurring costs are a major aspect of the budget of any corrections or criminal justice program. Ongoing costs are difficult to accurately forecast in the budget. Maintenance, food and other supplies, electricity, gas and water costs take large portions of the program budget, but more importantly, the amount involved can change from time to time or even regularly as a result of inflation pressures.

Unit of Analysis

All the costs associated with a program are analyzed during program evaluation. The key issue is the selection of an appropriate unit of analysis. In program evaluation, the units of analysis are the indicators or indexes which are calculated and used in costs analysis. The units of costs analysis must be compatible with the goals and objectives of the program. They must also be such as to allow itemized cost analysis. The following units of analysis continue to be adopted in program costs analysis:

1. Cost per specific output/outcome.
2. Overall cost per program participant.
3. Cost per day or per week.
4. Staff cost per program participant.
5. Administrative cost per resident or participant.
6. Administration expenditure as a proportion (%) of total program expenditure.
7. Non administration costs as a proportion of total program expenditure.
8. Ratio of administration costs to non administration costs.

The cost per specific output or outcome can be undertaken in various ways. The first method is to compute a ratio of program outputs/outcomes to program costs to give an indication of cost effectiveness. The second method is to identify key outcomes and estimate the costs per a specific outcome. With regards to overall cost per program participant, the index is obtained by establishing total costs and total number of participants, and dividing the total costs by the number of participants. This index is used in most costs analysis because it involves simple and easy computation, and also because the data required are readily available from program records. The next unit of analysis, cost per day or week, operates on the basis of the number of program days/weeks and the total cost of the program By dividing the total costs by the number of program days/weeks, the mean cost per day/week is derived. Program cost may vary from day to day or from week to week. What this unit of analysis does is to provide a mean index of cost per day or cost per week.

The other indexes are based on the sub-components of total cost, and provide refined units of analysis as they deal with specific items of expenditure. The unit of analysis, staff costs per participant, denotes the relationship between personnel costs and program participants. By dividing all personnel costs by the number of participant the unit analysis of staff cost per participant is obtained. Similarly, by dividing total administrative cost by the total number of participants, the index of administration costs per participant is obtained. Analysis of staff cost per participant, administration costs per participant, administration costs as a proportion of total cost and non administration costs as a proportion of total program expenditure provide very useful insights into how funding is used to deliver the program. In particular, it shows how much of the total funding was spent on administration costs. Funding agencies are usually prone to insist on more resources being directed at delivering the program rather than administration. The ratio of administration costs to non administration costs makes this vivid.

PROGRAM LOGIC

As indicated many times in this chapter, every program is set up with a specific purpose and defined expected outcomes. The ultimate expectations from a program are the outcomes that emerge at the end of the program. Program logic, also called the Logical Framework, demonstrates the logical and sequential relationships between program inputs and program outcomes. Program logic establishes the causal linkages between the resources which are used to start the program, how the resources are used, what outputs are produced and what outcomes the outputs yield. Thus, program logic has 4 levels, namely inputs, processes, outputs and outcomes. Inputs are the resources that are put into the program.

Every program needs some amount of resources to function. These resources are called the program inputs and include administration, professional staff and non professional staff and other resources that are put into the program. Processes denote what happens to the inputs, i.e. how the inputs are used, while outputs refer to the results the processing of the inputs produces. Processes are, therefore, the means for using the inputs to produce the outputs. Every output leads to an outcome which is the final level in the logical and sequential causal linkages between the 4 levels of inputs, processes, outputs and outcomes (figure 4).Funding agencies, program managers and other key stakeholders are particularly interested in the outcomes of a program, the final consequences of all the effort and investment that hves been made. Outcomes are the measures by which the program's success or failure is assessed In program logic the outcomes are often listed in a hierarchy Program logic, in essence, maps and provides a diagrammatical representation of the causal linkages between the 4 levels as follows:

To illustrate, suppose a community based rehabilitation facility is funded to provide programs to change the thinking (cognitive), attitudes, perceptions and practices of selected hard core offenders convicted of serious crimes including armed robbery, manslaughter and murder. The facility has to invest in human, administration, material and other resources to start operations. These resources constitute the inputs of the program and fall within the bottom box in the hierarchy of boxes (figure 4). The program is implemented by using the resources as a means of producing the outputs of the program. Counsellors and other professional staff deliver their functions, administration staff provide support and funds are invested, and other program beeds are mplemented (inputs). This then constitutes the second box called processes in figure 4. The outputs (3ed box) produced from processing the resources subsequently define the outcomes, which are the impact or consequences of the program over and above the tangible outputs.

In this example, the processes relate to the program components which are delivered using the inputs and may include counseling, cognitive skills development, group discussion, recreation, gymnasium and exercise. These activities may lead to a number of outputs such as program participation (number and proportion of participants commencing and completing all program activities).

The final consequences of the program are the outcomes from the outputs and may include changes in the thinking and attitudes or the participants, improvements in cognitive ability, reduced recidivism or cessation of recidivism etc. Outcomes are represented in the top box The outcomes must be represented in some form of hierarchy to show the importance of individual outcomes.

Additional illustration is presented in figure 5 which illustrates further the logical, sequential and causal linkages between inputs, processes, outputs and outcomes. Mapping the program logic in this way enables the evaluator to have a better understanding and knowledge of what resources were actually used, how the resources were used to produce the outputs of the program and how the outputs translated into outcomes.

Program Logic provides a picture of what has happened in the program at a glance and can be used to map out aspects of the program including issues and strategies. For example, program logic enhances the ability of the evaluator to pinpoint any issues at various stages or levels, issues which can then be diagrammatically represented in the appropriate box in the sequence of boxes. Issues about resources will be put in the bottom box, the inputs box. If the issues in resources cause issues in the implementation of the program, the implementation issues are recorded in the process box, while issues in the outputs and outcomes are represented in the output and outcomes boxes respectively.

The sequential causal linkages between the issues of the input level through to the outcomes level are pictorially shown in program logic. A glance at the boxes (filled with issues) shows clearly what issues were relative to the program, and facilitates the analysis of program issues, for example. Program logic is, therefore, very useful in program evaluation, and can be used to investigate and analyze any program subject matter of relevance to the evaluation goals and purpose.

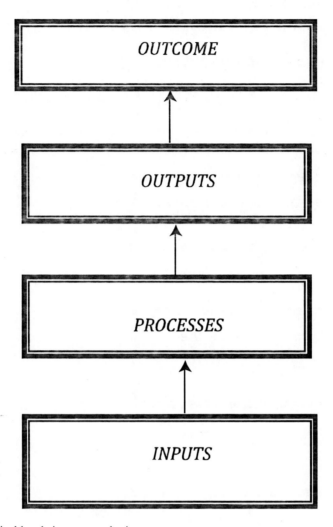

Figure 4. Hierarchical levels in program logic

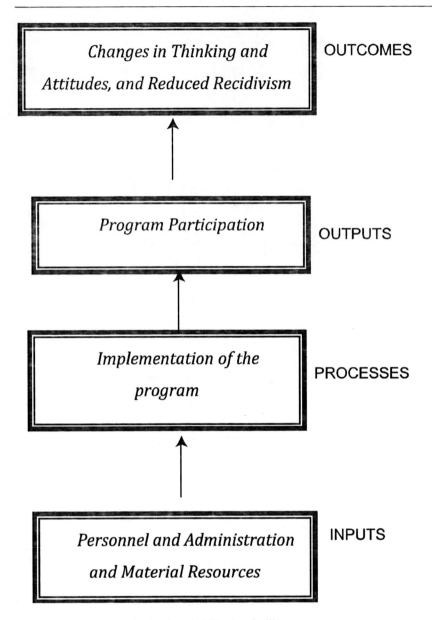

Figure 5. The program logic of a rehabilitation facility.

The usefulness of program logic extends beyond program evaluation. Program logic is useful in program planning and program development, and providers should plan and map the logic in their programs. Program providers can plot from the outset what inputs (human, administration and financial resources) will be needed to get the program functional, how the inputs will be used (program delivery), what are the likely or expected outputs and what outcomes the program outputs may lead to. Using program logic, program providers can establish a hierarchy of possible outcomes, identify which levels of outcomes are feasible as well as which levels of outcomes in the hierarchy can be achieved in the short, medium and long term or can be achieved after the completion of specific program components, together with which levels of outcomes can be achieved from the completion of the whole program etc.

FURTHER READINGS

Australian Department of Finance (1994): Doing evaluations. Canberra, Department of Finance.

Davidson, W., J. Koch, R. Lewis, and M. Wrensinski (1981): Evaluating strategies in criminal justice, New York, Permagon Press.

Dowell, D., C. Klein, and C Krichmar (1985): Evaluation of a halfway house for women. Journal of Criminal Justice, Vol. 13, 216-217.

Posavac, E. J., and R. G. Carey (1997): Program evaluation methods and case studies. Upper Saddle River, New Jersey, Prentice-Hall.

Windsor, R., T. Baranowski, and G. Cutter (1994): Evaluation of health promotion, health education and disease prevention programs. Mountain View, California, McGraw-Hill.

Yeboah, D. A. (2000): The evaluation of New Zealand's habilitation centres pilot program. Journal of criminal justice, Vol 28, No 3: 227=236.

Box 5.1. Types of program evaluation

1.	Process or Implementation evaluation.
2.	Formative evaluation.
3.	Outcome evaluation.
4.	Summative evaluation.
5.	Impact evaluation.
6.	Effectiveness evaluation.

Box 5.2. Selected models of program evaluation

1.	Traditional or fundamental model.
2.	Objectives and/or purposes based model.
3.	Funding based model.
4.	Accountability and performance model.
5.	Improvements based model.
6.	Open concept model.

Box 5.3. Practical steps in Program evaluation

1. What the evaluation was about – subject matter or topic.
2. Identification of the goals and objectives of the evaluation.
3. Review of the existing literature.
4. Selecting the evaluation design and related methodologies .
5. Identifying the main sources of data.
6. Identifying and consulting stakeholders, key organizations and individuals.
7. Carrying out the evaluation including data processing.
8. The main findings.
9. Minor findings.
10. Any conclusions drawn, especially as they relate to the evaluation goals and objectives.
11. Recommendations.
12. Any other items of relevance and interest to the evaluation.

Box 5.4. Some units of cost analysis

1. Cost per specific output/outcome
2. Overall cost per program participant
3. Cost per day or per week
4. Staff cost per program participant
5. Administrative cost per resident or participant
6. Administration expenditure as a proportion (%) of total program expenditure
7. Non administration costs as a proportion of total program expenditure
8. Ratio of administration costs to non administration costs.

Box 5.5. Questions for self reflection

1. What is program evaluation?
2. Why evaluate programs?
3. Why is consultation so important in program evaluation?
4. Why is cost analysis important in program evaluation?
5. Distinguish between efficiency and cost effectiveness
6. Identify the stages involved in evaluating a victims' support program in your locality
7. Distinguish between evaluation methodologies and evaluation models

Chapter 6

OTHER RESEARCH METHODOLOGIES

So far, three broad and big groups of methodologies for criminological research have been discussed in this book, namely qualitative research methodologies, quantitative research methodologies and program evaluation methodologies. Within each group a number of variations are discernible and have been presented. The criminological researcher can use any of these methodologies to investigate various issues in the criminal justice system including crime levels, fear of crime, victimization and corrections or rehabilitation programs.

There are a number of other methodologies which are used regularly by criminal justice system researchers, albeit not as widely as the so called big three. These other research methodologies are briefly presented in this chapter. Each methodology is introduced and discussed, followed by the identification of the strengths or advantages and the weaknesses or disadvantages of the methodology.

The other criminological research methodologies include:

1. Documentary research.
2. Case studies.
3. Experiments.
4. Analysis of existing data.
5. Comparative research.

DOCUMENTARY RESEARCH

Documentary research in the criminal justice system is the use of data in the criminal justice system documents to investigate various issues in that system. In contrast to survey and participant observation methodologies, documentary research methodology is, by and large, a source of secondary data as the data in the documents have been collected and recorded previously. Documentary research methodology usually involves data held in the documents of diverse agencies, in particular government agencies (official statistics), data held by non government organizations (NGOs), documents of corrections and rehabilitation program providers (community based statistics). Data for documentary research exist in documents, and can be in different forms including written or pictorial forms. By far the largest form of data for documentary criminological research is written information or text..

Other forms include histogram and related diagrammatical representation of data as well as photographs.

For example, the Courts, Police, Ministries and/or Departments of Justice, Corrections and Prisons all have a number of documents which contain much needed information for documentary research on various criminal justice topics, So also do community based program and service providers in the criminal justice system, agencies which keep relevant information on the servies and programs thay deliver as well as the beneficiaries of those programs. While much of the information held in the documents of these agencies is in written form, information is also held in photographs and other pictorial or diagrammatical representations. Documents in the Department of Courts have valuable data on sentences and sentencing patterns and trends, together with court room policies and practices, proceedings and, to some extent, the court room experiences of victims of crime, especially victims of sexual and physical assault who are often summoned to appear in court at the request of the defense.

Police documents contain data on both the offenders and the victims they offend. Unit record and aggregate data are usually available in the police records of most jurisdictions. They include demographic and personal data, such as age, gender, marital status and employments status, for example. The data in police documents may also include incidence and prevalence of crime, criminal history of offenders, leading crimes, patterns and trends in criminal activity, number and types of offences reported, number and types of offences which proceeded to prosecution, prosecution outcomes etc.

Prisons and Department of Prisons hold diverse data in their documents or records including number of prisoners and their demographic and personal data, their criminal history including the types of crime they perpetrate. These agencies also hold data on prison programs such as employment, education, training and other rehabilitation programs. Non government agencies of various kinds collect data on their clients and these are held in documents which may be accessed. Again the data include personal and demographic information, criminal history etc.

While the main sources of data for documentary research are those listed above, a number of research and international institutions hold useful data in their documents. Photographs and written comments on crime and the criminal justice system appearing in local dailies, magazines and related outlets tell a lot of stories about crime and criminal activity and, thus, constitute another source of data for documentary research.

Issues in Documentary Research

A number of issues are associated with using documentary research methodology. They include public versus private documents, access, document contents and classification, solicited versus unsolicited documents. Public documents are documents held by governments and their agencies. Public documents are often held by government agencies on behalf of its population. Some public documents are regularly published including prison census and crime statistics. Many documents are covered by Official Secret Laws and the public is refrained from seeing them. Others are stored for the exclusive use of the agencies and are not available to researchers except under special conditions and/or circumstances. In addition, permission is required for some government documents. In Australia, for example, official data held under the Official Secrets Laws/Acts are usually made public after a few decades in what is called declassification in some jurisdictions..

Private documents are diverse and include private documents held by individuals, groups of individuals or even community groups. An interesting example of private documents is the dairy of individual prisoners. In some jurisdictions with strong human right laws, prison officials are not allowed to see prisoners' dairies. Residents of community based corrections facility may also have dairies in which they record private information. Depending on the rules and regulations of the facility and the prevailing privacy laws in the jurisdiction, program managers may or may not see the residents' dairies.

Closely associated with the issue of public and private documents is the whole issue of accessibility. The mere existence of documents does not mean that they are readily available and accessible. Even where the documents are not restricted, access can sometimes be very difficult, time consuming and involve a number of procedures. In designing documentary research on any criminological subject matter, the researcher must not only conceptualize the issues and identify key sources of documents, but the researcher must also establish which documents can be accessed and used in the study.

That brings to mind the important issue of the content of the documents. The documents of interest to the researcher are those that contain the data that allow the researcher to analyze and answer the research questions. While the title of the documents provides a clue about its contents, the researcher may sometimes examine many documents before finding and selecting those documents which are of specific relevance and significance to the investigation. Public documents are also grouped in various classifications on the basis of content, importance, security interests, geographical or spatial categories etc. The onus is on the researcher to carefully identify the necessary documents and arrange to access them irrespective of the location of the document.

In examining information in documents, a further distinction is made between solicited and unsolicited documents. The difference between the two types of document is that solicited documents involve specifically asking for data to be recorded while unsolicited documents is the recording which occurs naturally without any request to do so. To illustrate, it was mentioned above that residents of community based corrections facility may record information in their dairies. A researcher or program evaluator investigating the program may specifically ask the residents to record certain events associated with the program in their dairy for a specified period of time, with the intention to use them later in the investigation. This is a solicited document. In contrast, the residents may on their own be recording daily events in their dairies without any request from the researcher.. These documents can be used in research depending on the rapport between the researcher/evaluator and the residents. This type of document is referred to as unsolicited. The decision to record is initiated by the residents themselves, not at the instance of the researcher or evaluator.

Documentary research methodology is rarely used as the only means of data collection. It is often used in combination with other methods. For example, an evaluator of a community based rehabilitation program may use documentary research with focus group, participant observation or survey methodologies. The researcher examines and obtains data from the program documents as well as from residents using any of the other methodologies.

Practice of Documentary Research

The practice of documentary research involves a number of stages. Some of the stages are identical to the other criminological research methodologies discussed previously, but a few are unique to documentary research.. Documentary research follows some of the stages outlined in the General Research Process (chapter two). The stages in documentary researtch include:

1. Identifying and establishing the subject matter or topic.
2. Reviewing the literature.
3. Other preliminary work.
4. Identifying the potential and actual sources of documentary data relevant to the study.
5. Implementing the research.
6. Data process, analysis and presentation.
7. Producing the report and disseminating the findings.

Identification of the Subject Matter

Consistent with the other research methodologies, the first step in documentary research is the identification and establishment of the research topic. The subject matter of the research has to be clearly defined so that subsequent steps can be taken logically and appropriately. The subject matter can range from criminal justice laws, policies and practices, crime levels and types, police policies and practices, specific crimes, special operations to combat crime etc. A precise definition of the subject matter is essential to facilitate the identification of potential sources of relevant documents for the research. The subject matter must be such that the required data are available in existing documents which can be accessed. If the subject matter is such that the needed data cannot be obtained from the existing accessible documents, another research methodology may be more suitable and should be considered.

Reviewing The Literature

The logical sequential stage after establishing the subject matter of the documentary research is to review the literature. This occurs basically along the same lines as presented in the General Research Process (chapter two). By reviewing the literature, the criminological researcher is able to discern what has been done on the topic, area and depth of coverage, the exact findings and so on. More importantly, the researcher is able to identify areas, within the broad topic, which are conspicuously missing in the previous research and plan and establish the priorities of the new study accordingly. Even where the researcher is replicating a previous study, a review of the literature on that previous work will provide ammunition for strong and informed decisions on hypothesis and data collection and analysis instruments and which parts of the results/findings should be emphasized. In the event that the researcher comes across a previous study using documentary research methodology, the literature will have added significance and provide the researcher with information on document sources, potential problems etc.

When reviewing the literature on previous studies involving documentary research, the object should be to find answers to a number of questions including the following:

1. What did the study investigate?
2. What documents were accessed?
3. Where were the documents found or located?
4. What problems were encountered in obtaining or accessing the documents?
5. How were the problems resolved?
6. What did the study find? What were the results of the investigation?
7. What conclusions were drawn from the results or findings?
8. Did the study identify areas for further research or investigation?
9. Are the identified areas for further study relevant to the current investigation?

As explained in chapter two, not every study will provide the necessary information to address the above questions. A few will provide information on areas for further research, some will mention problems encountered and how they were overcome, but most will present information on the problem, methodologies, results and conclusions. Answers to some or all of the above questions should assist in refining the subject matter for the documentary research and in defining the dimensions of the study. They may also help avoid potential problems in executing the study and improve upon the overall performance of the documentary research.

Other Preliminary Work

This is the stage where the documentary researcher plans and makes important decisions about the research. The researcher must decide the approach to the investigation. Decisions will have to be made on whether the research will be undertaken solely by the researcher or if it will involve other personnel. If other personnel are to be used to access the required documents in different locations, the personnel must be selected and trained for the purpose. The researcher must start talking to and contacting potential holders or custodians of documents. This is essential for the researcher to become familiar with what is available before the next stage. More importantly, it would inform the researcher about the requirements for access to various documents as prescribed by the custodians of the documents. It will also assist in decision making in the next stage of the research process.

Decisions on data processing including data entry, storage and management will have to be made in advance and planned for accordingly. The researcher must also decide how the data will be extracted from the documents and recorded for analysis, and plan accordingly. Reporting requirements must be recognized and planned for as well. Any other necessary consultations are made during this stage and momentum builds up for the other aspects of the documentary research to proceed. All materials required for the research, other than the documents, must be identified and planned for accordingly.

Identification of Sources of Documents

This is a crucial stage in the documentary research process. Documentary research operates simply on the access and use of data contained in documents. It is, therefore, crucial for the researcher to be able to identify and confirm potential and actual sources of relevant documents. Anything short of that could delay the research and also have other adverse impacts including a lack of adequate and appropriate data. This stage involves a number of steps:

1. The researcher must undertake research to indentify al sources of potentially relevant documents.
2. The researcher must make contact with the custodians of the documents and request possible access to the documents.
3. The researcher must define what type of access is required – full or partial.
4. The researcher must go through the various documents, thus obtained, and choose those documents that are of particular relevance, interests and appropriateness relative to the investigation.
5. Finally, the selected documents must be stored carefully.

As stated earlier in this chapter, documentary research methodology is often used in conjunction with other methodologies in some form of triangulation. An integral feature of this stage is that the researcher must decide which other methodologies will be employed. The additional methodologies will be determined by the goals and purpose of the investigation as well as what data are likely to be obtained from the potential documents. The point is that the data from the documents will reveal what data are needed for the study but which are not available in the documents. The researcher must then decide which of the other methodologies is best suited to providing the missing data to supplement and support the data from the documents.

Implementation of the Documentary Research

Closely following the selection of relevant documents is the implementation of the research. This is the stage of data collection, i.e. the stage of extracting data from the relevant documents. The main step at this point in the research process is for the researcher to delve into the documents obtained and stored, and identify and record needed data. Bearing in mind the purpose and goals of the documentary research, every document is read many times and relevant details noted and recorded.

If parts of the document are not clear, the research seeks explanation from the organization from which the documents were obtained. To allow for proper and effective analysis, the research must seek definitions for unfamiliar terminologies appearing in the documents. Even with familiar terminologies, it may sometimes appear appropriate to ask for definitions, as different agencies use their own definitions which may or may not be standard.

Steps will have to be taken to implement the documentary research methodology with any other methodology or methodologies selected for data collection. If the additional methodology is survey research, the steps identified in survey research implementation in chapter four must be followed. If focus group or participant observation methodology is used with the documentary research methodology, then the steps and procedures in chapter three must be followed to ensure successful completion of the study.

Data Processing, Analysis and Interpretation

The logical step following the collection of data from documents and other sources is to process, analyze and interpret the data. Data processing decisions made during the preliminary work or preparatory stage must be implemented at this time. Data must be entered into files, stored and managed depending on the type of data obtained (quantitative and/or qualitative). Measures identified for data analysis during the preliminary stage must be computed as part of the data analysis and interpreted. As usual the analysis must provide answers to the research questions and do justice to the subject matter. A lot of data could be obtained from numerous documents from diverse sources. The onus is on the researcher to identify, select, analyze and interpret data that have relevance to the goals and objectives of the study.

It should be noted that the analysis of documentary research data can be qualitative or quantitative, and the data analysis measures and procedures discussed in chapters three and four may apply as appropriate. For example, if data is obtained from documents on crime statistics, quantitative analysis may be in order, depending on the goals and objectives of the study.

Analysis of data on the criminal justice policies in a particular jurisdiction may attract qualitative analysis. In addition, depending on what methodology is used to obtain additional data to supplement the data obtained from documentary research, qualitative or quantitative analysis may be undertaken.

Documentary Research Report

Following data analysis and interpretation, the documentary researcher must put the evidence or findings together in a report which constitutes the end product of the documentary research.The report is prepared along the lines discussed in the section on General Research Process with modifications specific to documentary research, especially the goals and objectives of the investigation, methodology and sources of data. It is also usual practice to prepare an overall report containing and describing the following:

1. The subject matter or topic of the documentary research.
2. The goals and objectives of the research.
3. Review of the existing literature.
4. Main sources of documents.
5. Methodologies (if any) that were used alongside documentary research methodology and reasons for using them.
6. Problems encountered and how they were solved.
7. The main findings.
8. Minor findings.

9. Any conclusions drawn, especially as they relate to the goals and objectives of the documentary research.
10. Recommendations.
11. Areas for further research (if any).
12. Any other items of relevance and interest to the investigation.

STRENGTHS AND WEAKNESSES OF DOCUMENTARY RESEARCH

Documentary research can provide a great variety of data from diverse sources depending on the number and types of documents accessed. The data obtained can be large and in in-depth reflecting the wide variety of documents which were accessed. It is a very useful methodology for the investigation of past events and, in that respect, documentary research is similar to historical analysis. Documentary research is a very powerful methodology if combined with one or more other methodologies. In addition, the research methodology has a degree of flexibility to make selective decisions on which items to include and which items to discard from the documents.

The main weakness of documentary research methodology is that the event has already occurred, there are no study subjects for the research as such (unless a supplementary methodology is added) and the researcher cannot contact the persons involved. Another weakness is that the documents obtained may only provide partial information on the subject matter and the full picture is lost. Besides, conclusions drawn from partial information could be misleading, hence the need to combine documentary research with another methodology. The possibility of bias in the documents selected looms, as the documents are obtained on availability and access basis. Also, a very good source of data for documentary may be missed if the document is classified as restricted or access prohibited.

Despite these disadvantages, documentary research is useful for the analysis of historical events, and even more persuasive if combined with other methodologies (e.g. prison outbreak in the past or a previous government criminal justice police or practice).

Box 6.1. Steps in identifying sources of documents

1. Research to indentify sources of potential relevant documents
2. Contact with the custodians of the documents
3. Request for possible access to the documents
4. Definition of the type of access required – full or partial
5. Examination of the various documents, thus obtained
6. Choosing documents of relevance, interests and appropriateness to the investigation
7. Finally, the selected documents must be stored carefully, if obtained.

Box 6.2. Key points in data analysis in documentary research

1.	Decision on and selection of variables and associated data to include in the study.
2.	Variables and the associated data must be compatible with the study goals and objectives.
3.	Documentary research data may be analyzed qualitatively or quantitatively.
4.	If a supplementary methodology is added, the measures and analysis usually associated with that methodology must be applied.

CASE STUDIES

A case study research is the research which is undertaken to unravel facts and evidence on a specifically defined event, activity or program Similar to documentary research, case studies can involve a past event such as the 2005 prison riots of Barbados or the 1996 Port Arthur mass killings in Tasmania, Australia. With regards to corrections programs, a case study can involve a present or past program. For example, a case study may focus on the previous participants of the program or on the program's current participants. Either way, a specific criminal justice issue, practice, phenomenon .or activity is being investigated and, in this case, the corrections program.

The Role of the Researcher

Consistent with the other research methodologies, the role of the case studies researcher is paramount to the success or otherwise of the research. It is the responsibility of the researcher to determine the subject matter, methodologies to be used in the study, how data will be obtained, analyzed and interpreted. In short the researcher has the overall responsibility for the study. The research must plan the study, identify and contact key people or authorities associated with the case, event or program under investigation. The researcher is responsible for producing the final report, disseminating the findings, addressing any criticisms and defending the findings.

The researcher has to make further decisions on whether the study will be undertaken with other personnel including data collectors (depending on the methodologies to be used in the case study). Some methodologies yield a large amount of data which must subsequently be entered into data sets. In that situation, data entry personnel would have to be recruited and trained. It is the researcher's responsibility to make sure the recruitment and training occur.

STEP BY STEP GUIDE IN UNDERTAKING CASE STUDIES

Consistent with the other research methodologies previously discussed in this book, case studies research involves a number of stages including:

1. Selection of the case to be investigated and the definition of the specific subject matter
2. Planning or preparatory work
3. Literature review
4. Decision on research design or designs, i.e. what methodologies will be used to study the specific event
5. Implementation of the selected design
6. Data processing analysis and interpretation
7. Preparation of the report and the dissemination of the findings

Case Selection and Definition of Subject Matter

The first step in case studies is to establish which event, program or activity (called rhe case) is to be investigated. The point must be made that the specific case may have a number of dimensions and issues. Closely associated with the selection of the case for the study is the identification and definition of the subject matter, i.e. the aspects of the specific event or program that the researcher would focus on in the study. The point must be made urther that case studies can coer topics ranging from criminal justice policies through victim support and rehabilitation programs to special events in prison. Different illustrations are presented later in this chapter.

Planning or Preparatory Stage

This stage is crucial for the case study, and could pose difficulties depending on the researcher's knowledge, skills and motivation. A number of steps are envisaged at this stage of the case study. During this stage the researcher takes the necessary steps to identify the key people or authorities associated with the case or event. If the case study involves a criminal justice policy, the investigating researcher would contact the policy areas of the criminal justice sector agencies. In the event that the case study is on a specific victim support or rehabilitation program, the researcher would have to contact the program area, get familiar with the program, program activities or components and program personnel, especially the program providers and managers. The investigating researcher must provide adequate information on the research to the key people.

It is also very important for the researcher to hint at potential data needs, especially program records during these initial consultations. These initial consultations are critical to the case study eventuating. If, for any reason, the program providers refuse to participate or allow their program to be investigated or if the program providers refuse to make available pertinent documents, the case study is doomed and may have to be aborted.

It is also during this stage that the researcher makes decisions and plans on how to proceed with the case study in particular if other personnel would be involved, and takes the necessary steps to recruit and train as appropriate. Data processing and storage decisions are also made here including decisions on the potential use of data entry personnel, how many will be needed and how they will be recruited and trained. The researcher has to think carefully of the report and how the case study findings would be disseminated, as well as strategically identify potential problems and their possible sources. The preparatory and planning stage will not be complete without the literature review and the decisions on case study design. These two planning tasks are presented separately in the next two sections.

Reviewing the Literature

The 1 review the literature occurs basically along the same lines as presented in the General Research Process (chapter two), and documentary research. The chance of having a previous investigation of the same case study is not great and almost zero, but the researcher can and may review the literature on similar case studies and similar programs which were studied previously using other methodologies. By reviewing the literature, the criminological researcher is able to discern what has been done on the case study, topic, area and depth of coverage, the exact findings and so on. More importantly, the researcher is able to identify areas, within the broad topic, which have received limited attention in the literature and plan and establish the priorities of the new study accordingly.

When reviewing the literature on previous studies involving a case study, the object should be to find answers to a number of questions including the following:

1. What did the case study investigate?
2. What methodologies were employed?
3. What problems were encountered?
4. How were the problems resolved?
5. What did the case study find? What were the results of the investigation?
6. What conclusions were drawn from the results or findings?
7. Did the case study identify areas for further research or investigation?
8. Are the identified areas for further study relevant to the current investigation?

Answers to some or all of the above questions should assist in refining the subject matter for the case study and in defining the dimensions of the study. They may also help avoid potential problems in executing the study and improve upon the overall performance of the case study.

Decision on Research Design or Designs

The final step in the planning or preparatory stage is the identification and confirmation of an appropriate research design for the case study. This decision depends on many factors but more so the goals and objectives of the case study, the nature and type of program or policy being studied as a specific case, as well as relevant evidence from the existing literature. If the case study is the evaluation of a specific criminal justice or corrections program, the step by step guide to program evaluation outlined in the preceding chapter must be followed, and amended to suit where necessary. Similarly, if the researcher decides to interview key respondents, then focus group methodology (chapter three) or survey research methodologies (chapter four) must be employed. Research instruments must be developed in the event that the researcher decides to adopt interviewing as one of the main methodologies for the case study.

Implementation of the Research Design

After mulling various design decisions and settling on an appropriate design, it is logical for the researcher to proceed to implement the selected design as the next step. Data collection begins in earnest, the researcher either collects the data or employs trained personnel to assist with data collection (depending on the design decisions made in the identification of design stage). If participant observation methodology is the adopted design, the researcher makes arrangements to observe the behavior, event or activity. It is during this stage that the researcher takes the necessary steps to address all field problems associated with the case study.

Data Processing, Analysis and Interpretation

Once data collection is complete, data processing begins and the data processing, storage and management decisions made in the planning stages are implemented at this time. If decisions were made to employ data entry personnel, the recruitment and training of those personnel occur here and data are entered into data sets or files. Measures and data analysis techniques identified in the planning stages are now used to make a sense of all the accumulated data. The types of analysis depend on the types of methodologies used in the case study design. If survey research methodologies were used to obtain data, then the approaches to data processing, storage, management and analysis discussed in chapter four would have to be followed. Along the same lines, the data processing techniques for participant observation and program evaluation methodologies would be appropriate if those methods are used. All data analysis, measures, estimates and indexes, thus obtained, must be interpreted and plausible conclusions drawn from the interpretation.

Case Study Report and the Dissemination of the Findings

Following data analysis and interpretation, the next step is to prepare a case study report, which constitutes the end product of the case study..The case study report must definitely address the goals and objectives of the case study. It is also usual practice for the report to include analysis and information on the following:

1. The subject matter or topic of the case study.
2. The goals and objectives of the research.
3. Interesting findings from the review of the existing literature, in particular if the case study findings support or contradict the previous findings.
4. Main sources of data for the case study.
5. Methodologies employed and the reasons for using them.
6. Problems encountered and how they were solved.

7. The main findings.
8. Minor findings.
9. Any conclusions drawn, especially as they relate to the goals and objectives of the case study.
10. Areas for further research (if any).
11. Any other items of relevance and interest to the case study.
12. Specific interests of stakeholders

The completed report must be distributed to key stakeholders. Every effort should also be made to disseminate the case study findings in other ways including journal articles, local newspapers, conference presentations depending on the prevailing contractual obligations and agreements. Sometimes, funding agencies and contracts define how the findings are to be disseminated, and place restrictions on the researcher.

Advantages and Disadvantages

The main advantage of case studies is the potential to collect in-depth data on the specific policy, activity or program and provide further insights on the subject matter. Depending on the case study design, there is the flexibility to collect information on items of relevance which were not initially envisaged.

The disadvantages are that the scope is restricted to a specific case and external generalization is limited at best. Depending on the methodologies employed (qualitative or, quantitative), other advantages and disadvantages may apply.

Examples/Illustrations of Case Studies

Three examples from Australia, Barbados and New Zealand are used to illustrate what is involved in a case study. All the three illustrations are actual events which occurred in the past, but they are not previous studies. What is seen in this section is the examination of each case, describing the background to the example, methodologies that could be used, data analysis and interpretation and finally the report. All the stages described earlier in this section on case studies including the step by step guide are applicable and will not be described individually.

Case study 1. The Port Arthur Massacre, Tasmania, Australia

Background
In April 1996, Australians woke up to the shocking news of a massive massacre by one of their own in the popular tourist destination of Port Arthur. In all some 35 people died including children. The culprit indiscriminately shot many people who were visiting the tourist attraction at the time, and there was panic everywhere. As he escaped, the culprit forced people out of their cars and shot them as well. The culprit was later arrested in a nearby Guest House, a short distance from the scene of the crime.

Research Questions

A number of research questions may be developed depending on the goals and objectives of the case study. They may include:

1. What exactly happened at Port Arthur on that day?
2. Did the gunman give reasons or any indication for perpetrating the offence? Motive?
3. How many people were shot?
4. What was the death toll?
5. Any other consequences of the shooting?
6. What lessons resulted from the massacre?
7. What subsequent measures can be taken to avoid or prevent a recurrence of such a massacre?

Methodologies

In examining the Port Arthur massacre as a specific case study, various methodologies can be used. The most plausible methodology or methodologies would have to provide answers to the research questions. As many people were involved, the most appropriate methodology will be an interview of the victims, their families and other people who were present at the scene but escaped without any injury. A survey research methodology would appear very suitable and should be employed. This is particularly so because of the large number of people involved and the need to probe further to obtain detail information.

This criminal event occurred in a tourist destination and many of the people who witnessed the occurrence of the massacre may not be easily contacted, in particular overseas visitors will prove extremely difficult to reach, if at all. The survey would have to concentrate on the Australians at the scene during the massacre.

Data Processing, Analysis and Interpretation

The data obtained from the respondents must be processed, stored and managed with confidentiality and respondents/ privacy in mind. Various measures must be developed to analyze the data. In a case study such as the Port Arthur massacre where there are a lot of narratives and other qualitative and quantitative data, it is imperative to employ both qualitative and quantitative data analyses. Qualitative analysis will include personal accounts provided by the victims, their families and other witnesses of the massacre. Descriptive statistical analysis may also be employedl including frequency distributions (number of respondents by age and gender, number of actual victims by age and gender and by type of injury, total deaths). Measures of central tendency (mean age of injured victims, average age of the dead), and measures of dispersion (age range of injured victims, age range for dead victims) may be computed and analyzed. In more sophisticated procedures,   regression analysis may be employed. The data analyzed must be interpreted to address the research questions and to draw appropriate conclusions.

Case Study Report

The end product of the case study is the final report. The report describes the goals and purpose of the case study, relevant background information, key stake holders, methodologies employed as well as data analysis and measures relevant to the Port Arthur massacre. The report must address the research questions and, in the case of the Port Arthur massacre, provide recommendations to avoid a repeat of this heinous massacre.

Case Study 2. The 2005 Prison Riots of Barbados

Background

Barbados has only one prison facility known as Glendairy Prison. March 28, 2005 witnessed one of the most astonishing events in the history of the prison service in the country. On that day, riot started among a small number of inmates in one wing of the prison and spread rapidly to other wings of the prison. The most important aspect of the riots is the burning down of the dining hall and other essential parts of the prison, making the entire prison uninhabitable. The Barbados government acted very quickly to restore order and eradicate the security risk arising from the riots. The situation was brought under control after a few days and all the inmates were accounted for and transported to secret locations around the island A number of inmates and prison officials were injured and there were a few deaths. A new prison has since been built to replace the old dilapidated Glendairy Prison. The new prison is also called Glendairy Prison but is built in another location away from the old prison site.

Research Questions

In examining the 2005 Barbados prison riots as a case study, a number of research questions may be developed depending on the goals and objectives of the research. They may include

1. What exactly happened at Glendairy Prison?
2. What was the casualty level? i.e. injury and deaths?
3. What was the extent of damage to property?
4. What caused the riots?
5. Any other consequences of the riots?
6. What security arrangements were made to contain the situation?
7. What lessons were learned from the riots?
8. What subsequent measures can be taken to avoid or prevent a recurrence of such a prison riot?

Methodology

The selected methodologies must be appropriate to provide data and analysis to address the research questions. Given the nature of the event, the most appropriate methodology will be survey research involving the interview of inmates, prison officials and personnel of the justice sector Ministries and Departments. Some documentary research may be used to supplement the survey research, in particular the examination of government policy documents, prison documents on prison security, guidelines to contain riots etc. Prisoners constitute an engaged group and obtaining a sampling frame should not be difficult. A sample of inmates can be drawn randomly and interviewed for the case study.

Data Processing, Analysis and Interpretation

The data processing and analysis procedures are similar to those in the Port Arthur Case study, as interviewing are involved in both case studies. Confidentiality assurance and the maintenance of the privacy of respondents are critical as any leakages may result in attacks on the responding inmates. Various measures must be developed to analyze the data. In a case study such as the Glendairy Prison riots where there are a lot of narratives and other qualitative and quantitative data, it is imperative to employ both qualitative and quantitative data analysis, as discussed in the Port Arthur case study.

Case Study Report

After data analysis and interpretation, the next logically sequential step is to produce the case study final report. The report describes the goals and purpose of the case study, relevant background information, key stake holders, methodologies employed as well as data analysis and measures. The report must address the research questions and, in the case of the Barbados Prison riots, provide recommendations to avoid a repeat of the riots in the new prison.

Case Study 3. New Zealand's Habilitation Centres Pilot Program

Background

In the early 1990s, New Zealand experienced a large increase in crime and, in particular, recidivism was rising tremendously. The Government of New Zealand decided to tackle recidivism as a means of reducing the overall incidence and prevalence of crime. There was also increasing pressure on prison beds and related prison needs and facilities. After a series of discussions, research and policy analysis, two offender management proposals were put forward for trial, namely Home Detention Program and the Habilitation Centres Pilot Program. Both were to be piloted and evaluated before final decisions were made to include them as permanent sentences or features in the criminal justice system of New Zealand. This case study focuses on the Habilitation Centres Pilot Program.

Research Questions

Various research questions may be developed depending on the goals and objectives of the case study including:

1. What was the Habilitation Centres Pilot Program about?
2. What were the program components?
3. How many convicted offenders participated in the program during the pilot year?
4. What was the effect of the pilot program on the offenders?
5. Any other effects or impact of the program?
6. Was the pilot program successful in achieving its goals and objectives?
7. Should the program be adopted as a salient component of the criminal justice system and why?
8. If not, should the Habilitation Centres Pilot Program be abolished?
9. What subsequent measures can be taken to improve the performance of the program if it was retained?

Methodologies

In a case study, such as the Habilitation Centres Pilot program, opportunities exist to use various methodologies, Participant observation, focus groups and survey research methodologies may be used individually and/or in combination with one another. The researcher may decide to use survey research methodologies as the medium of data collection, interviewing policy makers, program and service providers as well as clients or residents of the Habilitation Centres. On the other hand, the researcher may decide to observe the participants at the Habilitation Centres and, therefore, employ participant observation methodology. Yet still, the research may decide to focus on a selected group of clients, in which case focus group methodology becomes paramount.

However, given the diverse program components or activities of the Habilitation Centres, a triangulation approach may be the most appropriate way forward. Program components such as group discussions are best examined using participant observation while clients' views on the program and its impact on them are usually assessed through the direct interview of the said clients , and focus group or survey research methodologies may be appropriate. A combination of participant observation and survey research methodologies may be in order.

Data Processing, Analysis and Interpretation

The data, thus obtained, from clients, program and service providers, policy areas (Ministry of Justice, Department of Corrections, Department of Courts, the Police etc in New Zealand) must be processed including storage and proper management to ensure that responses are not identified with respondents. The data must also be analyzed to address the goals and objectives of the case study as well as any predetermined research questions. Depending on the research goals and objectives and the methodologies adopted, a mix of quantitative and qualitative analysis would be required, as previously described.

Case Study Report

As indicated in the preceding case study, the end product of this case study is the final report. The report describes the goals and purpose of the case study, relevant background information, key stake holders, methodologies employed as well as data analysis, measures and interpretation. The report must address the research questions and, in the case of the New Zealand Habilitation Centres Pilot Program, assess the effectiveness of the program and make recommendations on whether the program should be retained or abolished.

Box 6.3. Some key points about Case study

1.	Case study methodology is useful for in-depth studies of specific events, issues or programs.
2.	The methodology may be survey research, participant observation, focus group or program evaluation.
3.	The role of the researcher is similar to the other methodologies.
4.	Steps or stages in case study research are consistent with the other methodologies.
5.	The difference between case study and the other research methodologies is that case study focuses on a particular event, activity or program called the case.

EXPERIMENTAL RESEARCH METHODOLOGIES

Another methodology used in criminological research is the experiment. In the natural sciences (physical and chemical sciences), experiments involve chemicals, molecules etc. However, in criminology, experiments involve interventions and human beings. In the natural sciences the product of experiments can be envisaged and is usually precise and predictable. In criminology the product of an experiment is not that precise because it involves human beings and human behavior is, by and large, unpredictable.For example, if two molecules of hydrogen are combined with one molecule of oxygen, water is produced regardless of location.

However, if a drug rehabilitation program is administered to two groups of offenders, the end result or outcome could be different, even where the two groups are from the same locality and have the same characteristics.

An experiment may be defined as the processes of testing the relationships between variables. In criminological research, experiment may be seen as the process of establishing the impact of an intervention, program or policy on a criminal justice group, such as offenders. Criminological experiments aim at identifying changes in behavior, attitudes and thinking arising from the impact of an intervention, program or policy.

Logic of Experimental Methodologies in Criminology

As alluded to above, the logic of experimental methodologies in criminology is that there is a relationship between one variable (e.g. an intervention) and another variable (the behavior of the recipients of the intervention). Experimental methodologies attempt to establish these relationships.

It may be argued further that this logic was similar to the underlying logic in survey research methodologies in the sense that both methodologies seek to identify the relationships between variables as well as thenature and extent of the relationships and how they are mearured and analyzed. The difference is that the main objective of criminological experimental methodologies is to change behavior of the subjects, whereas survey research methodologies do not aim at changing the behavior of the subjects. It should be noted that while the main object of criminological experimental designs is to introduce a variable and assess its effect on another variable, the study subjects., there have been instances where the intervention has had very little or no significant effect on the subjects.

The Practice of Experimental Research Methodologies

In experiment research, the process involves the establishment of two groups, namely the study group and what is called the control group. In most cases, a large group of subjects are initially selected and the members are randomly assigned to either the study group (also called the experimental group) or the control group.

The intervention is administered to the experimental or study group and not to the control group. The effects of the intervention on the study group are measured and compared with the control group which, by definition, did not receive the intervention. Randomness works best in circumstances where the subjects are engaged and/or where the subjects are in controlled or confined environments, such as the prison or another corrections facility or a rehabilitation center. This is because the engaged population serves as the sampling frame from which the random sampling occurs to select the study and ontrol groups.

For example to assess the effects of a new program component in a community based rehabilitation program, the entire clients of the program are selected initially. Half of the clients are randomly assigned into the study group and the remaining half automatically constitutes the control group.

In this way, the clients have an equal chance of being assigned into either the study group or the control group. The new program component or activity is administered to the experimental or study group only, and the effects of the activity on the study group are measured and compared with the control group. A diagrammatical illustration is found in figure . There is a potential for the changes in the behavior of the study group to be indirectly ransferred to the control group, as some members of the control group see the changes and adopt them. However, the point must be made that anyb such transfer is usually limited. The two groups can, therefore, be ompared appropriately at the end of the experiment.

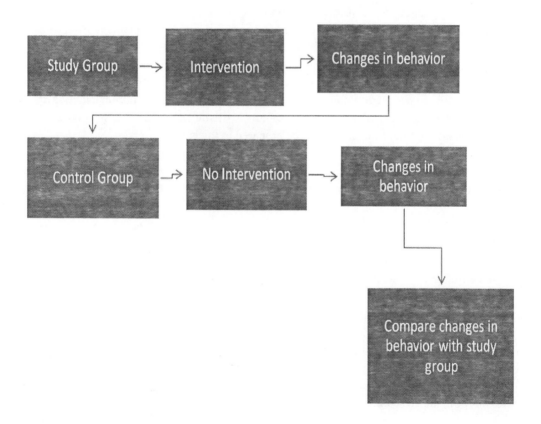

Figure 6. Illustration of experimental research methodologies.

Step By Step Guide to Experimental Research

Consistent with other research methodologies, a number of steps must be followed for successful completion of experimental research. They include:

1. Conceptualization and establishment of the subject matter.
2. Preliminary work.
3. Hypothesis or research questions.
4. Selection of the experimental research design.
5. Determination of Study and Control Groups.
6. Implementation of the design.
7. Data analysis and measurements.
8. Experimental research report.

The first step is to conceptualize the issues and identify the subject matter or topic for the experiment. Once the topic is identified, planning and preparatory work begin. The researcher must decide how the research will be done, who should be consulted and identify potential sources of data. If the experiment is to take place in a prison environment, the experimental researcher must contact prison officials for approval to undertake the experiment, but more so to familiarize themselves with the prison environment, prisoner movements as well as make arrangements for the experiment to be implemented.

It is also at this time that the literature review occurs, design options assessed and data processing, storage, and management decisions are made. The researcher must also decide whether to do the experiment alone or involve other personnel in the implementation of the research. If other people will be involved training will be required to ensure consistency. Training manuals and field manuals must be prepared at this stage.

It is critical during this stage to take steps to identify and establish the study subjects. Both the control and experimental groups must be identified and established before the experiment can take place. The instruments are also developed at this stage and piloted where possible.

Hypothesis and/or Research Questions

The researcher must consider the hypothesis or research questions that the study is expected to address. The hypothesis and research questions are usually dependent on the goals and objectives of the experimental research, and sometimes they are predetermined by major stake holders such as the funding agency. The hypothesis must try to establish some kind of relationship between the intervention (Variable 1) and the behavior of the subjects (Variable 2) The Null Hypothesis which states that no relationship exist between the variables must also be developed.

If research questions are developed, the data collection and analysis must provide for the addressing of the research questions. Consistent with survey research methodologies, experimental research is deductive and the hypothesis and research questions are based on pre-existing theories, ideas and preconceptions.

Selection and Implementation of the Experimental Design

One of the most important tasks undertaking during the preliminary stage is the mulling of design options and the identification and selection of the appropriate design. In criminological experiments, one aspect of the design is already known or fixed, i.e. the intervention. The design to be selected at this stage is the data collection design, involving how the data on the effects of the intervention will be collected. As indicated earlier, the usual practice is to adopt survey research methodologies, but the changes in behavior can directly be obtained using focus groups, while some specific behavioral patterns may sometimes be observed through participant observation methodology. Indeed, a triangulation approach including survey research is the best option.

Once the experimental methodology is confirmed, the experimental researcher proceeds to administer the intervention to the experimental group only. The relationships between the variables are tested through the collection and analysis of data using the pre-designed instruments together with any other methodology in the triangulation.

Data Collection, Processing, Storage, Analysis and Interpretation

The analysis and interpretation of experimental research data are the same as the analysis of data from survey research and the other methodologies. This is because survey research is the main methodology of experimental research. Detailed information on the analysis of survey data is presented in chapter four. As discussed previously for survey research, the dependent and independent variables must be operationalized and measured to allow the relationship to be examined thoroughly.If any specific behavioral changes are observed through participant observation, then the analysis asscociated with that methodology must be undertaken (chapter three)

Experimental Research Report

As demonstrated for other criminological research methodologies, the end product of experimental research is the final report. The report describes the goals and purpose of the experiment, relevant background information, key stake holders, methodologies employed as well as data analysis and measures. The report must address the research questions and report on the testing of the hypothesis, how and why the Null Hypothesis is disproved and why the hypothesis holds etc. The report must also clearly demonstrate the relationship between the dependent and independent variables and show the effect of the intervention or independent variable (Variable 1) on the behavior of the subjects or dependent variable (Variable 2). It must be pointed out that most of the time the analysis incorporates multiple variables in multivariate analysis of one kind or the other. Depending on the goals and objectives of the experimental research, the report would include some recommendations on the intervention.

Advantages and Disadvantages

Experimental research methodologies carry the advantages and disadvantages of survey research as discussed in chapter four. However, it has the added disadvantage that only a small number of subjects is often studied. Thus, experimental research can only produce standard data for a small number of subjects and external generalization is limited. There is also the flexibility for the researcher to control the influence of the variables but several aspects of the experiment remain outside the laboratory or study location.

Box 6.4. Definition of experiments in criminology

1.	In criminological research, experiment may be seen as the process of establishing the impact of an intervention, program or policy on a criminal justice group, such as offenders.
2.	Criminological experiments aim at identifying changes in behavior, attitudes and thinking arising from the impact of an intervention, program or policy.
3.	Criminological experiment is a process of establishing the relationship between the intervention and the behavior of the recipients of the intervention.

Box 6.5. Key points in criminological experiments

1.	Criminological experimental research involves human beings usuallyoffenders.
2.	The logic of criminological experimental methodology is consistent with the logic of survey research methodologies.
3.	Data analysis and measurements may be similar to those used in survey research methodology.
4.	Experimental research involves small number of study subjects.
5.	Experimental research methodologies involve two groups, namely study or experimental group and the control group.
6.	The intervention is administered to the experimental group.
7.	The behavior of the experimental group after the intervention is compared with the behavior of the control group.

ANALYSIS OF EXISTING DATA

Description

Analysis of existing data, as a methodology, involves the analysis of secondary data held by government organizations (official statistics) and non government organizations. Government organizations such as the Police, Departments and/or Ministries of corrections, Prisons, Justice, Courts collect and hold information on crime and criminal activity as well as the perpetrators of crime. Prisons hold data on inmates, courts have data on court proceedings, finding of guilt, sentencing and other outcomes of the prosecution process. Much of the data are quantitative but a lot of qualitative information may also be available, The quantitative data include demographic and related socio-economic background data, as well as criminal history. Non government agencies operating in the criminal justice system collect and keep data on their clients and those providing rehabilitation programs keep records of program components completed by each participant, breaches of rules etc. Program records constitute a useful source of data for program evaluation as noted in chapter five.

Step by Step Guide

The steps involved in the analysis of existing data are straight forward and include:

1. Identification of the problem.
2. Preparatory work.
3. Identification of types and sources of data.
4. Arrangements to obtain relevant data.
5. Data processing, analysis and interpretation.
6. Study report and dissemination of findings.

The first step is to identify the problem or subject matter of the study as described for the other research methodologies Preparatory work, data processing and analysis and the preparation of the study report are consistent with the steps involved in survey research methodologies. and the General Research Process. Identification of types and sources of data and arrangements to secure required data assume increased importance in the analysis of existing data and are discussed briefly as follows:

It is crucial in analysis of existing data for the researcher to identify the types of data needed to address the research questions or hypotheses as well as the potential sources for the identified data. A wide range of secondary data exists and most will not be of any relevance to the specific investigation. On the basis of the goals and objectives of the study, the availability of data and the ease with which the data can be obtained, the researcher determines what data are needed. Once data types have been determined, the logical sequence is to establish the potential sources for the identified data types. These sources may include official statistics and/or data held by non government organizations, regional and international organizations. The key point is the ability of the researcher to determine which sources will provide the best, accurate and reliable data without much difficulty. This can sometimes prove difficult as researchers find to their dismay and disappointment that the sources they identify do not have the information they need, or that the information is available but cannot be released for various reasons. Once the potential sources are identified, the next step is for the researcher to contact the appropriate personnel in the agency to arrange meetings to discuss the data needs and eventually secure the data where possible.

Advantages and Disadvantages

The main advantage is the large volume of potential data and the lower cost of obtaining the data compared to survey research and participant observation methodologies. The main disadvantage is that the data are secondary and may not be in the form required for the specific study. There are also the problems of some data being classified as restricted, as well as differences in definitions etc. Despite the difficulties, analysis of existing data is a commonly used research methodology especially in crime analysis using Police statistics.

COMPARATIVE ANALYSIS

Description and Definition

Comparative research is assuming increasing importance in criminology as different subgroups of the population and different societies are studied at the same time. In criminology, comparative analysis is the research process which is characterized by the examination of crime and criminal activity and other aspects of the criminal justice system in two or more countries or among various subgroups of the population, and involves the comparison of the situation in those countries. For example, a comparative research of crime victims can be undertaken within a specific country making comparisons by age and/or gender, geographical location and other characteristics. In the United States or Australia, such comparative studies may involve male and female crime victims of various ages for the country as a whole, and/or the distribution of crime victims in different States. It may even be refined further to cover victims of specific crime types such as the comparison of male and female victims of aggravated burglary.

Many other research methodologies including historical analysis, participant observation, focus group and documentary research tend to examine one society, a specific subgroup of the population or one society or country at a time. This is quite distinct from comparative analysis which involves at least two societies, subgroups or countries. That said, the point must be made that comparative analysis is often used to undertake studies across countries, and the methodology is most effective if it is used repeatedly across many societies or countries. The larger the number of societies or countries, the more persuasive and powerful comparative analysis becomes. When comparative analysis focuses on different countries, it is referred to as cross national studies. In other words it is exploring and comparing the issues in many different countries or nations.

Issues in Comparative Research

A number of issues can be identified with comparative research or analysis. The world is made of many countries with diverse cultures, languages, levels of morality, laws and criminal justice systems. This presupposes a need to examine and compare the situation in different countries to provide further insights into what is happening to crime and criminal justice around the globe, hence the place of comparative research in criminology. Even where the comparative research is internal to a country or society, comparative analysis throw more light on the subject and improve the knowledge and understanding of the subject matter relative to the different groups.

The advent of globalization has brought the countries of the world together and, with respect to crime and criminal activity, most crime types are found in each country. Besides, there have been many instances where criminal activity has transcended territorial borders of individual countries. Advances in communication, such as the internet, have served as a catalyst to stimulate information sharing across societies and countries and, in the process, facilitating the potential ability to undertake comparative analysis. The requirement for member countries of international organizations to provide information to the organizations has resulted in an increase in the availability and accessibility to crime and criminal justice data. For example, the United Nations Statistics Division holds a large amount of standard data on member countries of the United Nations Organization. In the domain of crime, even more data are held by the United Nations Office for Drugs and Crime. Much of the data are easily accessible from the websites of these organizations encouraging cross-national studies.

Besides, by learning about what is happening in different countries, improvements have been made in understanding crime, in particular the social and cultural factors that impact on the incidence and prevalence of crime, and lessons from one country may be adopted and used in another country. An examination of crime and criminal activity in different societies provides understanding of why crime levels are high in some societies and low in others. Using data from cross-national studies brings out differences not only in crime levels, but equally or more so differences in the factors that influence crime in different societies (laws, criminal justice policies and practices, norms, values, attitudes and perceptions). Despite these potential benefits, comparative analysis as a research methodology is plagued with a number of problems which are presented in the next section – advantages and disadvantages of comparative research.

Advantages and Disadvantages of Comparative Analysis/Research

The advantages of comparative research have been discussed in part in the preceding section. Its main advantage is the ability of the methodology to provide an analysis of a great variety of data on many countries. It is also important in allowing lessons from one country to be passed on to another country and, in the process, enhance the ability of individual countries to manage issues and problems in the criminal justice system It has the added advantage of facilitating repeated testing of the same hypothesis in many countries, or in asking and seeking answers to the same research questions in many countries.

Comparative research is not undertaken very often due to a number of problems associated with the research methodology. By definition, comparative analysis is the type of research which is undertaken across countries or subgroups of the population. Undertaking research in different countries entails a lot of expenditure and, thus, cost is a major disadvantage of comparative analysis. Cost is only part of the problem. There are methodological issues in comparative analysis, including definitions, measurements and sampling problems. The issue of definition stem from the differences in definition of various concepts in criminology across countries. More importantly, different countries tend to have different classifications of crime, so that what is classified as a major crime in one country may not enjoy the same status in another.

For example, in Barbados, reported crimes are classified into 5 broad categories as follows:

1. Major crimes against the person.
2. Minor crimes against the person.
3. Major crimes against property.
4. Minor crimes against property.
5. Other crimes.

The interesting and intriguing part of this classification is that serious offences such as firearm and ammunition crimes are classified as other not as part of major crimes. In many other jurisdictions, crimes involving firearms and ammunition including shooting of individuals will be classified as serious or major crimes. Undertaking a comparative analysis of crime using data from sources where the classification is inconsistent can prove problematic.

Another problem relates to measurements of data collected from different populations in different countries. As indicated time and time again in this book, all data collected using any methodology must be processed, the variables measured and analyzed. The problem arises from measuring data collected in different countries in the same way, regardless of the circumstances surrounding data collection, including levels of education and literacy. This situation is further exacerbated by problems of definitions and classification, as stated earlier Comparative analysis cannot be undertaken effectively if equivalent measures cannot be developed for the data collected in all the countries in the research. While it is possible for the most motivated or challenged researcher to achieve a degree of equivalent measures, the process can be very tedious, time consuming, costly and difficult.

The other source of problems for comparative analysis is sampling. Sampling in different countries or societies can be difficult, especially in areas where sampling frames are not easily available. In some societies, the lack of property addresses, incorrect and/or old addresses which have not been updated can aggravate sampling problems. Sampling size and, what sample size to use, can add to the problem, and cost can mount rapidly.

There is an outstanding problem associated with the ability of comparative researchers to be familiar with and have good understanding of diverse cultures and practices in different societies. No doubt, the level of crime and victimization as well as fear of crime, for example, depends on the norms, values, perceptions, attitudes and socio-economic characteristics in the study countries. These vary from country to country and a lack of knowledge, understanding and familiarization on the part of the researcher would impact adversely on the research.

Finally the issue of language and its associated problems must be recognized. Similar to cultural practices and beliefs, different countries have different languages which may be different from the researcher's own language. The usual practice is a series of translations of the instruments and the responses. Some of these translations may not be exact and the problem associated with that situation cannot be ignored. The issue of appropriateness emerges.

The problem in simple terms relates to what can be investigated or cannot be investigated in various countries. The basic tenet is that what is appropriate in one country many not necessary be appropriate in another country. For example, incidents of sexual assaults can be investigated or studied in western countries, but it will appear extremely problematic in Arab countries. Again in western countries it is appropriate for women to be interviewed by strangers, but this is inappropriate and culturally prohibitive in Arab societies and other Islamic societies.

Despite these weaknesses, comparative research is very useful, and and can be used to increase the existing knowledge and understanding of criminal justice issues in many countries.

Box 6.6. Definition of comparative research in criminology

1.	Comparative analysis is the research process which is characterized by the examination of crime and criminal activity and other aspects of the criminal justice system in two or more countrie or subgroups of the populations, and involves the comparison of the situation in those countries.
2.	The main definitional features are that comparative analysis involves:

   a.   Different societies or countries.

   b.   Standard data.

   c.   Comparison of the situation in the selected societies or countries (e.g. crime rates, fear of crime).

Box 6.7. Summary of strengths and weakness of comparative research/analysis

1. Strengths:

   a.   Comparative research covers many countries.

   b.   Provides standard data on many societies or countries.

   c.   Increases our knowledge and understanding of cross-national issues in the criminal justices system.

   d.   Lessons from one society can be passed on to another country.

2. Weaknesses:

   a.   Costly.

   b.   Appropriateness of the subject matter may not be the same in all societies in the study.

   c.   Problems of culture and language.

   d.   Problems of definitions, sampling and measurements.

FURTHER READING

Brathwaite, F. s. and D. A. Yeboah (2004): Victims of crime in the criminal justice system in Barbados. Journal of Criminal Justice, Vol. 32, No. 2: 431-442.

Giddens, A (1997): Sociology. Cambridge, Polity Press.

May, T. (2001). Social Research. Buckingham, Open University Press.

Teevan, J., J (1987): Basic Sociology. Scarborough, Ontario, Prentice-Hall.

Yeboah, D. A.. (2002): Crime and its solutions in Barbados. Journal of Criminal Justice, Vol.30, No. 5:409-416.

Box 6.8. Questions for self reflection

1.	What is documentary research?
2.	What is the difference between documentary research and case study?
3.	What is experimental research in criminology?
4.	What are the stages involved in experimental research?
5.	Distinguish between study group and control group in experimental research.
6.	Why is it important to add another methodology when using documentary research?
7.	Identify the strengths and weaknesses of comparative research.
8.	What are the differences between experimental research and survey research in criminology?
9.	In what way is experimental research similar to survey research.
10.	Identify the usefulness of case study.

Chapter 7

ETHICAL CONSIDERATIONS IN CRIMINOLOGICAL RESEARCH

In the preceding chapters (chapters 2 to 6 in particular), the various methodologies used in criminological research have been discussed. In this chapter, focus shifts to the norms, values and acceptable practices within societies, which guide the use of these research methodologies, i.e. the societal norms and values with which criminological researchers undertake their studies. These norms, values and practices determine what is morally sound in research and are usually referred to as research ethics. This chapter examines the ethical issues in criminological research with particular emphasis on:

1. Definitions and concepts.
2. Ethics and general criminological research.
3. Ethics of human subject research.
4. Professional ethics.
5. Ethics in program evaluation.

DEFINITION AND CONCEPTS

Ethics are the common set of norms, values and acceptable practices and behavior prevailing in any society at any one time. These norms, values and practices determine acceptable moral behavior within individual societies. Thus, ethics embody what society perceives and understands to be morally acceptable behavior and practices. Research ethics may be referred to as the guidelines for undertaking research within the confines of the acceptable moral behavior and practice in the society where the research is taking place. . The norms, values, beliefs, perceptions, practices, and morally acceptable behavior together constitute the culture of the society. Hence ethics is based on the culture of individual societies. A key ethics related attribute of research is the diversity of acceptable moral behavior that researchers have to work with within and across countries. A number of countries have different subgroups of the population, in particular ethnic and tribal groups. Different ethnic and tribal groups have different norms, values acceptable moral behavior, perceptions and practices, while different countries have different laws, norms, practices and moral behavior.

A distinction must be made between the concepts of morally acceptable behavior and legally acceptable behavior. Morally acceptable behavior is what the society has come to develop and accept as appropriate behavior with or without any legal connotations. Legally acceptable behavior is the behavior defined by law as perceived in the existing legislations in individual countries. Research ethics operates and are affected by both morally acceptable behavior and legally acceptable behavior. As various countries have different legislation in a number of areas which cut across research, ethical issues would vary across countries. The primary focus of these legislation and morals is to define and/or determine what is right and/or just and what is wrong and unjust.

What may appear morally appropriate or acceptable to one ethnic group may not necessarily be acceptable to another. In the developed countries of Australia, Canada, New Zealand and the United States of America, the population is mixed, but two broad groups are identifiable, namely the indigenous and non indigenous populations. In Australia, the indigenous population is called Aboriginal and Torres Strait Islander people, in New Zealand they are called Maori while in North America, they are called Natives (Native Americans and Native Canadians).What is acceptable to the non indigenous population in any of these countries as culturally and morally appropriate may not be seen in the same way by the indigenous population. Similar, a lot of countries, especially in Africa, consist of various tribes with different norms, beliefs, values and morally acceptable behavior. As discussed next in this chapter, these differences in ethics in different societies tend to impact on research methodology and practice especially in comparative research.

ETHICS AND CRIMINOLOGICAL RESEARCH

As part of the discussion of various research methodologies, the role of the researcher has been presented for each criminological research methodology. One more role is added here for all criminological researchers, especially criminal justice system researchers, regardless of the methodology employed. At every stage in the research process (from conceptualization to final report), the criminological researcher has a moral and legal obligation to adhere to acceptable moral behavior and consider ethical issues. The researcher must give ethical consideration to all research decisions, including the topic or subject matter, hypothesis, research questions, identification and implementation of research design right through to the production of the final report. By giving ethical considerations to the research process and all research decisions, a pivotal link is established between the research and the prevailing ethics of the society where the research is taking place.

Ethics are of particular importance in criminological research. Criminological research, by and large, involves direct or indirect contact with offenders, one of the most vulnerable and disadvantaged subgroups of many populations. There is always the potential and tendency to take advantage of the unique disadvantageous position of offenders during the research process, especially those incarcerated in prisons, hence the need to apply the prevailing ethical standards in research involving offenders. While they are classified as social outcasts with the associated stigma and while they may appear vulnerable, offenders have similar rights as other people involved in the research. The onus is on the criminological researcher to ensure that the respect of the offenders and the related ethical requirements of human subject research discussed later in this chapter are fully respected.

Closely associated with this is the whole concept of ethical judgments. Criminological researchers are continuously being called upon to make ethical judgments not just in studies involving offenders. Even where the studies involve victims of crime, ethical judgments must be made about the subject matter, what data can be collected and what should be avoided, how to ask the questions and what should go into the report, all with an inherent objective of avoiding the potential to hurt the victims in any way (perceived or otherwise). A useful illustration is where victims of crime are studied using a triangulation approach including direct face to face interviewing of selected victims. To ensure continued participation of the victims, ethical judgments have to be made throughout the study, especially in relation to what and how questions are asked.

Another way ethics relate to criminological research lies in the prevailing culture and other characteristics of the society in which the research is taking place. Questionnaire content and design, the way the interviewing is progressed or behavior is observed and measured must be guided by the society's norms, practices and acceptable behavior (moral and legal). If the research is taking place in Ghana, for example, the norms, cultural practices and morally and legally acceptable behavior should be considered and inculcated into the study, even where they are different from what is acceptable in the researcher's own society. Similarly, if the research is taking place in the United States of America, the ethical requirements of the United States apply. It is more complex in cross-national research where a number of countries are involved in the research. Many countries have different and sometimes contradictory laws and morally acceptable behavior. The researcher is obligated to conduct the research under the acceptable moral and legal behavior and practices in each country. The usual practice is to amend the research process to meet the ethical requirements of each country.

However, this is not always possible and sometimes the information obtained ceases to be standard and comparable. This is often the case where existing morals and sometimes legislation prohibit certain questions to be asked. For example, while it is normal in western societies to undertake studies on sex, including rapes and other sexual assaults, it may be morally unacceptable and culturally prohibitive to do the same in some societies Existing cultural practices and legislation in Arab societies prohibit women from talking to men unless they are related by blood or marriage. This means that, for a start, male interviewers cannot be used to obtain data from women. Even if an attempt is made to overcome the problem by using female data collectors, the fact still stands that the female subjects will not be interested in participating in studies involving rapes (marital and non marital) and other sexual assaults, with implication for sample size and composition. That is the culture and the rsearcher has to respect and adhere to it, eben it has adverse effects on the cross-national studies

It is completely impossible to get a sizeable number of sexual assault victims to study in some societies. This will adversely impact on cross-national studies on sex crimes involving those societies. The point must be made that there is nothing wrong with this cultural and legal position as every country is free to establish its own moral and legal requirements. However, it highlights some of the relationships between ethics and cross-national or comparative research. The point is that cultural practices and morals vary from society to society and what is ethical in one society may not necessarily be ethical in another society, points which must be given due consideration in cross national research.

Ethics have assumed more importance and significance in recent times because funding agencies now require criminological and other researchers to demonstrate that the proposed research meets existing ethical requirements to be eligible for funding. It is also due to efforts by government and research institutions to ensure that researchers give due respect to the study subjects and not take advantage of them. In some societies guidelines have been enshrined in law especially as they related to privacy and confidentiality as well as access to and use of unit record data. For example, it is a common and universal ethical requirement that analysis should be such that no response can be identified with any respondent. Some basic principles have been established and are universally applied or rather required to be met. Some of these are discussed in the next section, titled ethics of human subject research.

ETHICS OF HUMAN SUBJECT RESEARCH

As indicated earlier in this chapter, research subjects in the criminal justice system and other areas in criminology are, by and large, human beings. Criminological research generally focuses on crime, offenders, victims of crime, policies and programs in the criminal justice system. Even where the study focuses on Police practices and court room experiences of both offenders and victims, the human factor is still inherent. This presupposes a need to have core principles to guide researchers to achieve acceptable moral behavior and practice when undertaking research involving human beings, such as offenders or victims of crime. The acceptable and legal human behavior is embodied in what is called the ethics of human subject research.

Ethical Requirements of Human Subject Research

To achieve a total and complete fulfillment of the ethics of human subject research, the following requirements must be met:

1. Information for participants or subjects.
2. Rewards for participants if any.
3. Informed decision/Informed consent.
4. Voluntary participation.
5. Freedom to withdraw.
6. Confidentiality of responses and privacy of respondents.
7. Respect for the rights and dignity of the study subjects.
8. Aggregate analysis and reporting of data.

Information to Study Subjects
The first requirement is to give respondents as much information as possible about the research, the role of the researcher and what is expected of the study subjects. The information must be true, adequate and accurate. The respondents or study subjects must understand fully what is expected of them and they should be allowed or even invited to ask questions if they wish to do so (see Box 7.2) The researchers must also reveal their role to the

subjects and this is of particular importance in participant observation research where the researcher can hide his role in what is called covert participant observation research methodology. The role of the researcher is more obvious in focus group and survey research (especially face to face survey research methodology). Even in program evaluation, the subjects have to be given all the necessary information about the evaluation, its goals and objectives, the role of the researcher and the role of the subjects. It is also often the practice to inform the potential study subjects that their responses will be confidential and assure them of full privacy as discussed later in this chapter.

Rewards for Study Subjects

Closely related to the information given to study subjects is the disclosure of rewards to participants if any. After providing the study subjects with accurate, adequate and necessary information, the researcher has a responsibility to disclose predetermined rewards to the participants. Many researchers are now paying a fee to study subjects to encourage and/or entice them to participate in the study. This is completely legal and ethical as many subjects are becoming wary and skeptical about releasing personal information and spending a lot of time answering questions from strangers. In Africa, this reward is called "Kola", in western societies it is called a fee or tip and Asian and Caribbean societies have their own diverse terminologies. It is, thus, a common feature of research that a reward is provided to study subjects . If no reward is to be offered to the study subjects, they must be told clearly from the beginning to avoid confusion further down the line. Sometimes, the offer of rewards works to influence the decisions of the study subjects and convinces them to participate. In that respect it may be argued that the idea is unethical. This argument is counteracted by the fact that many potential subjects have refused to participate even when they were to be rewarded. Besides, research is becoming a business and people have to be paid not only the researchers, just as in any other business. In this respect, offering rewards to study subjects is completely ethical, normal and legal.

Informed Decision/Informed Consent

The requirement of informed decision operates on the basis that study subjects must be in a position to decide whether they want to participate without any pressure from the researcher or interviewer. After providing all the necessary information to the potential study subjects and offering them the reward if any, the researcher eagerly awaits their response to the question will you participate in the study. The potential study subjects are in a position to respond at this time. Following the provision of the necessary information and the offer of reward, the potential participants are well informed to make decisions on their participation. This is called informed decision making because the potential participants have the information to assist them with the decision making. Informed decision making is a very integral component of research ethics because no subject should be coerced or bullied into submitting to participate in the study.

Voluntary Participation

Closely associated with informed decision is voluntary participation. It is an ethical requirement that study subjects participate voluntarily in the study. Involuntary participation is unacceptable in research ethics. The study subjects must know, understand and feel that they are participating in the research voluntarily. They must also be made aware of the fact that participation in the research is voluntary. This is usually done with statements such as "you do not have to participate in the research if you do not want to, but your participation will be helpful and very much appreciated". Even with statements like this and rewards, some potential study subjects still refuse to participate in the study and the researcher must be prepared to accept and respect the decisions of the potential participants.

Freedom to Withdraw

Following the decision to participate, some study subjects change their mind and want to withdraw. Study subjects should be free to withdraw from the research for any reason and again that decision has to be respected by the researcher. Withdrawing from the study usually affects the sample size especially where many respondents decide to withdraw but, in practice, very few withdrawals if any occur in most studies (once the study commences). It is ethical for the researcher to make the study subjects aware that they are free to withdraw their participation, albeit the researcher would appreciate it if they don't. In practice, by telling the study subjects of their right to withdraw, many potential respondents are encouraged to participate in the study. Generally, unless something drastic or unexpected happens during the research or interview, the subjects do not exercise this right to withdraw once the research or interview begins.

Confidentiality and Privacy

To many ordinary people, research ethics mean respecting the privacy of study subjects and keeping their responses confidential.. Many respondents will only take part in studies if they are assured and if they believe the assurances that their privacy would be respected and their responses kept confidential. Privacy and confidentiality issues are very important in criminology because criminological research usually covers victims and offenders who may not be willing to divulge personal information. This is an important ethical requirement from the point of view of the study subjects as well. The subjects must be informed from the beginning about their privacy and the confidentiality of their responses, as this may encourage them to take part in the study. More importantly, confidentiality and privacy assurances given to the study subjects must be adhered to throughout the research.

Respect for the Rights and Dignity of the Study Subjects

A general ethical requirement is to respect the rights and dignity of the study subjects. Convicted Criminals, especially those serving prison terms, are usually looked down upon and associated with one form of stigma or another. Criminological researchers, undertaking studies involving disadvantaged and stigmatized groups such as incarcerated offenders and offenders who have been released after a term of imprisonment, must give the subjects due respect.

Their dignity and rights must be respected just as any other study group. Indeed, the offenders are willing to participate and divulge personal and other information if they can see that the researcher respects their rights and dignity. Respecting the rights and dignity of study subjects builds trust, with trust comes confidence and with confidence comes the provision of information by the study subjects.

Aggregate Analysis and Reporting of Data

A sure way of achieving the confidentiality of responses is to adopt a unit of analysis involving an aggregation of responses rather than unit record analysis. If the responses are put together as an aggregate of responses, no response is identifiable with any specific study subject and, thus, keeping their responses confidential. For example, instead of an analysis which goes like "subject A stated that the program was not effective and did not help, like or similar responses can be grouped into an analysis which states that 10 study subjects or 33.33% indicated that the program was not effective". A problem arises when the number of study subjects is small. Small numbers impair aggregation and make it difficult for responses o be disassociated from the study subjects.

PROFESSIONAL ETHICS

Criminological researchers are expected to work as professionals and in particular meet professional ethical requirements at all the stages of the research (from inception to final report). In so doing, criminological researchers are guided by what is called professional ethics. Criminological researchers belong to one professional association or the other, and all professional associations develop and maintain ethical guidelines in what is called the code of ethics. In this section, professional ethics are discussed in terms of:

1. Definition.
2. Code of ethics and its attributes.
3. General Principles.

What Is Meant by Professional Ethics?

Professional ethics is a common set of values, practices and acceptable moral behavior expected of all the members of the professional association. Members of professional associations usually work according to the ethical guidelines developed and maintained by the professional body. While differences in ethics are discrnible from one professional association to the other, most ethical requirements are similar across the professions and, in some cases, the differences are marginal. For all associations the instrument for maintaining professional ethics is the code of ethics.

Code of Ethics

In its simplest definition, the code of ethics consists of statements outlining the acceptable moral behavior, practices and general conduct that the professional associations require their members to adopt. The code of ethics embodies professional ethics. It can, thus, be defined also as the common set of values, practices and behavior upon which members of professional association undertake their professional work.

In addition, the code of ethics provides principles and rules to enable members to function in acceptable manner in the various professional situations they work in. Each code of ethics may have specific objectives related to the specific professional body. However, all codes of ethics aim at:

1. Protecting the welfare of its members.
2. Ensuring professionalism.
3. Guiding professionals in diverse situations and, for the purpose of this book, diverse research environments and circumstances.
4. Protecting the study subjects.
5. Protecting the community.
6. Ensuring the highest professional standards.

In general, the code of ethics of most professional associations consists of a document which contains an introduction, preamble, statements of required ethical standards for professional work and what is called the general principles.

Attributes of the Code of Ethics

Common attributes of most codes of ethics include the following:

1. Enforcement of the document.
2. High standards.
3. Obligation on members to adopt.
4. Restricted to professional situations only, not private activities.
5. Imposition of sanctions for failing to oblige.
6. Regular review of the code.
7. Personal commitment.

A key attribute of the code of ethics is that the document is enforceable. Most professional bodies make it obligatory for the members to adopt and practice the tenets of the code of ethics, and there are provisions to impose sanctions if the requirements are breached. The point must also be made that some of the requirements in the code of ethics may also be legal requirements in some society, and professionals breaching those requirements could have legal problems to contend with. Needless to say the code of ethics is of high standard to withstand scrutiny and to meet public approval. A key issue is the tendency to assume that the professional code of ethics covers the private circumstances and private situations of members.

It is worthy to mention that the code of ethics is developed for professional situations and is not intended to cover the researcher's private non professional activities. Most professional bodies review the code of ethics from time to time. This is critical to meet changing values, public demand, legislation and professional environments. Finally, all members of professional associations must demonstrate a high level of personal commitment to the code of ethics.

The General Principles

The general principles are statements which serve as a guide to provide ethical courses of action to address specific demands of diverse professional situations. As a rule, the general principles address the following topics:

1. Professional competence.
2. Responsibility to the community.
3. Integrity.
4. Disciplinary and scientific responsibility.
5. Respect for the rights and dignity of clients, study subjects.

Professional Competence

Most professional associations (including criminological societies and associations) expect their members to exhibit the highest level of competence in the discharge of their functions, including the way and manner they conduct research. A related point is that most professional bodies encourage and usually expect their members to undertake work in areas they have been trained, educated, registered and competent to function effectively in. In so doing, professionals are expected to undertake, and most professional bodies subject their members to, regular training and retraining in what is called continues education or continuous improvements, to ensure that members are abreast with new developments in the profession. For example, medical associations subject their members to what is called continuous medical education (CME). The bottom line is that professional bodies encourage and require their members to know their limitations and function with those limitations in mind.

Responsibility to the Community

The underlying philosophy of this principle is that criminologist and other professionals work in the community and are, therefore, responsible to the community. As discussed earlier in this chapter, ethics are basically the acceptable norms, values, practices and acceptable moral behavior in the community Professional associations require their members to be responsible to the community in which they function and to abide by the norms, values, cultural practice acceptable moral behavior and the laws of that society. If a criminological researcher is undertaking cross-national research about concern about or fear of crime, the prevailing norms, values, cultural practices, acceptable moral behavior and laws may change from one country to the other. They may also be different to the situation in the researcher's home country, but the professional associations require their members to adapt to the changes as they undertake research in different countries and societies. In addition, criminological professionals must work to achieve the public good.

Integrity

A critical principle in all the previously discussed principles is integrity. Integrity is the key to behaving professionally, building trust and winning the confidence of study subjects, in particular offenders and other parties in the criminal justice system. Integrity requires professionals (criminological researchers, for example) to be honest, fair and show respect for their study subjects or clients at all times.

Scientific Responsibility

While the principle of professional responsibility to the community has been discussed, sight should not be lost of the overarching responsibility to the discipline or what is called scientific responsibility. Criminological researchers have to adhere to the highest scientific, disciplinary and professional standards. They must also accept responsibility for their work, and respect each other.

Respect for the Rights and Dignity of Clients

Criminological researchers have to respect the rights and dignity of the study subjects as applicable in the society in which the research is taking place. By the mere fact that criminological researchers deal with disadvantaged groups such as prisoners and other offenders, there is an ethical requirement not to demonstrate discrimination of any sort, shape or form. In undertaking studies, criminological researchers should respect all their study subjects and not discriminate by age, gender, race, color of the skin, nationality or disability. The point is also made here that criminological professionals (researchers etc.) have to accept the right of others to divergent views, values, norms beliefs and cultural practices.

ETHICS IN PROGRAM EVALUATION

The ethical issues outlined in this chapter apply to all criminological research methodologies. There are certain specific ethical requirements for the successful undertaking of program evaluation, and they are presented briefly in this section. Evaluators are often faced with ethical dilemmas of various kinds. A common ethical issue is the pressure and persistence of stake holders seeking amendments to the evaluation findings because it adversely affects them. The dilemma here is that the criminological researcher, evaluating a program, can either manipulate the findings and please the stake holders but lose their professionalism, or stand firm on their evaluation findings and lose potential future funding or consultancy services from the stake holder. Evaluator, especially those external to the organization,s are usually faced with the dilemma of being asked to provide information for service and program improvements while being perceived as auditors or professionals looking for faults, inadequacies and failures at the same time.

Informed consent and confidentiality are particularly important in ethics of program evaluation. The clients of the program and all study subjects must give consent to participating in the study largely because the evaluator wants the subjects to provide accurate information willingly and freely. Program evaluation involves sensitive, commercial and private program records The evaluator has an ethical responsibility to keep all the evaluation data confidential, but more so information obtained from program records and funding agencies.

Program evaluation usually included identifying areas for improvement, outcomes and assessing the effectiveness or efficacy of programs. Evaluators are professionals and have their own views on issues such as the effectiveness of specific programs to address crime and other issues in the criminal justice system. There is an ethical requirement for evaluators to ground their conclusions and recommendations on the findings of the evaluation not on any preconceptions, personal views, biases and opinions.

FURTHER READING

May, T (2001): Social research. Buckingham, Open University Press.
Posavac, E. J., and R. G. Carey (1997): Ptogram evaluation: Methods and case studies. Upper Saddle River, Prentice-Hall.
Yeboah, D. A. (2000): The evaluation of New Zealand Habilitation Centres Pilot Program. Journal of Criminal Justice, Vol 28. N0 3: 227-236.

Visit the website of your professional association and read the code of ethics.

Box 7.1. Key points in research ethics

1.   Ethics are about norms, values, and acceptable moral behavior.
2.   Ethics are also about the cultural practices and beliefs.
3.   Ethics are not universal in all societies and must be strongly considered in cross-national research.
4.   While ethics is generally based on morally acceptable behavior, some ethical requirements are also legal.
5.   The highest level of ethics is important in criminological research because criminological research involves disadvantaged and vulnerable groups such as offenders.

Box 7.2. Typical information given to research subjects

I am D.J. and I want to invite you to participate in the research we are doing by answering a few questions. The research is about crime, the level of crime and concern about crime. The objective is to collect and analyze adequate data to support policy and program development to fight crime. As you know, crime is every body's business. I want to ask you a few questions during the next 15 to 20 minutes if you agree to participate. You do not have to participate but your participation will help a lot and it will be much appreciated. The information you provide will be treated with the highest level of confidentiality and no reader of the research report can identify you or associate any response with you. All participating people will be paid a reward of $10.

Box 7.3. Key points in ethics of human subject research

1.	Adequate and accurate information about the research must be given to all the potential study subjects.
2.	Study subjects must be advised if there is a reward or fee for participating in the study.
3.	Study subjects must be allowed to make an informed decision to participate and give their consent without any pressure.
4.	Study subjects must voluntarily agree to participate.
5.	Study subjects must be made aware of their freedom to withdraw from the study.
6.	Study subjects must be assured of their privacy and the confidentiality of their responses.

Box 7.4. Key points in professional ethics

1.	The main instrument of professional ethics is the code of conduct
2.	Most professional bodies have a code of conduct/ethics
3.	The code of conduct is a document which contains guidelines to assist professionals to behave appropriately in diverse professional situations.
4.	The code of ethics protects both the professionals and their clients
5.	The general principles of the code of ethics usually include:
	a. Professional competence.
	b. Responsibility to the community.
	c. Integrity.
	d. Disciplinary and scientific responsibility.
	e. Respect for the rights and dignity of clients including study subjects.

Box 7.5. Questions for self reflection

1.	What is ethics?
2.	Why are ethics so important in criminological research?
3.	If you were to undertake a study of victims of crime in your community, what information will you give to the study subjects?
4.	Can an ethical requirement be moral and legal at the same time?
5.	What are the main ethical requirements for human subject research?
6.	What do you understand by the code of ethics?
7.	List the general principles usually found in the code of ethics.

Chapter 8

DESIGNING QUESTIONS AND INTERVIEWING IN CRIMINOLOGICAL RESEARCH

In many methodologies used in criminological research, designing questions and interviewing are integral components. Methodologies such as survey research (face to face and telephone survey methodologies), focus groups, case study and program evaluation provide opportunities for questionnaire design and interviewing. This chapter discusses:

1. Types of questions:
   a. Leading questions.
   b. Pressuring questions.
   c. Hypothetical questions.
   d. Personalized questions.
   e. Embarrassing questions.
   f. Memory questions.

2. Questionnaire design:
   a. Content.
   b. Principles.

3. Interviewing:
   a. Processes.
   b. Usefulness.

QUESTIONNAIRE DESIGN

The design of the instruments or questionnaires has various aspects, namely the types of questions, content and the principles involved in questionnaire design. It is usual practice to vary the types of questions in the instrument and include different types of questions in the study. To obtain accurate data using questionnaires, the questions must be such that they are adequately understood by the study subjects. To obtain data to test the research hypothesis and/or address the research questions, the content of the questionnaire must cover topics and provide data necessary to test the hypothesis and/or address the said research questions. For the instruments to be effective, a number of principles have to be adopted and adhered to. More details on the types, content and principles of questionnaire design are now presented.

TYPES OF QUESTIONS

Open-ended and closed questions were discussed in chapter four Each of these two broad types of questions can take the form of leading, pressuring, hypothetical, personalized, embarrassing and memory questions. Leading questions point the respondent to a particular direction, and usually to a particular answer. It usually follows an initial question which the respondent may be having problems answering. In situations where the respondent is finding it difficult to answer a question or answers the question in a way not expected by the researcher, the researcher can ask further questions which may include clues to lead the respondent to a specific response. Leading questions are usually used in probing to have the respondent respond in a particular direction. For example, a criminological researcher is investigating recidivism among a selected sample of Australian youth. The researcher asks the question "how many times have you reoffended since you were released from the juvenile detention center. One of them states only once, but the research knows of another occasion. So the researcher asks the leading question, what about the case of the handbag you took from the old lady?. This leading question is intended to prompt and remind the offender to think again and provide a more correct response.

Pressuring questions seek to coerce a study subject to answer a particular question which the respondent may not want to provide a response. In the example of the hand bag above, the respondent may refuse to answer, and the researcher can put further pressure on the youth by asking more questions such as "you took the hand bag? Did you not? Don't t you know somebody saw you? Don't you know that your court appearance was in the paper? Tell me how many offences have you committed since your release? One area in the criminal justice system where pressuring questions are used is questioning of suspects by the Police. Statements such as give us a confession, you did it, so accept it. Why don't you want to confess and make it easy for every one? Why don't you confess and we can give you a deal etc? In court room practices it is often the case for defense attorneys to put pressure on victims of rape and other sexual assault to accept partial or full blame for what happened. You went to his home willingly. You consented to sex, didn't you remember? I put it to you that it was consensual sex, you agreed to do it.

In hypothetical questions, the respondent is asked to imagine a situation which is not actual or real, and asked to answer a specific question. The researcher presents the situation to the study subject as follows: Suppose a researcher is investigating the potential for recidivism for offenders who have just completed a sex offender rehabilitation program involving therapy, counseling, confession, self-assessment and group discussion as well as relapse prevention programs. The researcher puts the following situation to the study subjects Suppose you were walking through a quiet alley one afternoon and you saw a young beautiful lady walking by herself. You look and there is nobody around. Will you be able to restrain yourself? Or will you take advantage of the absence of other people and the quiet surroundings and attack the young woman? This scenario places the study subject in a situation which is not real and which the subject is being asked to imagine.

Personalized questions, as the name suggests, are those questions which are designed to relate to a particular individual. You were convicted last June and again in April this year. How many times have you been convicted throughout your criminal history? Personalized questions are tailored to allow for the collection of information on a particular individual or individuals. Now tell me, were you personally involved in the break and enter? Or were you just the mastermind behind the crime but did not actually participate in the break and enter?

Embarrassing questions are uncomfortable or difficult to answer because they usually ask the study subject to come up with information which may be too personal, intruding, or shameful. They include questions which make the study subject uncomfortable or even stupid as in the case of repeated victimization. Why is it that you keep leaving your door unlocked despite being burgled four times? You complained that the suspect sexually assaulted you but you kissed the suspect. Didn't you?

Finally, memory questions seek to obtain information on something which happened in the past. The study subjects are expected to remember what happened and answer the questions posed. Memory questions are therefore recall questions and most survey research methodologies use memory questions. For example, a researcher studying the economic impact of criminal victimization asks the respondents "can you tell me what you lost when your house was burgled? What was the cost? How much was the insurance reimbursement? How much did you personally lose? How much did you have to supplement the reimbursement so as to replace the stolen item? Was any of the lost items recovered by the Police? These questions are soliciting answers on a past event and the study subjects have to think back, remember what happened and respond accordingly.

Content of Research Instruments or Questionnaires

Types of questionnaires were discussed in preceding paragraphs and how to deal with the content of the questionnaire to make it useful for the research objectives and goals is now presented. The first step in designing the research instruments is to define the problem and identify the research goals and objectives together with any defined or stated hypotheses and/or research questions. The next step is to establish the items or variables which have the potential to provide information to test the hypotheses and address any research questions, i.e. the content of the research instruments. The following are the key points or issues in determining the content of the questionnaire:

1. Goals and Objectives of the research.
2. Research Hypotheses or Research questions.
3. Knowledge of the study subjects.
4. What key stake holders want to know?
5. What the researcher envisages for inclusion in the final report?

Goals and Objectives of the Research

The point must be made that the goals and objectives of the research are the principal determinants of the content of the instrument. It is often the practice to include variables which will provide information to achieve the research goals and objectives. The achievement of the research goals and objectives is critical for the success of the research or program evaluation and it is imperative for data to be obtained to meet the need to address the research goals and objectives. For example, a criminological researcher may be investigating the impact of crime on their victims by examining the physical, economic and emotional or psychological impact of crime. The researcher settles on face to face survey research methodology. A questionnaire is required in face to face survey research methodology and, to achieve the goals and objectives of the research, data must be obtained on the physical and economic impact of the criminal victimization on the victims. The instruments must also allow for data to be obtained on any emotional or psychological problems from which the victims may be suffering as a result of the criminal victimization.

Various questions can be developed and used to obtain the necessary data to address the physical, economic and psychological or emotional impact of criminal victimization. Common questions may include:

1. What crime were you a victim?
2. Did you sustain any injuries? Please list all injuries arising from the criminal victimization.
3. Did you suffer any economic losses? Please list all economic losses including medical and health costs, loss of personal belongings and/or valuables including money, cost of repairs (vehicle, building, other).
4. Are you encountering any emotional difficulties as a result of the criminal victimization?
5. Are you having problems in relating to other people as a result of the assault?
6. Are you afraid to leave home?
7. Aare you afraid that you will be burgled again.
8. Are you having difficulties in your sexual relationships as a result of the assault? i.e. in the case of sexual assault victims.

Answers to these questions will provide data that may be analyzed to denote the extent of physical, economic and emotional or psychological impact of crime on the victims of crime.

Research Hypotheses or Research Questions

The above questions will not only provide data to achieve the goals and objectives of the victimization study, but it will also provide data to address the hypotheses including the null hypothesis, as well as any defined or stated research questions. Most studies will have stated hypotheses or stated research questions. The content of the instruments must provide data to addresses the hypotheses or the questions, otherwise the study will be considered to have failed, not useful and lacking strong contribution. Remember it is in addressing the hypotheses or research questions that the study makes its point and/or contribution.

Knowledge of the Study Subjects

A key issue in questionnaire design is the need to pitch the questions to the level, knowledge and understanding of the study subjects. There is no point in asking questions the study subjects cannot answer for any reason. For example, the questions must not be technical and beyond the understanding of the respondents. In addition, a researcher undertaking a victimization survey should not ask the study subjects if they know of any criminal victimization involving their neighbors. The respondent may or may not have an answer to this question, the answer they provide may be incorrect and it is difficult to obtain a large amount of standard data. The study subjects must be in a position to use their knowledge to respond, and they are better able to do so if the questions related to their own personal situations.

Interest of Stake Holders

What stake holders want to know from the research is critical for the acceptance of the research report. Stake holders define which aspects of the subject matter they want to learn more about, which specific questions they want answers to, and where they would like the research to focus on. It is important for the researcher to design the instruments so as to obtain data to address the issues raised by stake holders Stake holders' interests are of particular importance in program evaluation. Funders of the program want to know if the funds have been used as agreed, if the program has been effective and efficient and if funding should continue. Program and service providers want to know areas where the program can be improved, if the program components or activities have been helpful in achieving the program objectives etc. Clients of the program want to put forward suggestions on which program activities were helpful and need to be maintained and which activities were unhelpful and need to be abolished etc. It is critical for the content of the instruments to allow for the collection and analysis of data for appropriate and useful feedback to stake holders of the program evaluation, for example.

Researcher's Vision of the Research Report

Supplementing the stake holders' interests and program goals and objectives is the researcher's vision of the final report. What the researcher envisages should be included in the report determines to some extent the content of the instruments. Questions must be asked on the variables and items the researcher envisages will be discussed in the report. What the researcher wants in the report is determined by the stake holders' interests and the nature, type, goals and objectives of the research. What the researcher sees as essential for the report is also partly determined by the subject matter and the problem associated with the subject matter that the research set out to investigate.

Principles of Questionnaires Design

The logical step following the determination of the content of the questionnaire is to set the questions. Setting questions is not as simple and easy as perceived by many people. In setting or developing the questions, a number of principles exist to guide the researcher. These principles are essential because their use allows for the development of questions which can be understood by the respondents and, thus, improve the data obtained by soliciting the correct responses. The adoption of the principles also improves data quality and enhances the capacity of the instruments to achieve the research goals and objectives. These principles include;

1.   Simple straight forward wording.
2.   Clear and unambiguous sentences/questions.

3. Questions should be concise, and not unduly lengthy.
4. One question sentence, not two questions in one sentence.
5. Items must follow in a logical sequence.
6. Pitching questions to the level and understanding of study subjects.
7. Focus on the subject matter of the study.
8. Clarity about which questions will be answered by whom.
9. Efficiency and effectiveness of the questionnaire rather than its appearance.
10. Layout and printing should enhance coding and editing.

Simple Straight Forward Wording

A key element in developing questionnaires is to use simple and easy to understand wording. Non essential technical terms, jargons and other terminologies should be avoided as much as possible. Essential technical terms and terminologies when used should be defined and explained to the understanding of the respondent. To illustrate, imagine a researcher is investigating recidivism among a group of convicted criminals who have just completed a period of residence at a rehabilitation facility. The research asks them are you sure that you will not be a recidivist in the near future? Instead, the researcher may ask are you sure you will not commit another crime in the future? Again, a researcher studying victimization in a community decides to use focus group methodology to obtain the needed data. The researcher puts the following question to the study subjects: What criminal victimization did you suffer? Instead, a simple straight forward question should be asked, such as what crime was committed against you?

Clear and Unambiguous Questioning

A related point is that not only must the questions be simple and straightforward, they must also be clear and unambiguous. The principle of clarity and unambiguousness operates on the basis of the underlying philosophy that study subjects will understand clear and unambiguous questions better. With better understanding of questions comes the ability to respond correctly and with correct responses comes the collection of accurate and relevant research data. The principle of clarity and unambiguousness cannot be overemphasized in focus group and survey research methodologies. They are also critical in program evaluation in which the research methodologies include focus group and/or survey research.

Concise Questions

A closely related point is the principle of concise questions. The instruments must be such that no question is unduly lengthy. Long questions have the potential to confuse study subjects and attract inaccurate and/or missing responses. The tendency is for the respondent to forget the earlier part of the question especially in face to face survey, telephone survey and focus group methodologies. Inaccurate responses, by and large, adversely impact on the study data, analysis and conclusions. Wrong conclusions lead to wrong recommendations and affect the overall value and significance of the research. Lengthy questions should be broken up into concise parts or completely rewritten in short sentences.

For example, in the criminal victimization study, the researchers ask one study subject this question: Is it true that, on the day the crime was committed against you, you left home in the evening and was walking to the shop when suddenly you felt somebody was creeping behind you and as you turned to look, the person attacked you?

This question must be broken into various parts as indicated in the next section, or replaced by the simple question – Were you attacked as you walked to the shop in the evening?

One Question Sentence

The point must be made that asking multiple questions in one sentence can be problematic. Many a time, there is a potential tendency for researchers who design research instruments to include more than one question in one sentence. Having two questions in one sentence means the respondent must provide two possible answers. However, in practice, the study subjects usually provide one answer. For example a researcher investigating family interactions between recently released prisoners and their family members asks the released convict the following question at the beginning of the meeting: How are you and how is the family? The respondent responds fine. This is ambiguous, misleading and confusing, Fine to what, the first part of the sentence (how are you?) or fine to the second part of the sentence (how is the family?). To resolve potential problems such as those arising from asking two questions in one sentence, two questions must be asked in two separate sentences as follows:

1. How are you?
2. How is your family?

In the previous victimization illustration the following question was asked: Is it true that, on the day the crime was committed against you, you left home in the evening and was walking to the shop when suddenly you felt somebody was creeping behind you and as you turned to look, the person attacked you? This question should be broken up into a number of related questions including:

1. Was the crime against you committed in the evening?
2. Were you walking to the shop at the time?
3. Is it true that you felt there was somebody behind you?
4. Did you turn to look?
5. Was it at that point that you were attacked?

Logical Sequence of Question Items/Variables

The items or variables in which information is sought using questions should follow in a logical sequence. In criminological surveys some variables come first in particular bio-0data or personal information. Demographic and social data such as age, gender, marital status, employment and/or occupational status, family background and related variables appear early in the questionnaire before the actual criminological survey subject matter. In, a study of fear of crime or concern about crime, the respondents should be asked questions on the above stated personal information before proceeding to ask other questions such as have you ever been a victim of crime? Are you afraid of crime? Are you afraid to go out alone in the evening? Are you afraid to leave home? Again, it is inappropriate to ask "when was you car stolen?" before asking "have you ever been a victim of cime?

Questions Must Be Pitched O the Level and Understanding of the Study Subjects

Pitching questions to the level and understanding of the respondents may result in appropriate feedback from the respondents. The respondents are able to provide accurate information because they understand the questions. The researcher must have a fair idea about the study subjects, their education etc. A researcher investigating offenders convicted of serious white collar crimes can actually work on the basis that the study subjects may be well educated and intelligent. In the situation where the research focuses on prisoners with little education, the researcher should be able to design the instruments using simple and easy to understand language that is pitched to the characteristics and understanding of the study subjects. There is a potential problem where the study involves subjects of mixed backgrounds such as victimization studies. Victims of crime can come from any background and there is usually a mix of educated and uneducated, wealthy and poor victims as well as intelligent and other respondents. The standpoint taken in this chapter is to follow the basic principles of questionnaire designat all times to obtain the required information.

Focus on the Subject Matter of the Study

The ultimate objective of the instruments is to secure the collection of appropriate, relevant and accurate data to achieve the research goals and objectives. The research goals and objectives are determined by the subject matter of the research and the problem under investigation. It is no doubt a matter of utmost importance that the instruments must be developed to reflect the subject matter and any associated problems identified in the research goals and objectives. Focusing on the subject matter will improve the potential to test the research hypotheses including the null hypothesis and/or address the stated research questions. It will also give the final report a defined focus.

Clarity about Which Questions Will Be Answered by Whom

The researcher must be clear about who will answer what questions. In survey research methodology this may appear irrelevant as the object is to obtain standard data on all study subjects. In focus group methodology and program evaluation, it is sometimes necessary to distinguish between study subjects and pose some questions to some groups only. For example, in the evaluation of a community based rehabilitation program, such as New Zealand's Habilitation Centres Pilot Program, program managers, service providers, policy makers, staff of the corrections facility and the beneficiaries or recipients of the program may be asked different questions. Some fundamental questions may be put to all study subjects, but it is often the practice that some study subjects will be in a better position to answer specific questions which are more related to their experiences. For example, program managers are better positioned to respond to questions on program rationale and itemized cost against expenditure etc, while program recipients can express their views about program activities and their effects on their lives.

The issue is more complex in focus groups. The researcher must be clear about who will answer specific questions and address the questions at them accordingly. The point is that members of the focus group may have different backgrounds, training and education, together with diverse experiences. In victimization studies, questions should be addressed to the members of the household who are able to provide the necessary responses. The onus is on the researcher to identify these differences and direct specific questions to those whose backgrounds and experiences will allow them to answer the specific questions.

Efficiency and Effectiveness of the Questionnaire Rather Than Its Appearance

Effectiveness and efficiency to produce the required data should be the principal objective of the instruments, not the appearance of the instruments. The appearance of the instruments by itself cannot provide the required data and should not be the point of emphasis. Fancy appearances could serve as a source of distraction for the study subjects, resulting in inaccuracies in reporting by the said study subjects. The content of the instrument is what matters and the questions must appear neatly but not fanciful. Having beautiful designs along the edges of the questionnaire is not the way to go, as it has the potential to distract interviewers and respondents, and also add unnecessarily to the cost of printing.

Layout and Printing Should Enhance Coding and Editing

Closely related to the above principle are the effects of layout and printing on coding, editing and data processing and storage. It is crucial for the layout of the questionnaire to reflect the coding and data processing needs of the research, especially where optical mark reader or other automated data entry is envisaged or used.. These days the use of automated data entry involving scanning and the other approaches identify earlier in this book. The layout and printing of the questionnaire must not inhibit or hinder the automated entry, editing and coding of the data on each questionnaire. The size of the questionnaire when printed must not be bigger than what the scanner can take, for example, otherwise data entry, editing and overall processing may be impeded or delayed.

INTERVIEWING

Interviewing is the process by which a researcher or trained interviewer poses a number of predefined questions to selected respondents to obtain data on identified variables. It is one of the most widespread medium of data collection used in criminological research, and can be used to collect data on a wide range of topics in criminology and/or the criminal justice system. Interviewing is an integral component of survey research and focus group methodologies, but interviewing is sometimes used in program evaluation as well. By definition, interviewing cannot be used with participant observation as this methodology involves the direct observation of behavior. Interviewing usually involves asking questions on past or future events as previously discussed in chapter four.

Types of Interviewing

Chapter four identifies various types of interviewing including:

1.   Face to face interviewing.
2.   Telephone interview.

Face to face interviewing is the most widely used interviewing methodology. This type of interviewing can be structured, semi-structured or unstructured (chapter four). Another type of interviewing involves focus group methodology. Focus group interviewing involves the selection of a group of respondent to whom questions are posed and data obtained (chapter three). All these methodologies have been discussed elsewhere in this book as indicated and only their interviewing aspects are presented in this section.

Step by Step Guide to Successful Interviewing

The process of interviewing has a number of sequential steps that can lead to a successful interview. These steps are:

1. Identification of the respondents.
2. Familiarization with the respondents.
3. Familiarization with the interview venue.
4. Familiarization with the questions.
5. Pose the questions in a culturally and linguistically appropriate manner.
6. Note responses carefully to avoid complications in coding, editing and analysis

Interviewing has two main parties, namely the researcher or trained interviewer and the respondent. The object is for the researcher or interviewer to solicit and obtain data from the respondents, hence the first step is to identify and select the interview respondents. It is crucial for the interviewer or researcher to know the study subjects by familiarizing themselves with the respondents. This will allow the questions to be pitched to the level of the respondents. It also helps the researcher or interviewer in knowing how to approach the whole interviewing process.

The following illustration will suffice. Suppose a researcher is examining fear of crime by interviewing both the perpetrators and victims of crime. The level of education, training, employment history and family and socio-economic backgrounds of the perpetrators and victims may not be the same Different approaches may be required for these two groups involved in any criminal activity. As convicted crime perpetrators are usually disadvantaged and vulnerable, care should be taken in approaching them and soliciting the information. This is particularly true if the researcher wants to obtain their full cooperation. With regards to the victims, the researcher or interviewer must recognize their plight, the impact of the crime, their anger and other emotions arising from the criminal victimization as well as their backgrounds, and approach them accordingly. Depending on the types of crime perpetrated against them and its impact and whether the victim perceives that they contributed in some way to the crime (through their actions), the victims may or may not want to participate and where they participate they may not want to respond to certain questions.

The need for the researcher or interviewer to familiarize themselves with the interview venue may not be recognized by many researchers. The surroundings including noise levels, potential interruptions (especially prison interviews), can impact on the degree of comfort of the respondent to answer the questions. For example, prisoners are not readily open to cooperating with researchers where a guard is standing close by, or where another person can possibly hear the conversation between the researcher and the prisoner etc. High noise venues may impair the ability of the parties to hear each other properly. In addition, interviewing crime victims at the scene of the crime may prove emotional, affecting their responses and the collection of accurate responses.

The logic in the researcher familiarizing themselves with the instruments and their specific content cannot be overemphasized. Knowing the questions not only enhances the process of eliciting basic data or initial information, but it also enables and prepares the researcher or interviewer for further probing for detailed responses. Under no circumstance should the researcher or interviewer fumble with the act of questioning. Fumbling does not help the respondent and, in some instances, may turn them off and/or hinder the collection of accurate data.

The next step is to develop and ask questions in a manner appropriate to the linguistic and cultural backgrounds of the respondents. This is essential to ensure that the respondents understand the questions and are not offended by the said questions. With understanding comes the ability to respond correctly and hence the collection of accurate data. It will be very challenging to find prison populations or victims of crime who do not have differences in cultural and linguistic backgrounds. It is critical for the researcher or interviewer to be sensitive to the backgrounds of the respondent as well as discern potentially sensitive linguistic and cultural issues before and during the interview. This is particularly important where the investigation focuses on victims of rape and other sexual assaults, or where the study involves study subjects who have different linguistic and cultural backgrounds to those of the researcher or interviewer.

The final step, the logically sequential step to asking the questions, is to record the responses carefully and truthfully. The responses must be recorded as provided and no prejudices and/or preconceptions should be entertained. Any errors made in recording interview responses will impact on editing, coding and data quality as a whole. To avoid recording errors, the responses must be recorded immediately. Further probing should occur after the initial responses have been recorded, unless the initial responses are not clear. Delaying the recording of response can lead to memory lapse and inaccuracies as the researcher or interviewer attempts to remember what was said previously. That said, the point must be made that the researcher must be very clear about the response or politely ask for a repeat of the response. This is what works in practice.

Advantages and Disadvantages of Interviewing

The advantages and disadvantages of interviewing are similar to those of survey research (see chapter four). It would suffice to say here that the main advantage is that interviewing facilitates probing for additional information while serving as a catalyst for the collection of standard data. The main disadvantage is cost as interviewers have to be paid, potentially in addition to payments to or rewards for the study subjects.

FURTHER READING

May, T. (2001): Social research. Buckingham, Open University Press.
Brathwaite, F. S., and D. A. Yeboah (2005): Victims of crime in the criminal justice system of Barbados. Journal of Criminal Justice, Vol. 32, No. 2: 431-442.
Yeboah, D. A. (2000): The evaluation of New Zealand's Habilitation Centres Program. Journal of Criminal Justice, Vol.28, No 3: 227-235.
Yeboah, D. A. and F. S. Brathwaite (2007): The nature and impact of criminal victimization in Barbados. Journal of Ethnicity in Criminal Justice, Vol.5, Nos. 2/3: 55-77.

Box 8.1. Principles of developing questions

1.	Simple straight forward wording.
2.	Clear, unambiguous.
3.	Questions should be concise, and not unduly lengthy.
4.	One question sentence, not two questions in one sentence.
5.	Items must follow in a logical sequence.
6.	Pitching questions to the level and understanding of study subjects.
7.	Focus on the subject matter of the study.
8.	Clarity about which questions will be answered by whom.
9.	Efficiency and effectiveness of the questionnaire rather than its appearance.
10.	Layout and printing should enhance coding and editing.

Box 8.2. Sequential step in interviewing

1.	Identifying the respondents.
2.	Familiarize yourself with the respondents.
3.	Familiarize yourself with the interview venue.
4.	Familiarize yourself with the questions.
5.	Pose the questions in a culturally and linguistically appropriate manner.
6.	Note and record the responses carefully to avoid complications in coding, editing and analysis.

Box 8.3. Questions for readers self reflection

1.	Why is the content of the questionnaire important?
2.	Distinguish between content and principles in questionnaire design.
3.	Why should the principles of questionnaire design be followed?
4.	Why does the researcher's knowledge of the study subjects help in questionnaire design?
5.	What research methodologies involve interviewing?
6.	What are the advantages and disadvantages of interviewing?
7.	Identify the role of language and culture in interviewing

Chapter 9

FINAL WORDS

In this concluding chapter, attention is refocused on the content of the book together with the general implications of research. The object is to refresh readers memory about what is available elsewhere in the book and provide insights nto what tyupe of methodology to adopt in various situations and circumstances etc. Three broad headings have been identified to achieve this objective, namely:

1. Summary.
2. Type of methodology to adopt.
3. Implications of research.

SUMMARY

The main sources of data for criminological research is found in chapter two and include administrative or official records and special studies..Administrative records consist of data held by various government departments as well as data held by non-government organizations working in the criminal justice system. Departments or Ministries of Justice, Prisons, Corrections, Courts and the Police in various jurisdictions collect and keep crime and related data which are of particular relevance to criminological research. Many community based non government organizations provide services for offenders including rehabilitation, accommodation support and employment assistance services and programs. These organizations keep data of relevance to criminological research (chapter two).

A number of research methodologies which are available to criminological researchers have been presented in this book. In chapter two, the General Research Process is presented to introduce the general step by step guide to undertaking criminological research. This is followed by a discussion of qualitative research methods. Two main qualitative research methodologies are presented, namely participant observation and focus groups (chapter three). In participant observation, the researcher directly observes the behavior of the study subjects by looking, listening and recording what is observed. In Focus group research, the researcher identifies and establishes a small number of study subjects who are called or rather constitute the focus group. The researcher obtains data from the group by asking them a number of questions including probing questions. Following the chapter on qualitative research methodologies is the chapter on quantitative research methodologies. The main quantitative methodology is survey research. The point was made that survey research may be face to face, telephone, postal or observational and, that, face to face interviewing can be structured, unstructured or semi-structured (chapter four).

Program evaluation is discussed in chapter 5, with a presentation of the different types of program evaluation, the importance of program evaluation, program evaluation models and methodologies, and the step by step guide to undertaking program evaluation. The main types of program evaluation has been identified as process or implementation, formative, outcome, summative, impact and effectiveness evaluation. Other criminological research methodologies presented in this book are documentary research, case studies, experimental research, analysis of existing data and comparative analysis (chapter six). The advantages and disadvantages of the various methodologies are discussed. Ethical issues in criminological research, asking questions and interviewing supplement the research methodologies (chapters seven and eight).

WHAT TYPE OF RESEARCH METHODOLOGY DO YOU ADOPT?

As indicated previously, there are different research methodologies each with its individual strengths and weaknesses. The question arises as to which of the research methodologies should be used in an investigation. The decision about the most appropriate methodology or methodologies (in the case of triangulation) to adopt is the prerogative of the individual researcher. However, certain conditions and factors work individually and severally to guide the decision-making process. These include:

1. Goals and objectives of the study.
2. Types of data needed to achieve the research goals and objectives.
3. Issues of funding and related resources.
4. Agreed timelines and deadlines.
5. The strengths and weakness of the methodologies relative to the specific study.
6. Researcher's skills and knowledge.

The primary focus of any study is to address the subject matter or problem identified for the study. The subject matter determines to a large extent the goals and objectives of the study, which in turn determine the types of data required for the study. The types of data required for the study, by and large, determines the type of methodology, other factors being equal. Specific research methodologies lend themselves better to the collection of certain types of data. For example if the objective is to obtain standard data in large volumes, then survey research would appear the most appropriate methodology.

Funding is a "sine qua non" for most research activities, i.e. no research activity occurs without some degree of funding or resources allocation. In that respect, funding appears to be the ultimate determinant of research methodologies. Some methodologies, such as participant observation and the analysis of existing data, are less expensive than survey research. In making decisions on which methodology or methodologies to use in the study, the researcher has to give serious consideration to the funding and related resources available for the study. Agreed timelines and deadlines are also important. Research activities have a start and finish timelines, while many commissioned research projects have firm deadlines that have to be met. Some research methodologies, such as survey research methodologies, are time consuming and take a long period of time to complete. Depending on the agreed timelines, the researcher has to determine the most feasible methodology or methodologies which will allow for the collection of relevant data and which will, at the same time, allow for the research to be completed on time.

Yet another factor to consider is the plus and minuses involved in the strengths and weaknesses of individual research methodologies. The strengths and weaknesses have been identified for the various research methodologies presented in this book. The onus is on the researcher to weigh the strengths and weaknesses of the methodologies and determine which methodologies have advantages for the specific research. Closely related to the discussion in the preceding paragraph are the skills of the researcher. It is important to mention that the knowledge and skills of the researcher is paramount and can override many other factors. For example, a researcher may have adequate funding to undertake survey research, but if that researcher has limited skills and knowledge in quantitative research methodologies, other methodologies may become more attractive. Researchers have their strengths and weaknesses. Only a few are all round researchers grounded solidly in both quantitative and qualitative research methodologies, for example. Naturally, most researchers tend to lean towards methodologies with which they are very familiar and, about which, they have the necessary knowledge, understanding and skills.

It must further be pointed out that a number of factors work together to determine the most appropriate research methodologies for a specific study. Using the factors discussed in this chapter can help determine the said appropriate methodology. The circumstances of each investigation are different, even where the study involves the same researcher or researchers. The circumstances of each research must be separately appraised to make decisions on appropriate methodology or methodologies.

IMPLICATIONS OF RESEARCH

As indicated in chapter one, research is undertaken for a purpose and this presupposes a need to identify and establish the purpose of each specific research activity and the implications of the research findings for that purpose. As research increases in importance especially in ever day life, so also grows the need to establish the implications of research. The implications of research are of particular interest to program and service providers, policy makers, funding agencies as well as related research activities, The main avenues or instruments for unveiling the implications of research are the conclusions and recommendations. Recommendations provide a summary of the implications so formulated to allow the necessary actions to be taken. Besides, it is often the practice to have a section on the implications of the research, especially where the research findings have policy and/or program development and funding implications. While implications of research may be discerned for various areas, the following are identified for further discussion:

1. Planning.
2. Policy formulation.

3. Program and service development.
4. Funding.
5. Further research.

IMPLICATIONS OF RESEARCH FINDINGS FOR PLANNING

Depending on the topic or subject matter, the implications of research for planning can be tremendous. Planning Divisions of criminal justice sector organizations rely on evidence from research for the planning analysis and planning decisions. While it is not normal practice for criminological research to specifically identify the implications of research for planning activities, the analysis and recommendations usually provide ammunition for planning analysis and decisions. For example, research into prison numbers, accommodation and related logistics would provide the necessary information for the modeling and planning of future prisons and other corrections facilities. Research findings from investigations of crime levels, patterns and trends will assist law enforcement agencies such as the Police to undertake evidence based planning to tackle crime.

Policy Implications of Research Findings

The interrelationships between research and policy can be discerned in a two-way process. Research usually provides evidence and support for policy formulation, development and implementation, while policy tends to define and stimulate research activity on the subject matter covered by the policy. In these days of scrutiny and assessment of policy impacts and effectiveness, research has become an integral component of the policy development process with implications of research findings serving as a useful source of evidence for determining and defining policy directions in many jurisdictions across the globe. .Research is now one of the first stages in the policy process and occurs before the initial policy draft. The bottom line is that policy directions vary, even for the same subject matter, and policy makers can go in one direction or the other. Research findings and their implications clearly indicate the most appropriate course of action and policy direction, empowering policy makers to confidently subject their policies to scrutiny.

In the illustration above on crime levels, the evidence from research will show not only how high or low crime is, but also the patterns and trends. Inherent in the patterns and trends are the indications of the distribution of crime by type of crime. Data from this distribution will show the common or leading crimes and this will have implications for crime policy. For example, if aggravated robbery and grievous bodily harm appear to be the leading criminal activities, there are clear implications for crime policy to direct efforts at addressing those crimes. If the study crime study findings new patterns and/or emerging trends in criminal activity, policy makers can use that evidence to support their policy decisions. In addition, research on support for victims of crime may provide evidence to support policy on victims support in particular what type of support should be provided and so on. A research into court room practices can produce findings to stimulate a range of changes in the policies governing court room practices and related aspects of the criminal justice system.

Implications of Research Findings for Program and Service Development

The implications of research findings for program and service development operate along the same lines as the policy implications of research findings. However, research findings have more implications for program and service development and delivery. Research can lead to the establishment of new programs, new corrections facilities and even refined approaches to offender management. Program evaluation has resulted in improvements in program development in many jurisdictions, especially prison and community based rehabilitation programs. Evaluation findings and their implications for program performance improvements continue to be used by program and service providers to seek support for their activities and to underscore the importance of their activities.

A research into the effectiveness of a community based corrections facility would produce evidence to support decisions on whether the facility should continue to operate. The findings could also have implications for improvements and new services provision as the research identifies unmet needs for rehabilitation of offenders. In addition, program evaluation has the potential to identify which program activities are efficient and effective and which activities are not useful, with further implications for program development.

FUNDING IMPLICATIONS OF RESEARCH FINDINGS

Research implications and funding are interrelated. Funding supports research while research findings have implications for funding decisions. In the prevailing situation of limited funding and many competing demands for the limited research funds, the implications of research for funding decisions cannot be overemphasized. First research findings provide essential data for modeling and the development of funding models. These models play effective roles in decision on funding allocations, especially the direction and level of funding. The second point which must be considered is that funding agencies are keen to learn from research and in particular program evaluation if the funding provided has been used as agreed, if the funded activity has been effectively and efficient. For funding agencies, the ultimate objective is to obtain evidence to support decisions to continue or stop funding for the specific program.

The third point relates to funding of research as a whole not just program evaluation. Local, national and international agencies providing financial assistance for research rely on research finding to establish firm or core areas for research funding, usually called areas of interest or concentration/focus. These agencies undertake their own research and rely on findings from existing and new research to identify emerging research issues and to establish areas which become classified as suitable or priority for funding and seek applications for research funding on those subject matters.

Further Research

As indicated earlier in this section, research can have implications for further research. One research activity may unveil areas of relevance which could not be included in the specific study but which could be undertaken in another research activity. Thus research may arise from a previous study and at the same time stimulate further research on aspects of the subject matter in the future. For example, a researcher investigating fear of crime finds that a particular reason takes a disproportionate share of the reasons given by respondents for their answer to the question about fear of crime. The scope of the research does not permit further investigation of the specific reason and the researcher may note it as an area for further research in the future. Sometimes the implications of research for further research are clear as the researcher identifies and states them. Other times areas for further research are discerned from the findings of a previous research, where the said areas have not been specifically identified or stated.

Box 9.1. Factors to consider in selecting the research methodology

1.	Goals and objectives of the study.
2.	Types of data needed to achieve the research goals and objectives.
3.	Funding and related issues of resources.
4.	Agreed timelines and deadlines.
5.	The strengths and weakness of the methodologies relative to the specific study.
6.	Researcher's skills and knowledge.

Box 9.2. Key areas where research implications are important

1.	Planning.
2.	Policy formulation.
3.	Program and service development.
4.	Funding.
5.	Further research.

Box 9.3. Questions for readers self reflection

1.	How does cost influence the selection of appropriate research methodology?
2.	In what ways are the goals and objectives of the research important for selecting the research methodology?
3.	What are the implications of research for:
	a. Funding.
	b. Policy formulation.
	c. Program development.
	d. Further research.
	e. Planning.

REFERENCES

Aldridge, A., and K. Levine (2001): *Surveying the social world*. Buckingham, Open University Press.

Bayda, E. D., (2000): Restorative justice in Canada. *Forum of Corrections Research*, Vol. 12: 28-31.

Brathwaite, F. S. and D. A. Yeboah (2004): Victims of crime in the criminal justice system of Barbados. *Journal of Criminal Justice*, Vol. 32, No. 2: 431-442.

Cramer, D. (2003): Advanced quantitative data analysis. Philadelphia, Open University Press.

Davidson, W., J. Koch, R. Lewis, and M. Wrensinski (1981): *Evaluating strategies in criminal justice*, New York, Permagon Press.

Dowell, D., C. Klein, and C Krichmar (1985): Evaluation of a halfway house for women. *Journal of Criminal Justice*, Vol. 13, 216-217.

Dyer, B. (1994): The hyabilitation of offenders. New Zealand Mental Health Foundation.

Giddens, A. (1997): *Sociology*. Cambridge, Polity Press.

Kennedy, L., and V. Sacco (1998): Crime victims in context. Los Angeles, Roxbury Publishing Company.

Laub, J. H. (1990): Patterns of criminal victimization in the United States of Ameraica. In Victims of Crime: *Problems, policies and programs lurigio*, A. et al.,(Eds), 23-49.

May, T., (2001): *Social Research, Buckingham*. Open University Press.

Mayhew, P., N. Maungn, and C. Mirrlees-Black (1993): The 1992 British Crime Survey. Home Office Planning and Research Unit Report, London, Home Office.

McKenzie, J. F., and J. L. Smeltzer (2001): Planning, implementing, and evaluating health promotion programs. *Needham Heights*, MA (USA), Pearson Education Company.

Palmer, K., and D. Farrington (1999): Criminal victimization in a Caribbean Island. *International Review of Victimology*, Vol 6, No 1: 1-16.

Posavac, E. JU., and R. G., Carey (1997): Program evaluation: Methods, and case studies. Upper Saddle River, Prentice-Hall.

Teevan, J. J., (1987): Basic Sociology. *Scarborough* (Canada), Prentice-Hall.

Utts, J. M., (1999): Seeing through statistics. *Pacific Grove*, CA (USA): Duxbury Press.

Windsor, R., T. Baranowski, N. Clark, and G. Cutter (1994): Evaluation of health promotion, health education and disease prevention programs. *Mountain View*, CA (USA), Mayfield Publishing Company.

Yablonski, L., (1989): *The therapeutic Community*. New York, Gardner Press.

Yeboah, D. A., (2000): The evaluation of New Zealand's habilitation centre pilot programme. *Journal of Criminal Justice*, Vol. 28, No. 3: 227-235.

Yeboah, D. A., (2001): Proposed strategies for reducing crime in Barbados. *Caribbean Dialogue*, Vol. 6, Nos. 1 and 2: 93-106.

Yeboah, D. A., (2002): Crime and its solutions in Barbados. *Journal of Criminal Justice*, Vol. 30, No. 5: 409-416.

Yeboah, D. A., and F. S. Brathwaite (2007): The nature and impact of criminal victimization in Barbados. *Journal of Ethnicity in Criminal Justice*, Vol.5, Nos. 2/3: 55-77.

INDEX

Q

T